BLACK WOMEN OF AMHERST COLLEGE

BLACK WOMEN *of* AMHERST COLLEGE

by Mavis C. Campbell

Amherst College Press

AMHERST, MASSACHUSETTS

1999

Contents

ॐ

Foreword

～

When Mavis Campbell first proposed to write and compile this book, the idea appealed to me immediately. The idea of a companion volume to Harold Wade's remarkable *Black Men of Amherst* made perfect sense. After all, Wade's book was published in 1976, the year that Amherst became coeducational, and in that sense it marked the end of one era but did not account for the beginning of another. More than 20 years had elapsed since then; surely, we agreed, it was time to correct the imbalance. Even so, there was concern that the work might be premature. As Professor Campbell has noted, Wade surveyed a tradition that went back 150 years; he was able to describe lifetime achievements of his extraordinary subjects—to name a mere sampling, men like the passionate editor George Washington Forbes of the Class of 1892, the great desegregationist Charles Hamilton Houston of the Class of 1915, and the celebrated jurist William H. Hastie of the Class of 1925. Most of our women graduates, on the other hand, are still under 40 years of age, less than half way into their careers. Surely the story of their highest accomplishments is yet to be told.

Happily, Professor Campbell's book puts that worry to rest. For one thing, with her meticulous historian's eye and ear for narrative, she has given us the story of the coeducation movement not only at Amherst College but elsewhere in the United States. That provides a context for all that follows: the impressive, individual accounts of the many black women who have graduated from Amherst since women's admission. Here Nicole M. Moore '90 speaks very frankly, and no doubt for many other black alumnae, when she writes that "black women can claim Amherst as their own because of what we have brought to the table academically, athletically, culturally and socially. We should be proud of our tenacity," she writes, "our ability to excel in an environment that has not always been welcoming or comfortable."

Amherst, too, should be proud. These women have now begun to make names for themselves in their communities, their professions, and even the world. Like the Forbeses, the Houstons, and the Hasties before them, each brings honor to Amherst's name as well as to her own.

TOM GERETY
President, Amherst College

Preface

ॐ

Some two decades ago, before his tragic early death, Harold Wade, an Afro-American Amherst graduate from the class of 1968, largely completed the writing of a book which he titled *Black Men of Amherst*. It was a remarkable book written at a remarkable time in the history of the nation and of the College. With this volume Harold Wade raised to the consciousness of all those interested in Amherst a fascinating dimension of the College's history which had been largely neglected in previous chronicles.

I had myself read every book and article on the history of the College which I could find. I also had some seventeen relatives over four generations who had graduated from Amherst and who had filled my ears with the oral traditions of the place. I did know that Edward Jones, a free black man from Charleston, South Carolina, had been a graduate in the class of 1826 and that he had gone on to become president of a college in Sierra Leone. But only with the reading of Wade's book did I learn about Charles Houston from the class of 1915 who as Dean of Howard Law School had trained a generation of black lawyers, planned the strategy, and argued the cases which made it possible and logical for the Supreme Court to render the Brown decision desegregating public education in America. Only with Wade's book did I learn about that quartet of black "Supermen" who had come from the Dunbar High School in Washington to the classes of 1925 and 1926 at Amherst: Charles Drew who pioneered the process for storing blood plasma just in time to save thousands of lives in World War II; William Hastie who went on from being Editor of the *Harvard Law Review* to become still another Dean of Howard Law School, Governor of the Virgin Islands, and Chief Judge of the Third Circuit Court of Appeals; Mercer Cook, distinguished Professor of Romance Languages at Howard; and Montague Cobb, who from his post as Chairman of the Department of Anatomy at Howard University trained a whole generation of black physicians.

Pursuing research into the College's records from its founding in 1821 to his own class of 1968 Harold Wade compiled a list of some 93 black graduates over these years, nearly a century and a half. Not content with chronicling what he could find about their lives, Wade acted vigorously both to increase dramatically the number of black men at Amherst and to enhance their presence on the campus. He helped to found an Afro-American Society and to secure permission for a Black Studies Center to be located in the historic building of the Octagon. Working with Dean Wilson's Admission office, Wade and other black students managed within the seven classes between those of 1968 and 1975 to more than double the number of black graduates from the 93 during the first century and a half to the 200 or so whose names finally appear in *Black Men of Amherst,* published in 1976. Harold Wade and his generation had truly seized the momentum generated during the civil rights movement of the '60s to enrich our awareness of the role Afro-Americans had played in Amherst's past as well as to provide a firm base for their role in Amherst's future.

What, then, can we expect from a book on the *Black Women of Amherst College* appearing over two decades after Harold Wade's pioneering volume? Since the first black women to graduate from Amherst entered in 1976 and ordinarily will be just beginning to reach the age of 40, one cannot reasonably expect full accounts of lifetime achievements. Nor can one look for the same level of heady excitement at the discovery of an Afro-

American dimension in Amherst's history which greeted the publication of *Black Men of Amherst*. The late 1990s are a more complex and confusing time for racial stories in America than was the mid '70s: affirmative action is facing serious challenges. The President has called for a national dialogue on racial matters so that we may understand better how the actual lives of Afro-Americans are working out in contemporary America.

At the same time the women's movement of the '60s and '70s has opened the way for major changes in the lives of American women. How can we understand more accurately what those changes have been in the career lives and the family lives of American women and especially American black women over the last two decades? How have they responded to the educational opportunities opened to them? What kinds of careers have appealed to them? How frequently have they chosen to provide services to the larger black community and to the nation? Have they been willing and able to try to carry out Amherst's missionary motto, *Terras Irradient*, by making some impact on the world beyond our borders? Our present need is for some more precise answers to these questions, for an understanding of how an Amherst education may have helped or hindered them in reshaping the world they have inherited. This is what we can expect from the publication of Mavis Campbell's *Black Women of Amherst College*.

Professor Campbell, of Jamaican extract, received her higher education up through the Ph.D. from the University of London. She has published widely and is presently engaged in writing a social history of Belize, Central America.

Professor Campbell joined the faculty at Amherst in 1976, the same year when eighteen young black women came to the College as members of Amherst's first fully coeducational class. Over the next two decades she served as teacher, advisor, mentor and friend to many of this first generation of black women at Amherst, encouraging them to fulfill the high standards of the British educational system in which she had been trained.

In a lengthy introduction to the book, Professor Campbell adds a number of interesting items to our understanding of Amherst's history. She reveals that some of the College's founding fathers, including particularly the Reverend David Parsons, came from families that had owned slaves in the days when slavery was legal in Massachusetts. She tells us a bit more about Edward Jones '26, Amherst's first black graduate, based on her own knowledge of the history of Sierra Leone. The main question which she undertakes to answer is why Amherst took so long to admit women, why it was the *last* of the prestigious male colleges in New England to do so. Her answer to this question leads her to reveal some amusing passages from the 19th century discourse on the topic.

The other central theme of this introduction is to explain *how* she chose to gather and present the material for this book. If she could not rely upon the longer historical perspective and the records of completed lives which Harold Wade could bring to his book, she did manage to take maximum advantage of the simple fact that her subjects were still alive. With remarkable persistence she has secured direct written testimony from a large proportion of the 256 black women in the twenty Amherst classes from that of 1980 to that of 1999—a larger number than the 200 black men Harold Wade found in Amherst's first century and a half.

Here, then, often in their own words are accounts of how their Amherst education influenced them, how for example a course in "Japanese Theater and Film" led to an Amherst-Doshisha Fellowship, to a Ph.D. program in "Film History, Ethnic Representation, and Cultural Performance Studies," to responsible posts in the film industry and to teaching posts. Although this testimony is generally enthusiastic, it does not ignore difficulties encountered at the College, the departments which seemed formidable to black women as well as those which were supportive. A black woman with an A- average in her Physics major even tells how she handled a request from a white male athlete to help him cheat on a course exam.

Professor Campbell has supplemented this evidence on the students' educational experience with testimony from professors about their impressions of some memorable black women students. The net result of these combined testimonies means that this volume on black women students gives the reader a far more complete, complex and intriguing sense of what Amherst was like for these black women students than Harold Wade could provide for his black men.

Beyond that, any reader browsing for a time among all these biographical sketches can gain some clearer understanding of the new world opening up for black women in America. Many of them choose to follow the traditional paths of Amherst men into the law and medicine. Yet within these fields, whether by personal inclination or some covert channeling process, there is a tendency toward governmental, non-profit, public service agencies. There also seems to be a tendency to continue expanding horizons by further graduate study and the piling up of JDs, MAs, MBAs, and Ph.Ds. Their career lines demonstrate a heightened sense of responsibility for committees to combat racial or gender bias within the professions. The popularity of a college major in Psychology is paralleled by subsequent careers in clinical psychology or psychoanalysis.

In soliciting, compiling, and ordering all this wealth of information on the first classes of black women to graduate from Amherst, Professor Campbell has made a major contribution to the history and to the community of Amherst College. She has seized upon a historic moment to record more about the lives of these Amherst graduates than we could have known otherwise. And she has urged that the work begun here and by Harold Wade two decades ago should be continued and updated every twenty years or so. I hope the College will find it possible to do so even after the lives of Amherst graduates of all races have merged still more fully into a common destiny.

THEODORE P. GREENE '43
Emeritus Professor of
History and American Studies

BLACK WOMEN OF AMHERST COLLEGE

Introduction

꒰

Black Women of Amherst College, although altogether a labor of love, was not an easy book to write. Indeed, when the decision was made to write it, I thought that I could have breezed through it in no time, underestimating the extent to which it would have been time-consuming and frustrating at times.

It was difficult, first, in terms of structure and organization. In his *Black Men of Amherst,* Harold Wade, Jr., had a time span of over one hundred and fifty years dating from the time the first black man entered Amherst College (1822), to the time of the publication of his book in 1976. In this work, we have scarcely more than twenty years to deal with, representing the period since the College became coeducational in 1976 to the present. Wade could thus chart the *full* lives of some impressive black alumni of Amherst, many of whom distinguished themselves in medicine, the legal profession, education, music, diplomacy and the like. For our part, these black women can hardly be considered as having lived out their full lives during these twenty-odd years. Indeed, when we can say this, it is with sadness and grief: from the class of '81, we must report the untimely death of Julie Keith (Jarrett), for whom her brother, Dr. Stephen Keith, '73, has written a most moving dedication (pp. 93–94).

When I finally discovered a structure for a part of this book, it was quite unwittingly. It came to me after a conversation with Professor Edward Belt of the Geology Department, where he talked enthusiastically of a woman—who happened to have been black—who wrote an excellent Senior Honors thesis in geology under his supervision. And it was sometime later that I found my Eureka! Why not ask some professors to tell me something about this category of students that they have taught here and then include their response in the book? In asking them, I merely made some very general stipulations: that the students they wrote about need not be "stars" receiving "straight As," although this is very important too, but they could also have been impressed by a student because of some special characteristic—strength of character, leadership capabilities, motivation, community service, and so on. The response, for the most part, was enthusiastic and incredibly useful. Only a few of those I asked (not more than three) were unable to contribute because of pressure of work, a few did not have the relevant recollection in order to participate, and a small number agreed instantly, promising to send information in no time, but despite my many reminders, I still have not heard from them (not more than three). Altogether, the contributors were given a free hand, with some writing two or three pages, others a page, or, in some cases, just a pertinent paragraph. But I did issue one caveat to them: they should write only if they had a clear memory of a student who stood out to them; their statements should not appear forced in the manner that so many of us as teachers at one time or another had perforce to write references for certain students—as of duty bound. And those who responded, including the tough-minded Professor Bill Kennick, certainly conformed to this. I am tempted to give some samples here but since they are *all* to be found in the main text when dealing with the relevant students, then, I shall refrain.

But if I singled out the piece by Professor Robert (Kim) Townsend and mention a part of it here, it is because he replied on a philosophical/reflective level before dealing with the particular black female student who impressed him most. "Upon being asked," Townsend said that his "immediate reaction was cowardly. What was I to say? Or *who* was I to say?

But almost immediately I thought of one woman, one woman who in fact I often recall when I ask myself what it is I do as a teacher. I have been asking *that* question for almost thirty-five years now and obviously have yet to come up with a satisfactory answer. By one route or another I always end up thinking of Henry Adams' famous summation of his experience teaching at Harvard: 'A teacher affects eternity,' he says in his *The Education of Henry Adams*. 'He can never tell where his influence stops.' The idea is—even for Adams—too grandiose. I know of no evidence that could support it. ('Eternity'?) A humbler version of it, though, has always proven helpful. You never know, I say to myself."

The student Professor Townsend went on to write about in deservedly glowing terms is Kimberlyn Leary '82 now with a Ph.D. in Clinical Psychology (see the class of '82 for her biographical sketch).

Yet, from the voices of these women in this book, I unexpectedly learned how much these black women have gained from their teachers here even under some very trying circumstances, and wondered if Townsend is not too modest. And it was interesting to note that the professors most praised were not those riding on the backs of blacks to enhance their professions or to satisfy some urge for supremacy. Some of these women spoke in general terms about the Amherst experience while others singled out some of their professors who most affected their lives and careers. Karla Fuller, of the true pioneer class of '80, for instance, was uncertain about career goals when she entered Amherst, until she took a course with Professor Robert Tyler (no longer here) on "Japanese Theatre and Films," and "when we got to the films," she said, "my life was changed forever, though I did not know it yet." She soon became the first *woman* (not to mention *black*) to have been awarded the highly competitive Amherst-Doshisha Fellowship under which she spent a year in Japan studying the language and culture and also teaching English at the Doshisha University. Her statement to me on her exciting stay in Japan (see class of '80) is written with wit and charm. She is now completing a Ph.D. at Northwestern University, after a Master's (M.A.) Degree from Columbia University—all dealing with film making (Japanese and the United States). Karla writes that every time she faces an audience or a group of students while lecturing on Japanese films, she would begin by telling them that "it all started in a course at Amherst College."

Then there is Barbara Smoot (Liggon), class of '84, Phi Beta Kappa (1983-1984), who majored in Physics. She spoke enthusiastically of some of her professors in the Physics Department—Gordon, and Jagannathan, and Professor Denton from the Mathematics Department. When she took the first tough actuarial examination in 1985, one year after graduation, and received the highest possible score, she credited this to Denton's classes and to majoring in Physics at Amherst: "Professors Gordon and Jagu's exams made the actuarial exams seem like 'cake' by comparison. . . ." Barbara is now in the rarified actuary profession—where there are relatively few women of any ethnicity—and for this she credits her overall experience at Amherst College. She is grateful that she "had the good sense to keep at it at Amherst and the wits to follow the advice of my professors." For much more on Barbara and more of what she has to say about her professors (including this author!), as well as some of the difficult situations she encountered here, see her biographical outline under the class of '84.

Crystal Brown of the class of '89 is grateful to Professor Cody of the English Department. She was "uptight as a freshman and wanted to do well but there was so much that I had to get used to. I had such problems with my English 11 class. I used to go to see Professor Cody after every class. He devoted so much time to helping me understand Shakespeare and polishing papers. I owe a great deal to Professor Cody. He was always so patient with me." These and many more attributions to professors on this campus are to be found in the text of this book and even if they do not necessarily have eternal implications, we can, however, associate with Townsend when he went for the middle road and said, "Better than Adams is Walt Whitman on teaching":

> He that by me spreads a wider breast than my own proves the
> width of my own,
> He most honors my style who learns under it to destroy the
> teacher.

The other component to the organization of the book was, of course, the obvious one of contacting all the black women who graduated since the first class of '80 (including a few transfer students). And this was the part which gave me the mixed feelings of frustration and excitement. The frustration resulted from the difficulty of getting responses from some of these women. Even though Douglas Wilson '62, Secretary for Public Affairs, had warned me (from his own experience) not to expect more than about a third in response, I still was not prepared for the frustrating delays. I simply was not in control of my "material," and in this sense this was the most difficult book I have written. Closely associated with this frustration was the fact that my ongoing academic projects had come to a halt and, indeed, during this period I only managed to have refereed a manuscript for *The William and Mary Quarterly,* and a project for a grant-giving foundation. In addition, the research for this book drew my attention to the important parts played by New England women—of all classes—in the early establishment and development of Amherst College and on this topic I have also written a short pioneer article, to be published elsewhere.

Altogether, I sent out three letters to every black alumna of the College, in addition to making numerous telephone calls. More than a dozen of the letters have returned to me either with directives stating that the addresses were not known or that the forwarding orders have been expired and these will be found in Appendix A, with the hope that these women will contact the Alumni Office here to update their addresses. Just about four of the subjects told me on the telephone that they did not want to be included, two of these citing "bad experiences," here as their reasons, while the other two said that they did not think that they had done anything "important enough" to be entered in a book. In some cases I succeeded in persuading this category to respond, because there are many "out there" who felt this way. Even Janet Buckner, M.D., class of '84, told me this! Many whose addresses are current, did not even bother to respond to the letters and the many telephone messages or messages given to roommates. There is yet another category. This "type," upon hearing about the project, was excited and enthusiastic about it, and was most anxious to participate—but nothing further happened; no information followed. This "type" is the Procrastinator Incarnate! There was one (whose name I will not reveal here but you will meet her in the class of '94) who confessed to a faculty member here on campus that two of my letters were "magnetized to [her] fridge. Every time I reach in for a beer [she was then in Japan] . . . I feel a twinge of guilt, but no more." These two letters are dated May 31, 1995, the first, asking for a reply by June 30 (1995), (See Appendix B) and the second was dated July 20, 1995. Then after a third letter and the active intervention of a faculty member, I have the satisfaction to state that she did respond—finally, as did many more like her, albeit much beyond the deadlines.

There is yet another category which turns out to be among the best when it comes to responding to my letters. This is from the few, eight in all, who replied to Mrs. Janice Denton of Frost Library. During the Spring of 1995 Mrs. Denton displayed a photographic exhibition of black women who graduated from Amherst College, and for this she had written them not only for photographs but also for some account of themselves since their graduation. In my second communication to them, I asked them to advise if I could use the material they sent to Mrs. Denton and all but one replied positively. Kelly Jones was the only one who did not respond to this as well as to other letters and numerous telephone calls and telephone messages to roommates; therefore I must conclude she did not want to be included in the book on black women at Amherst College. Some of these women—Amina Merritt, Margaret Vendryes, Sonya Clark, Crystal Brown, among others—have all sent me much additional information, most useful for the book. It was Janice Denton's exhibition that gave her the idea that became the genesis for this book—a logical one since there is already a book on black men of the College (since 1976).

But the thrilling side to the writing of this book—the labor of love aspect—was to see the impressive achievements of these black women within the relatively short period of coeducation at Amherst. I found that, like Harold Wade, despite my measly time span, I too could (should I wish) begin this book in his words—only changing the gender: "Listen to My Story. It is a story of fascinating black [women] who in various ways have left their mark on society. These [women] did not rule over nations. They did not command armies or wage wars. Theirs is the record of [woman's] struggle for existence against nature and the oppressions of human society."[1] In *Black Women of Amherst College*, we will find that a number of these women, some we mentioned above, are already leaving their marks on society. We could mention many here but will identify only a few of those who are in unusual positions or those positions not typically held by women *qua* women or by African Americans in general. There is, for example, Susan Prattis '80, the "fiercely independent" young woman, with a V.M.D. and a Ph.D. in Veterinary Medicine, who is holding her own in her field, publishing scholarly articles, making her mark on society, and, as would be expected, also struggling "for existence against nature and the oppressions of human society."

There is also Bonnie Jenkins '82—"Lady," as she was fondly called on campus, by everyone including President Gibbs—already with a J.D. degree, a master's in public administration (M.P.A.) and is now going for the Ph.D. But it is the type of work she is doing and the awards she is accumulating that place her in this context. For the past six years, she has been involved in high politics and diplomacy, working as an attorney in the Office of the General Counsel at the U.S. Arms Control and Disarmament Agency. In this complex high- powered situation, she provides legal advice to many, including U.S. Ambassadors and U.S. delegations negotiating arms control treaties, as well as to the Senate, etc. The most recent treaty in which she was involved was the Bosnia Agreement about which she has even written a very technical article published in the *Fordham International Law Journal* (vol. 19, no. 5, June, 1996), and this is just one of her publications. Her overseas travel in this position is enormous as you will see later. Among her numerous awards are the "Meritorious Unit Award," which she gained in 1995 as a Special Duty Officer (Intelligence), the "Defense Service Medal," and the "Arms Control and Disarmament Agency Meritorious Honor Award," among many of this kind, and not including the academic scholarships and fellowships she has also received—all of which will be found in her biography below, under the class of '82.

Consider, too, Allison Moore-Lake '82, "out there" (1983–85) with the Peace Corps in Senegal, West Africa, in a small village busily building an irrigation system and vegetable and fruit garden/orchard with several other surrounding villagers. And, as if this was not enough, there she was again, working with some other village women's group on a "chicken co-op," helping also, in the process, to improve their diets and in the building of fuel conserving stoves. This very public spirited young woman continued with outreach community programs upon her return to the U.S., as her biographical sketch will show under the class of '82.

Lisa Evans must also be mentioned in this context. True, she has done law which is a popular subject among graduates—but how many ended up in the U.S. Department of Justice, working closely with the present Attorney General, Janet Reno, and receiving an award from her? The award, given October 8, 1996, was for special achievements and appreciation and recognition for her service to the Department of Justice (see p. 160), and what is more, a picture of her with the Attorney General and the Assistant Attorney General for Civil Rights, Deval Patrick, will all be included in this book.

But, in looking at the achievements of black women who graduated from Amherst College within a wider context, I soon discover that this was not an isolated phenomenon, but is, in fact, a pattern throughout this country, and there is a good deal of attention given to this subject in recent times. *The Journal of Blacks in Higher Education* (JBHE), for instance, has carried a number of articles in different issues on this subject. A main focus of these articles is the extent to which black women have gained in higher education on just about every measurable level: in enrollment, in staying on and graduating, in going to graduate schools, in receiving awards, and so on.[2] This subject has even caught the attention of the prestigious British journal, the *Economist.* The negative side, though, to the great improvement of black women in higher education is that the black men are not even keeping apace but have fallen behind alarmingly. The *Economist*, in its issue of November 4, 1993, said that in 1993 there were 226,000 more black women in university than black men, while the *JBHE,* in its spring issue of 1994, said that this disparity "today" saw "over 300,000 more black women enrolled in college than black men," which explained what the *Economist* meant when it said that the enrollment of black women was increasing "twice as fast." In very crude arithmetical terms, I have also discovered that the number of black women who graduated from Amherst College up to 1996—that is, beginning with the class of '80—has exceeded that of the black men from the class of 1826 to that of 1975, by Wade's calculation even though his figures may not be entirely accurate. And, of course, with higher education, black women have also increased and improved their position in the upper end of the labor market. The *Economist* of the same issue said: "Between 1984 and 1994, the number of black women executives more than doubled;

black men progressed only half as fast." All this happened only since the whole issue of coeducation came to the forefront in the 1960s, but the literature on the subject may be somewhat too sanguine. Although time and space will not permit a full analysis of the dramatic increase of the participation of black women in higher education and better job situations, nevertheless, we would do well to look at another view which is less rosy. Beverly Lindsay, for example, has found the great proverbial "glass ceiling" blocking meaningful advancement to black women in their positions, especially in the field of administration in higher education.[3]

Equally, when we identified the positive testimonies of some of these black women at Amherst College, it is not for a moment meant to cloud over the real difficulties and discriminations many of them encountered here. The single most common criticism they made of their experience at the College, we are sorry to say, came from those who ventured into the sciences and economics. It is noted that the black male students had also grappled with this situation. In visiting the "House" (Drew House later) in 1975, Amina Merritt was struck by the serious concerns and anxieties that the black men displayed with respect to this problem. Many of them, she recounted, "were attempting to be economics or science pre-med majors. I say 'attempting to' because it was a topic of discussion . . . among many students whether there was a conspiracy to keep us out of the sciences or whether we should just give up. . . ." With coeducation, women in general, but particularly black women were to have similar complaints, as their biographical sketches will show. Yet, I am pleased to give another side to this very real problem. Apart from Barbara Smoot's ('84) excellent experience with Professors Gordon and Jagannathan of the Physics Department, and Professor Denton of the Mathematics Department, in recent times, many black students have expressed to me, their appreciation of Professor Patricia O'Hara of the Department of Chemistry. They speak with delightful gratitude of her encouragement and interest in their work, giving them the confidence to work hard and succeed. Some confessed to me that they would have dropped "the sciences" had they not "discovered" Professor O'Hara. One such is the gifted Anastasia Rowland '93, just about completing the M.D. at Columbia University in New York City, receiving, in the process, numerous national awards. For more on Pat O'Hara and her black alumnae in Chemistry, see, particularly, the biographical sketches of Akinyi Adija '92, Anastasia Rowland '93 and Amani Brown '97.

In identifying the positive testimonies of some of these women, therefore, it is meant in great measure as a paean to their good grace, resilience and their indomitable will to succeed. And, in going through the statements of those who responded to me there is no doubt that the pioneer class of '80, and those immediately following, possessed a great deal of these qualities—qualities that are still guiding them in their careers and helping them to make their mark on society.

In this work, I am making an urgent entreaty that Harold Wade's admirable work, *Black Men of Amherst College*, be revised and updated; this is long overdue. It was a pioneer work and as such, certain modifications, additions and corrections are necessary (some of these I have mentioned in the text of the present work). In like manner, I am suggesting that *Black Women of Amherst College* be also updated periodically. This volume should therefore be seen as a *beginning* and those whose biographies are not entered herein, because they did not receive or did not respond to my communications, or for any other reasons, would thus have other opportunities. It would seem appropriate that the first updating be done to celebrate the next twenty years of coeducation at Amherst College, and thereafter, making it a vicenary endeavor. Not only have I spoken to many of these women about this, but in order not to let the recommendations lapse, I have also suggested that a small committee be instituted to oversee this enterprise.

The work is arranged in roughly two parts. The first section takes a quick look at coeducation—or higher education for women in general. I wanted to place the book in context, bearing in mind that coeducation at Amherst College and elsewhere involved not just black women, but *all* women of whatever creed or color. In order not to write in a vacuum, therefore, and to give some background to the work, I found it necessary to review the main arguments particularly *against* higher education for women (which was so universal, stubborn and well established in the social structure of just about all known civilizations), and, to an extent, to examine why Amherst College was not among those in the vanguard for coeducation in the '60s. This question was asked me repeatedly by both men and women on this campus who knew that I was writing this book.

Acknowledgment

It was a real delight to have received so much support from the College authorities in the writing of this book. It represented that traditional community spirit that can be associated with the College at its best. The President, Tom Gerety, must first be thanked for his enthusiastic support for the writing of *Black Women of Amherst College*. From the beginning he gave both institutional support as well as personal inspiration and encouragement to me. It should be noted that the writing of this book has not gone unnoticed by these alumnae and a large number of black alumni also, many of whom had not been returning to the College over the past few years, but have now pledged new interest in participation. Alice Middleton Merrick '87, for instance, felt "compelled to write for two reasons." One was to "applaud and appreciate your work on this undertaking," and the other was because "the current president of the College made me proud to be an alumna when he articulated Amherst's support of Affirmative Action during the commencement of 1996," and Alice is among those we can expect to see on campus again. But what is even more gratifying is the extent to which black alumni like Stephen Coleman '78, Stephen Keith '73, Wayne M. Wormley '72, among many others, became interested in this companion piece to their *Black Men. . . .* They viewed the work with satisfaction and expressed their gratitude to Tom Gerety for supporting it.

So far as other institutional support is concerned, Douglas Wilson, of the Public Affairs Office, has always been there, willing to assist with advice, as mentioned earlier, and with information. Many were the moments when I called him hurriedly asking for his help in supplying some explanation, a date, some information, and even if he did not always have some of the answers at hand, he could be relied on to point to other sources. His very witty work, which he generously made available to me, *Now and Then: The Class of 1962*, I also found very useful. I am also grateful to those staff members and officers of the Alumni House who have so willingly supplied me with useful information—my special thanks to

Hubbard Smith (now retired) and to Michele Stokes-Mattera on whom I could always rely for quick and cheerful service; I am also most grateful for the gracious and efficient assistance from the Registrar, Gerald Mager, and the Assistant Registrar, Louise Westhoff. The urbane Mager, time and again, went the extra mile in support, supplying me with critical information without which the book could not have been possible. Thanks also to Daria D'Arienzo, Archivist of the College, and her Senior Archives Associate, Carol Trabulsi. They have been unstinting in their assistance. There were times when I felt that I had taxed Carol's patience to breaking point with my numerous requests, but she was always helpful, willing and cheerful in serving and I am indeed grateful to her. To the Smith College Archivist, Margery Sly, I owe a great debt for her initiative and help especially for some rare primary documents she made available to me. Associate Dean of Students and Director of Residential Life, Charri J. Boykin-East, was marvelous when I called her hurriedly for some information on the organization on married and transfer students first established by Margaret Vendryes '84. In no time I received from her a beautiful piece on the life and progress of this organization.

My gratitude, too, to the Board of Trustees for granting me permission to reproduce for the book some documents issued by them. Dorothy W. Hertzfeld's (interim Secretary to the Trustees), letter to me is included in Appendix C. It is because of the magnificent institutional assistance I received from the College that I did not find it necessary to employ a research assistant. However, my numerous telephone calls especially this last summer (1996), to solicit responses from the women, were both expensive and time-consuming. Our College Photographer, Frank Ward, went much beyond the call of duty in helping me to contact the black women on campus to have their photographs taken. We are grateful to him.

Then there is Emeritus Professor of History and American Studies, Theodore (Ted) Greene, whose advice has been invaluable. As an alumnus and one who has written extensively on Amherst College and the Amherst town and community, I used his work often for historical background of the College and his support for this project was enthusiastic.

Finally, I must thank Mrs. Rhea Cabin, Assistant to the Chair/Secretary to the Department of History, Amherst College, who typed the entire work. But her assistance went much beyond this because, in most cases, she was even more successful than I in tracking down those procrastinators who held up the work. She did this with good humor and efficiency and we are grateful to her.

Part I

Black Women of Amherst College is meant to be a companion piece to *Black Men of Amherst*, written by Harold Wade, class of '68 and published in 1976. Wade was a product of the 1960s, and the strident tone of his book encapsulates the turmoil of that period. He experienced what must have been an emotionally wrenching ordeal for any young, intelligent black then—the assassination of Martin Luther King—and the consequent race riots across the country on different college campuses. But the work also captures Wade's ideals, his uncompromising integrity and strong sense of values, combined with the passionate urgency that characterizes his concerns for his people. "If the reader" he said, in reference to the book, "still finds moments of emotional excess it is because not only does the author take great pride in the subjects but, furthermore, sometimes excess is necessary to counteract the sin of omission concerning black American history."[1] Wade and other black men at the College were already involved in activities designed to improve their condition but King's death acted as a catalyst for more heightened and concrete demands, particularly through the newly formed Afro-American Society.

The Afro-American Society, Wade tells us, was an offshoot of an original organization of the early '60s, called Students for Racial Equality (SRE), consisting of a campus coalition of what he terms "liberal whites," faculty and students, as well as blacks. The coalition, however, did not seem to have survived for very long: "As whites lost interest in SRE, its membership became increasingly black. The SRE charter was rewritten by the new membership and it became the Afro-American Society." This Society in which Wade was to play a pivotal role was instituted in 1967 and the original officers consisted of Cuthbert Simpkins '69 (now Dr. Simpkins), who was elected its first president, Adrian Johnson '68, Vice President, Rick Simms '70, Secretary, and Francis Griffin '70, treasurer.[2] These black students—all men, of course—then proceeded to effect changes at the College, and they saw their first task as dealing with enrollment. In making enrollment a central issue it should be noted that these students were not just idly engaged in playing the number games, for, as Wade pointed out, black enrollment at the College at this time, starting with the 1920s, was pretty dismal. He cited records showing that during the decade of the 1920s, only 16 blacks graduated from Amherst, while the decade of the 30s saw only five such graduates, and between 1939 and 1947, "no blacks graduated."[3] Wade thought that the Depression had a great deal to do with it, but William H. Hastie, class of '25, the distinguished jurist, pointed out another factor that existed here at the College. Judge Hastie found that: "On the campus itself there was one decade during which the then President of the College adopted a practice of inviting successive groups of seniors to social evenings at the President's House until this hospitable gesture had been extended to all seniors who were not black. One can only speculate how much this attitude at the top contributed to the circumstance, noted in this book, that from the middle 1930s until the late 1940s so few blacks attended or graduated from Amherst."[4]

The "then President" was none other than Stanley King, president of the College from 1932–1946, the period roughly coinciding, if Wade is correct, with the time when no blacks graduated. As if a twin of his kind, there was also Richard McMeekin, Assistant Dean of Admission, 1936–1939, and Dean of the same office from 1939–1946, who completely shared King's racially exclusionist policy. This type of morally flawed leadership not only kept out blacks and other ethnic groups, but it also had the tendency of making racial discrimination acceptable on the campus, coming as it did from the top. To be sure, hate also pervaded the entire country as exemplified by the brutal lynchings of the 1920s and '30s, dramatically presented, for instance, in *The Journal of Blacks in Higher Education* (Winter, 1994/1995, no. 6, pp. 74–75).

Fortunately, as Judge Hastie said, while not wishing to condone or minimize the harmful impact of Stanley King's behavior, nevertheless up to the time he wrote, it was a "rare" act from a President. And certainly the next President, the enlightened Charles Woolsey Cole (president from 1946–1960) class of 1927, and one of the most outstanding scholars to have held this position, was to prove the very opposite to the likes of Stanley King and Richard McMeekin. One of Cole's first appointees was Eugene Wilson, class of '29, as Dean of Admission and together they were to transform the base of the student body. Between them, they soon set the tone for a positive vision for the College. "More Catholics and many more Jews entered as Amherst freshmen,"[5] one author said, but the response from blacks, despite Wilson's tremendous efforts, was not very successful, largely because of the Depression and the hostile racial environment. One source also attributed this to the lack of sufficient scholarship grants.[6]

Although Wade and his fellow students did not have the enlightened President Cole as their president, they were, however, fortunate to have had Calvin Plimpton in the '60s as president of the College. By all accounts, President Plimpton responded with sensitivity and fair mindedness in dealing with their concerns. He cooperated fully with the Afro-American Society toward a commitment to the recruitment of more black students on campus. It is noteworthy that the Afro-American Society published a recruiting booklet, *The Black Student at Amherst*, which was circulated throughout the eastern part of the country with the purpose of attracting black students to the College. Apparently the effort was effective and the result could be seen from the increased number of blacks from the class of 1972. Wade and the other members of the Afro-American Society worked assiduously on this recruiting pamphlet, considered the first of its kind in this country, and they estimated that some 3,000 copies were printed. Some were circulated to admission offices of colleges throughout the northeast, and soon a number of other colleges, determined to increase the enrollment of blacks on their campuses, imitated this recruiting device[7] This booklet also prompted Wade to write his book on black men at Amherst College. He tells us that it was while "editing and writing a portion of that pamphlet, it became apparent to me that there was much to be told concerning the history of the blacks who have attended Amherst since 1822." Wade had a pleasant surprise when he discovered how much Amherst College had contributed to the advancement of black men, "unique" among white schools, he said.[8] But up to this point, we still hear nothing about enrollment of women of whatever race, creed, or ethnicity to the College—from black and white men alike.

WOMEN IN HIGHER EDUCATION: A SHORT REVIEW

In looking at blacks at Amherst College since 1822, Wade's work has necessarily dealt with black *men* since the College was an all-male institution up to 1976. It is indeed tempting here to respond immediately to the fact that the College was opened to blacks in 1822. This is saying a great deal about Amherst College considering the historical background of the period. But before we examine this—that is, the racial dimension—let us first deal with the gender component of the question, since *Black Women of Amherst College* is, in a sense, an update of Wade's work, to include in this case the whole notion of co-education, before we focus specifically on black women.

At the time when Amherst was established (1821) the question of coeducation or even higher education for women was hardly considered here or just about anywhere else. Indeed the very notion was fair game for satire and some pretty bawdy humor as exemplified, for instance, in many of the works of Gilbert and Sullivan. That they belabored the subject so often in their comedic lines meant that they were not writing in a cultural vacuum, but were, in fact, pandering to representative sentiments, even in the 1880s. In *Princess Ida* (1884) replete with gender and racial slurs, for example, when the prince complained that his wife had left him,

> And, with a band of women, shut herself
> Within a lonely country house, and there
> Devotes herself to stern philosophies!

the king's telling reply,

> Then I should say the loss of such a wife
> Is one to which a reasonable man
> Would easily be reconciled—

reflected the same sentiments of the "wisecrack" who quipped: "The woman who *thinks* is like the man who puts on rouge, simply ridiculous."

It is no wonder that the prince proceeded, nostalgically, to reminisce on the time when his wife was his "blushing bride" with "bib and tucker, frill and furbelow!"

Indeed, higher education for women was considered if not incongruous, a useless and expensive ornamentation ("furbelow!") as long as women were viewed merely as destined to perform domestic functions. In this country the issue has been raised intermittently (after the Civil War, for instance) but it became insistent during the 1960s. The decade of the '60s familiar to Harold Wade, was easily one of the most vociferous in recent times. It saw other political and social issues foremost of which were the wider Civil Rights Movements and the Vietnam War. Together these issues seemed as if they would tear apart the very fabric of society: there were protests everywhere, violent demonstrations, both within the general public and on college campuses across the country. Like Wade and his group, students were making numerous demands: there were "sit-ins" and altogether there appeared a pervasive atmosphere of distrust and disrespect for traditional authority. And what was more, "most college authorities, likewise frustrated by their inability to redirect national policies though distressed at the tactics and self-righteousness of students, found themselves morally and politically disposed to countenance a variety of change within their institutions."[9]

But within the general cacophony of this historical moment two major themes emerged, at least so far as the institutions of higher education were concerned: one was the new awareness of "student-power," perceived among themselves as well as by the outside world and the other was that the days of the cozy homogeneity of most elite colleges in this country would seem to have been numbered. Ted Greene has summed up this latter trend when, reflecting on the heady days of the '60s, he observed "a new atmosphere of cultural pluralism." This pluralism expressed itself in a preference for diversity and "respect and appreciation of difference."[10] Indeed the term diversity has become a veritable code word for colleges in this country, including Amherst, up to the present.

Coeducation was to become a part of the new diversity "philosophy." Many all-male colleges, therefore, began to take a close look at themselves and to initiate studies to investigate all the issues involved with the whole question of coeducation. Princeton University was among the first of these colleges to have responded when, in June of 1967, its Board of Trustees authorized a committee to look into the "desirability and feasibility of Princeton's entering significantly into the education of women," and then subsequently it was agreed that the study should be limited to the undergraduate level—reflecting the caution with which the matter was approached.[11] A year later a very impressive report emerged that argued for coeducation and this was to set in motion a process in this country, that, in all probability, is irreversible. Other institutions of a similar kind especially in the northeast followed the coeducational path: Yale (1969), Williams (1970), Trinity (1970), Bowdoin (1971)—to mention a few.

Princeton's rationale for taking the bold initiative of coeducation—as it was then considered—is worth considering since its study (The Gardner Patterson Report) was to become "the classic study of the issues, the model consulted by all other colleges," as an Amherst committee was later to admit. The Princeton committee examined the likely effects coeducation would have on wide-ranging issues such as costs, size and quality of male applicants (does coeducation necessarily mean expansion—and at what monetary cost—or a cut in male enrollment?); on the faculty and the curriculum; on the social, intellectual and cultural aspects of undergraduate life; on alumni relations within the institution; on whether the change should be based on the model of a quota system or equal access from the start, and perhaps, even more important, what were the broader effects of coeducation on the competitive capacity of the institution within the nation's system of higher education, and the like. (These are the same kinds of questions that Amherst would be grappling with later.) After due deliberations the committee voted solidly (one opposition) for coeducation. It was a clear-sighted, rational evaluation based on the positive results that would accrue to the college should it begin to educate both men and women. "We believe that for Princeton to remain an all-male institution in the face of today's evolving social systems would be out of keeping with her past willingness to change with the times: it would be to go back on her tradition of seizing every opportunity to improve the quality and relevance of the education she provides. In our opinion it would also mean that within a decade, if not sooner, Princeton's competitive position for students, for faculty, and for financial support, would be less strong than it now is. The issue, then, is crucial to Princeton's future,"[12] the Gardner Patterson Report intoned.

Meanwhile, what of Amherst College? Harold Wade has shown us earlier how this College was in the vanguard with respect to responding to black students' demands especially for increased enrollments of blacks at the College. Ted Greene has also given us a more detailed account of the activities of both the College and the town—town and gown working together on issues coeval to the '60s, particularly with respect to the civil rights movement and opposition to the Vietnam War.[13] Certainly we should not forget the efforts of Amherst in its participation in the struggle for civil rights.

After the assassination of Martin Luther King, as Wade already mentioned, all college activities were increased, as they were with the town of Amherst where issues of racism "in all areas of Amherst's life from the schools to the economy" and housing were addressed. The College's sustained protests against the Vietnam War soon became famous and were even seen as a model for emulation elsewhere. Greene mentioned that the *New York Times* gave this Amherst initiative front-page coverage and editorial commendation.[14] And it gained more national attention when the activities gravitated from symbolic politics to symbolic civil disobedience, involving the newly appointed president in 1972, John William Ward, who was destined to deal with the question of coeducation at Amherst College. Ward, impatient with the more sedate protests consisting of debates and letters to the President of the United States, expressed his irritation by claiming that composing letters to the nation's President was "like launching paper airplanes against a wall," and he promptly joined students, faculty and some townspeople in committing peaceful civil disobedience by sitting down somewhere along the entry roads of the Westover Air Base from where B52s were flying to join in the bombing of Hanoi and Haiphong.[15]

Thus Amherst College was not backward in responding to and even taking the leading roles in many issues of the '60s. But on the question of coeducation, we see nothing happening. It withstood the '60s as an all-male liberal arts college, and resisted the issue when it was considered at this time. Harold Wade, for instance, despite the activism of his group, is completely silent on the subject of coeducation in his *Black Men of Am-*

herst. The increased enrollment he and his fellow black male students sought was for a new addition of black men to the College.

Although this work is by no means a history of Amherst College, nevertheless it may be useful to take a backward glance at the College before the 1960s to see if we can find clues that would give some insight into Amherst's resistance to coeducation.

We find that, in fact, the question of coeducation for Amherst College was discussed at its semi-centennial celebration in 1871. Among those recorded as having participated in the debate are two prominent alumni: Alexander H. Bullock, class of 1836, then governor of Massachusetts; the Rev. Henry Ward Beecher, class of 1834, an early exponent for the abolition of slavery, and brother of Harriet Beecher Stowe the author of *Uncle Tom's Cabin*; and a non-alumnus, Professor Edwards A. Park, who taught at Amherst College between 1835 and 1836 before accepting a professorship at the Andover Theological Seminary. Both Beecher and Bullock, the two Amherst alumni, favored coeducation, with Beecher arguing for what he called universality in education at Amherst. Indeed, only he, as far as we know, combined at this time the issues of gender and race. "If a man be black, and is fully prepared, or if a woman is fully qualified, its doors will open to them. Amherst should lead in this march of progress, and if she does, it will not be the first time that she has led in progress and philanthropy."[16] Bullock, for his part, in arguing for coeducation, made a concrete offer "as a fit memorial tribute to the occasion" by sending to the Amherst Board of Trustees his "humble offering of a scholarship endowment, with the condition that its benefits shall be appropriated to a woman upon the basis of equal fitness in the examination. In that direction it is offered—and may Heaven grant it a blessing."[17] Apparently, the amount of money he gave was $1,500[18] and it would be interesting to know what became of this Bullock Scholarship.

Professor Edwards Park, on the other hand, was against coeducation in general, and he was to prove, as we shall see, not only consistent on this issue but also influential. In arguing against coeducation for Amherst, Park brought to bear his most clever rhetorical devices. He would not speak on the proposed question of admitting women into the regular classes of the college, but would, instead, since the occasion was also one for reminiscences at its bicentennial, repeat a story from President

Humphrey "who has been fitly extolled this afternoon as a wise and sound man."[19] The story was about a student (as told by the wise and sound Humphrey, second president of the college). This student was neglecting his studies. So noticeable was this that it necessitated a prolonged meeting of the Amherst Faculty where the discussions tried to locate the cause of the student's remissness. One professor thought that the young man was troubled with the headache; another thought that he had a fever; yet another thought that the problem had its basis in pecuniary embarrassment, and so on. At length "the President" (presumably Humphrey) uttered, with a pause after almost every syllable, these suggestive words: "I have reason to believe that the remissness of the young man is owing to a shock which he has received from a *gal*–van–ic (sic) battery," and without another word the Professor took his seat.[20] What was the response from the august gathering to the professor's nicely veiled bawdy joke replete with its multiple metaphors? It was one of "uproarious laughter and prolonged applause which . . . showed clearly enough that the audience made the obvious application of his illustration, and the attempt to make Amherst coeducation failed."[21]

If we are to believe Park's story—apocryphal or not—then the attempt to make the College a coeducational institution failed because of what was conceived as the inconvenience women would have created for men: their presence would result in distractions from their manly scholarly pursuits. Whether or not it was this type of argument *alone* that settled the question of coeducation at this period, we cannot be certain, but there is no doubt that many contemporaries felt it to be so. This may seem odd to modern thinking. But it should be borne in mind that the Amherst Academy founded in 1814, and the "mother of Amherst College," had, what was then a common practice—a section called "the ladies department"—which was doing exceedingly well, even surpassing the male section in some cases, and together they contributed to the great reputation of the Academy, maintaining a high "standard of Scholarship and Christian culture." Yet the ladies' section was soon abolished. Why? Partly "to avoid some difficulties and some scandals which at length arose from educating the two sexes together. . . ," Professor W. S. Tyler delicately tells us.[22]

Thus Smith College, founded by Miss Sophia Smith of Hatfield, Massachusetts, was to prove central to this discourse. Indeed we shall see that

Smith played a very important part—directly and indirectly—in Amherst's attitude to coeducation.

When Smith College was established in 1871 (first class in 1875) and the Trustees were casting their nets around for a suitable president, one who should be "a first-class *man . . .*, a *man* of taste and culture fully equal to the presidents of our best New England colleges,"[23] (my emphasis) they were certain they found their man in the person of L. Clark Seelye. The Rev. L. Clark Seelye was first appointed to teach at Amherst College as the Williston Professor of Rhetoric and Oratory and English Literature in March of 1865, and, although he had intended to return to the ministry, by 1872 he was contented at Amherst, proving himself, according to W. S. Tyler, "more and more the right man in the right place,"[24] and resisting many attractive offers elsewhere. He also refused Smith's overtures for the presidency. But the fledgling college had certainly set its heart on Seelye and in the spring or early summer of 1873 a committee was formed with a view to persuading Seelye to reconsider and accept the presidency. The two most prominent members of this committee were the Rev. John M. Greene, and Professor Edwards A. Park mentioned above. The Rev. Greene was the pastor of Sophia Smith who founded Smith College as expressed in her last will and testament of May 1870. But it is interesting to note that many male writers hereafter gave the credit to pastor Greene, an Amherst graduate of the class of 1853. L. Clark Seelye himself, in writing the early history of Smith, referred to Greene as the one who "implanted in her mind [Miss Smith's] the seed-thought of a woman's college,"[25] while W. S. Tyler, of the Amherst class of 1830, referred to Greene as the "father of Smith College at Northampton"[26] without even mentioning Sophia Smith's name. Professor Park too, had earlier said that the college, though endowed by Miss Smith, "would probably never have been devised, had it not been for an alumnus of this institution [Amherst],"[27] referring also to the Rev. Greene. No doubt Greene was receptive to and he may even have encouraged Sophia Smith, but it would seem strange that such an independent and tough-minded woman did not know what to do with her money and had to wait for someone else to tell her what to do with it. Even the type of institution she wished to establish would seem to suggest independent thinking on her part.

However, the Rev. Greene's sincerity and commitment to the establishment of Smith College was undeniable and he wrote a most moving letter (a copy in his own handwriting, I have in my possession) to Seelye encouraging him to accept the presidency of the College. He reminded Seelye that:

> The enterprise is the most important educational movement of the age. It is to organize for the better education of more than half of the race. It is to restore to women her lost rights; i.e., the right of equal knowledge with men & all the influence that comes with it. The great surplus of women in Mass. makes this State the place of all others to attempt this great work. Our New England girls are just the best material for it— and you can show to the women, through Smith College, what woman is capable of; what she can do for its church, the family, the state, the women. . . .
>
> I think we have a fair prospect of turning into Smith College the interest in and about Boston on the Higher Education of Women. Of course we cannot and would not compromise in the least the religious character of the College. The College must be for Christ. To make its graduates thoroughly educated Christian women will be its work. But we can welcome as co-workers any who sympathize with that object. There are many so-called liberal men and women here who are very desirous of seeing . . . for women just what Smith College proposes. And if we are courteous (as of course we shall be) but firm and consistent they will work with us. . . .
>
> Now, dear sir, my only apology for writing this letter is my very strong desire that you become the first President of Smith College. It would afford me great satisfaction to know that you were to stand at the helm and give distinction to affairs as this College launches out to do its work in the world.
>
> I might write much more but I do hope that even this is not needed to secure from you a favorable response to the wishes of the Trustees. Ours is a most important work, a truly Christian work, and I do not know where we shall find a man whom

the Master has so fully qualified for it as yourself. It seems to
me that He calls you to it.

Please pardon my earnestness if I am too earnest, but I feel
every word that I say. . . .[28]

It was an age of earnestness indeed, but it was also an age noted for its
double entendre and Professor Park, as we already saw, was a master of this
art. In trying to influence Seelye to accept the position, Park first pointed
out the pioneer nature of the venture; it represented "a new era in the education of women," and Smith would certainly be the model for future
colleges of a similar nature; and it appeared to him "a rare privilege and a
great honor" for the new president engaged in this pioneer undertaking.
Then, one could almost "hear" a change in the tone of voice as Park pon-
tificated on another reason why Seelye should accept: "If you should take
the presidency of this institution, you would, I think, be an important
agent in settling the present dispute with regard to female education and
would be a means of preventing well-established colleges from introducing women into their existing course of study and would thus save the
community from a great amount of evil,"[29] making him consistent in his
opposition to coeducation, and the "evil" he referred to here does not re-
quire any explication.

The "present dispute" regarding female education that Park mentioned referred to that which was taking place during the decade following the American Civil War, and the debate turned, substantially, on two
major questions: first, should women simply be admitted to the existing
male colleges? Or, second, should separate new all-women colleges be
founded? Coordinate colleges or coeducation, and it is clear that the pre-
dominant thinking then argued for the former. Alexander Bullock and
Henry Ward Beecher were therefore of the minority view on this question, while Park was among the majority.

Was Seelye influenced by Park's argument that if he accepted the presidency of Smith it would be "a means of preventing well-established colleges from introducing women into their existing course of study . . ."?
We cannot be certain. But it is certain that his attendance of his niece's
graduation at Vassar while the Smith presidency was being considered,
confirmed his opinion that the Smith fund was inadequate for a "real"

college, and this helped him to decline the presidency initially. But it also made him more favorably disposed to a good education for women. He had "a clearer vision of what a college for the higher education of women might accomplish and the vision grew more attractive."[30]

In New England, at this time, the most popular form of higher education for women consisted of the usual Female Academies, Ladies' Boarding Schools or Female Seminaries of which the Mount Holyoke Female Seminary was one of the most representative. But in her will, Sophia Smith had explicitly stipulated that the college she wished to found should be on a par with the best of the existing men's colleges in New England. The institution must be designed "to furnish for my own sex means and facilities for education equal to those which are afforded now in our Colleges to young men," a part of her will read. The requirements for admission therefore, the trustees maintained, must be "substantially the same as Harvard, Yale, Brown, Amherst and other New England colleges," since she did not wish to replicate the usual female institutions. But this required more than her endowment could afford as Seelye also knew, and efforts were therefore made to increase the endowment simultaneously as efforts were made to urge Seelye to accept the presidency, and both were successful. It is tempting to guess that Greene's very sincere letter, dated May 7, 1873, a month before Seelye accepted, probably wielded as much influence as Park's. There are those who think that Smith's example prevented the continuation of the Wellesley Female Seminary founded and chartered in 1870, but changed to Wellesley College by legislative enactment in 1873. Seelye accepted the position of President of Smith College in June of 1873 although his formal inauguration did not take place until July of 1875, and he held the position for the next 37 years. It was a distinguished career and even today he is remembered with respect and affection on that campus.

His very success, however, served to put a stop to the discourse on coeducation, making Park's words prophetic. Coordinate colleges separate and at safe distances apart from men's colleges to save the community from "a great amount of evil," not coeducation, was to become the order of the day—at least in New England, while Old England was making a slightly different kind of compromise just about the same time. In the establishment of Girton College (founded 1869, one year before Sophia

Smith's will, and opened in 1873), although a part of Cambridge University, Girton was nevertheless built some convenient miles away—much away from the delightful architectural cluster of the main colleges. But even such notions were ridiculed by Gilbert and Sullivan:

> A Woman's college! maddest folly going! What can girls learn within its walls worth knowing? I'll lay a crown (the Princess shall decide it). I'll teach them twice as much in half an hour outside it.

Well, this woman's college, Smith, had a great deal to do with the lateness of Amherst's decision to admit women within its educational program. Amherst's closeness to Smith—six miles across the river, and to Mount Holyoke—ten miles over the mountain—made the college develop the concept of itself as occupying an ideal situation, unlike, for instance, Williams or Dartmouth away out there in the wilderness—*vox clamantis in Deserto* with no one in sight to respond. So the geographical nearness of the women's colleges influenced the social life of the Amherst men.

Even while a Female Seminary, Mount Holyoke contributed to the social life of Amherst College. On their different excursions, geological, mountain climbing, mountain naming or pleasure trips, the Amherst men were often entertained by what they called "the ladies of the Seminary 'over the mountain,'" George Cutting tells us in his book, *Student Life At Amherst College*. . . . On July 4, 1845 for instance, after a strenuous mountain construction of a path "to the top of Mount Holyoke," these ladies of the Seminary "provided a repast for the undefatigable toilers."[31] There also appear many other meetings with these ladies "over the mountain," which Cutting called "coincidences." One such was a pleasure excursion in 1852 by Amherst to Mount Holyoke, and here, "by a curious coincidence, they met the Ladies of Mount Holyoke Female Seminary, who had selected the same day for a visit to the mountain." Then in 1863 the Amherst freshmen made an excursion to Mount Holyoke and, "as luck would have it" there were the ladies of a Northampton Female Seminary, in this case, and, "After a 'social hour,' the class, as in duty bound, escorted home their fair friends."[32] After 1871, these "coincidences" would certainly have included Smith College.

Closer to our period, during the debate over coeducation, in the '60s, we find an Amherst College Report—the Greene Report—pointing out that the geographical nearness of the women's colleges made Amherst's "social life more 'natural', less calculated and spasmodic than was possible for the other men's colleges. For these reasons Amherst men came to accept as an article of faith the axiom that Amherst enjoyed 'the best of both possible worlds'. It shared the prestige which, in that era, accrued to the model of an eastern men's college while finding much easier access than its brother institutions to the pleasures of feminine companionship."[33] And who better to understand this than the author of the above words, Emeritus Professor Theodore P. Greene (Ted), class of 1943, who is a walking example of this fruitful relationship. His father and grandfather were alumni of Amherst, while his mother and grandmother were alumnae of Smith College. After Smith College was instituted it soon became the tradition for the "Amherst man" to marry the "Smith Lady"—then— now "woman." Smith, therefore, with its reasonably safe distance from Amherst College prevented the inconvenience of which Park spoke.

At Smith's first commencement in June of 1879—eight years after the "experiment"—for so this college was initially considered for a number of reasons—the keynote speaker, President Eliot of Harvard, considered then "one of the foremost educators of the day," was to touch on many of these points. He was pleased with the "experiment" of a collegiate education for women "without being complicated with the social experiment of bringing scores or hundreds of young men and women into intimate relations in the same institution at the excitable age of eighteen to twenty-one."[34] Smith also passed the test regarding higher education and women's health. Strange as it may seem to us, it was common currency then that higher education would seriously endanger women's health— some seeing brain fever a strong possibility, while there were those who were convinced that it would interfere with their reproductive capabilities. At his inauguration as Smith's first president, in July 1875, Seelye felt called upon to confront this burning issue, admitting that it would certainly constitute a serious objection if higher education would destroy women's health. But he did not think so. He was convinced that there was "no more danger in an intelligently arranged system of higher education for women than there is for men. Imprudence in study is subject to the same penalty as imprudence in other things, but study properly pursued is healthy."[35] But now, eight years later, at commencement, although the experiment was of short duration, Smith College was commended by President Eliot and others, for averting any serious health problems. In fact, the students were considered very healthy—"most of them stronger physically than when they entered college."[36]

The intellectual health of the college was also considered to have been in perfect form. Indeed it was said that the professors from Amherst College who were teaching certain classes at Smith had found that "the average scholarship of the young women was higher in the same studies than in the Amherst classes."[37] But what was even more important to the men was that the fear they had that higher education would have rendered the women less "eligible" was proved unfounded. So prevalent was this "fear" that, as with the issue of higher education and women's health, Seelye, at his inauguration, also dealt with this anxiety. "We wish," he declared, "it to be distinctly understood, that it is neither the aim nor the tendency of the higher education to make woman less feminine, or less attractive in those graces peculiar to her sex. It is to preserve her womanliness that this College has been founded; it is to give her the best opportunities for mental culture, and at the same time, the most favorable conditions for developing those innate capacities which have ever been the glory and charm of true womanhood. . . ."[38] Seelye's words soon became prophetic. The Smith women had not become "less womanly or less winsome" as a result of higher education; on the contrary, they had developed very "ladylike" qualities and were very desirable—witness the pairing habits the Amherst men were to pursue for instance. By 1918, at the inauguration of Smith's second president, it was stated unambiguously that Smith "sends year by year into American society a stream of young women well-fitted to be the equal mates and effective comrades of *pure, vigorous, courageous, reasoning, and aspiring* young men . . . !"[39] (My emphasis.)

Thus within the first two decades of the discourse on higher education for women, the conventional wisdom of the educated classes at least in the northeastern section of the country, considered that the matter had reached a most satisfactory conclusion thanks in large measure to Smith College. Perhaps no one has expressed this better than President Eliot of Harvard, in his commencement speech: "The discussion about the best means of giving a collegiate education to women has sprung up, raged, and been settled in New England within the past twenty years; that the conclusion in favor of separate colleges for women has been so quickly reached is in large part due to the timely munificence of Matthew Vassar, Sophia Smith, and Henry Fowle Durant"⁴⁰ (*i.e.*, for Wellesley College which followed Smith's example and established a full-fledged college, as noted above, instead of a Ladies Seminary).

The matter of coeducation was indeed so settled—at least within the northeast—that it was hardly debated again until the 1960s—nearly a century later. And, as we saw above, most of the elite colleges responded with Princeton in the lead. Amherst therefore resisted largely because of its "ideal" geographical location—close to and with institutional and other ties to neighboring women's colleges.

To be sure there were other variables that influenced the College at this time. By the '60s, Amherst had a strong institutional reluctance to expansion as it was thought that coeducation inevitably meant growth in size. By this time also the College had an acknowledged tradition of a very successful institution worthy of emulation. Witness the number of colleges that were being established elsewhere in the country, referring to themselves at times as "the Amherst of the Mid-West" or "The Amherst of the West Coast." The College was experiencing no decrease in the number of highly qualified candidates knocking at its doors for admission; nor did it have problems recruiting and maintaining good faculty. Its financial condition was sound, and, what was more, there were no legal or moral imperatives for the College to admit women. Indeed, the status quo adherents argued that to make such a drastic change would be to jeopardize most of the things prized by the College: the advantage of its small size, its ties with the sister colleges, the loyalty and generosity of its alumni; and then there were the nonquantifiable affective considerations, based on the very special rapport of a long tradition of fraternal brotherhood of the "Amherst men." And it should be noted that this transcended race lines. In reading Harold Wade's book—despite his criticisms of Amherst, when he thought it was justified—one is bound to recognize his profound sense of confraternity with the college at its best. It was generally thought that this male *esprit de corps* would be adversely affected by the presence of women and, it was those who felt this strong bonding with a male *qua* male college who argued perhaps most passionately for the status quo. Since, to this group, there were so few excellent colleges for men (at the pace co-education was going), then Amherst should remain a model of its kind and qualified males who would prefer this model should surely have the opportunity to make such a choice—especially when its geographical nearness to the women's colleges was considered.

But a closer examination of the Princeton Report we mentioned above will show that (with the exception of the desirable ties to the women's colleges) this institution shared similar favorable attributes with Amherst at the time it took the vanguard position in coeducation. Princeton took heed of the writing on the wall emerging from the social tumult of the '60s and saw in it a script for change. One eschews the notion of historical inevitability but it would seem that Amherst's options were narrowing, as the decade of the '60s came to an end and serious debates on coeducation began in 1970.

It is clear that President Calvin Plimpton, class of 1939, understood the temper of the times perfectly but whether or not he was prepared to preside over the coeducation of his *alma mater* was quite another matter. He had already left his mark on the College in many positive ways, including his favorable response to Harold Wade's recruiting policy for black men, and to the Civil Rights movement on campus. Perceiving that a radical new order was approaching, Plimpton tendered his resignation in 1971 after ten years as president. But in making this announcement, he appointed a special Long Range Planning Committee to deliberate on Amherst's future over the decade of the 1970s. The new President, a faculty member of the College, John William Ward, Professor of History and American Studies, has already been mentioned. With superb leadership, Ward took a central position on the subject rather than ducking behind delegated committees. Ted Greene observes that the President "chose to put himself at the center of the deliberations and of the controversy over this issue. Elsewhere college presidents had appointed either a faculty member or a trustee to head the committee studying coeducation, to make the recommendation to the president and the trustees, and thus to incur most of the wrath of disgruntled alumni while the president tried to maintain a mediating function throughout the process of institutional decision. Bill Ward, however, presided over all the meetings of the Select Committee on Coeducation. . . ."[41]

At the end of Ward's second year as President, he recommended to the Board of Trustees that Amherst should become a College for men and women. This was most remarkable, because, as Ted Greene tells us, Ward was not, initially, an adherent of coeducation at Amherst. But it was only after he was seriously involved in the arguments for and against the change that his doubts left him and he became committed to it, making his position resemble Patterson's at Princeton, who also was skeptical at first. But he, too, was soon strongly convinced that the change was "vital" for Princeton's future. The Amherst Board of Trustees, however, was unready for Ward's recommendation. The voting proved indecisive and a counter recommendation was made by the Trustees for a moratorium of five years before further discussions of the admission of women to Amherst be considered. The Board, for instance, felt that it would benefit the College if, during this period, more was known about the experience of other men's colleges that had recently changed to coeducation.

The moratorium period, however, was considered much too long by the faculty and students who were more amenable to coeducation (80 percent of each category, it was estimated). After heated confrontations and discussions, it was finally decided that committees be established to take into consideration different aspects of the questions raised by the Board. Thus during the academic year of 1973–74, five college committees were instituted for this purpose. They were the Committee on Educational Policy, the Committee on Priorities and Resources, the Admission Committee, a Committee on Five-College Relations, and a Visiting Committee to inquire into the experience of other comparable institutions.

After a most agonizing and divisive series of debates, the committees, for the most part, recommended coeducation for the College. The Visiting Committee, for instance, with its comparative perspective, in its impressive 67-page Report, concluded that: "The question is not whether a significant college like Amherst can with justice continue to exclude women. The question is whether Amherst can remain as significant and vital a college in the future if it does not admit women" (p. 56).

A practical answer to this proposition turns on admission. Most of the all-male colleges that were consulted reported that prior to coeducation they were losing some of their best potential freshmen, those they would most wish to keep, to other institutions. The Director of Admission at Princeton, for instance, reported that his institution lost "one third of its admitted students to other colleges. These students all too often are the very people we want most. There is no doubt whatsoever . . . that coeducation is very much a factor in their decision not to attend Princeton."[42] The college arrived at this conclusion after sending out questionnaires particularly to those who declined to attend after acceptance. Yale also had a similar experience, while Amherst's Visiting Report could find only a "very small proportion of the most promising students" who would prefer an all-male college (p. 53). But it was the Amherst Admission Committee that pronounced confidently on the relationship between coeducation and the intellectual life of the colleges: "The directors of admission at Princeton, Wesleyan and Williams unanimously agreed," it tells us, "that the quality of their applicant pools has markedly improved by the inclusion of women. They point out that not only have women brought increased excellence and diversity to the student body, but also there are indications that the institutions have become more attractive for many first-rate prospective male applicants as well" (Admission Committee, p. 5 in Casebook).

The reports of these committees are now contained in "The Casebook on Coeducation at Amherst College" and can be found in the Archives of the Frost Library. But the "Casebook" is more than the sum of the committees' report. It is, in Ward's words, "an effort to say what there is reasonably to be said on the question of coeducation at Amherst College. Before formal presentation to the Board of Trustees, the Casebook in its present form is being submitted to the scrutiny of alumni, faculty, and students of Amherst College to insure the effort is complete, that the Casebook is a thorough and fair presentation of what is at issue in the important question which the Board of Trustees will decide."[43]

As we all now know, the Board of Trustees decided in favor of the admission of women to Amherst College, after a protracted period of decision-making. In admitting that it was a "long and exhaustive" exercise, the Board felt that it was, "perhaps the most important question to come before the Trustees of Amherst College in the twentieth century"; and this is easily understood in the light of our study of the subject since 1871.

But in agreeing to coeducation the Board hoped that the College would maintain all its special features that made it a pre-eminent liberal arts college. It was hoped, for instance, that the alumni would not be estranged from the decision. The Board knew that the College would continue to need the strong support of its alumni, and was hopeful that such a support would continue.

In making their recommendations the Trustees voted that from the academic year of 1975–76, the College would admit women as transfer students in the sophomore and junior classes, while in the academic year of 1976–77, they would be admitted in the Freshman Class. (See Appendix D, pp. 1 and 2).

Part II

Women were now admitted to Amherst College after well over one hundred and fifty years of its existence, without any stipulations based on race, creed or color. The College thus continued to demonstrate its capacity for self-reform, evolving first from a narrowly-focused evangelical institution, established for the training of young men for the Christian ministry, and then to a liberal arts institution. As a Christian establishment designed for the Classical Education "of indigent young men of piety and talents for the Christian Ministry," it excluded not only women in general, but, although it did not, technically, exclude all other religious faiths, nevertheless, its orientation was Puritan orthodoxy, making even Catholic males of whatever color not automatically welcome. In effect, therefore, only Protestant males were welcome, and these were, for the most part, given the nature then of American society, of white Anglo-Saxon extraction. To be sure, Protestant black males were also eligible to be admitted from the beginning of the college—other things being equal. But other things were certainly not quite equal because America was then a slave society where blacks were held as property, and in the eyes of the law were viewed as non-persons.

Slavery was a common practice in Amherst and its environs at least up to the end of the American War of Independence. Most of the very prominent people of "Quality," the pillars of society—in the manner of

Ibsen—owned slaves. Among the most distinguished of this class was the Rev. David Parsons, Jr., first minister of the First Congregational Church in the "Third Precinct of Hadley" (as Amherst was called until 1759). Although his appointment was not formalized until 1739, nevertheless he began his ministry from 1735 until 1780, when his son of the same name succeeded him. The son, the Rev. Dr. David Parsons, was one of the founders of Amherst College.[44] As President of the Board of Trustees of the Amherst Academy which together with the First Church established the charitable fund for the founding of Amherst College, he presided over the ceremony of laying the first cornerstone for the College, and his contribution of $600 to the charitable fund was among the most generous. James Avery Smith, in his elegant, pioneer article, "Age, Estate, and Quality," reminds us that: "The members of the church, in prewar Amherst, owned African slaves. Between 1737 and 1770 there were twelve *identified* slave owners (all men) at Amherst . . . three . . . were Parsons and the two sons of Isaac Chauncey, the pastor of the First Church of Hadley . . . ," and then he pointed out that, in Amherst, "Slave ownership raised the perception of one's Quality," and, like "other slave owners in town," men like the Rev. Parsons speculated heavily in lands. He bought large tracts of land in Vermont, sold about 100 acres in Belchertown in 1769 and "dabbled in Amherst real estate." He used his slave labor to farm his land, and, as a man "wise in the ways of earthly Mammon," he also operated a "tavern with the aid of his slave family which was headed by a man called Pomp [Pompey]."[45] New England's peculiar morality at this time saw to it that slaves attend church. Indeed there were special seats "reserved" in church for them. Pompey and his family (a wife and a son) attended church and Pompey was a communicant member of Parsons's church, where his wife, Rose, and his son Goffy were baptized by the Rev. David Parsons, Jr., himself, and, what was more, this was done at the same service (in January 1749) when Parsons baptized David, his own son![46] But the analogy stopped there. Goffy was Parsons's property who would soon be toiling on his estates, while David, his son, would soon be sent off to Harvard (from where he graduated in 1771, and by 1800 was awarded the degree of Doctor of Divinity from Brown University and was destined to be, as noted above, the first president of the Board of Trustees first of the Amherst Academy and therefore of Amherst College before resigning in favor of Noah Webster immediately after the laying of the first cornerstone).[47]

Parsons died leaving a large fortune. His extensive real estate in Amherst alone, we are told, included the large home farm "(which extended South from near Snell Street to the present Amherst Golf Course) [which] contained his large dwelling house, a Tavern house, a barn, and the 'old house' (this last house being on or near where the Amherst College President's house now stands)."[48]

It appears, however, that Parsons clerical democracy did not extend to the world of Mammon, for in his detailed will we see nothing left for Pompey and his family, and his other slaves.[49] In that, therefore, the Parsons's great wealth (father and son) was enhanced by slave labor, facilitating the son's contribution of $600 initially (in addition to more later) to the *permanent* Charity Fund that established Amherst College, then blacks in this country could safely claim to have contributed to the establishment of the College—even if indirectly. It is somewhat surprising that Harold Wade has mentioned the historical fact of slavery in Amherst only in a footnote, when he said that the first recorded blacks in Amherst were 3 slaves mentioned in 1738.[50] Without a doubt the history of slavery in Amherst is yet to be written.

PIONEERS: EDWARD JONES, CLASS OF 1826, AND BLACK WOMEN, CLASS OF 1980

Yet, by a strange quirk of history, it can truly be said that Amherst College had no official discrimination policy based on racial grounds at its inception. And the living example of this is to be found in the person of Edward Jones, a black man—visibly black and not "passing"—who entered the college in 1822, one year after its establishment. It was this that prompted Harold Wade to exclaim that Amherst College had a long tradition of "black history"; it was a history the College could "be proud of; it 'discovered' the black American long before it became fashionable to do so."[51]

Edward Jones is therefore as much a pioneer—perhaps much more so—than the black women who first entered Amherst College in the freshman class of 1976–77. We are certain that these black women would be curious to know something of Jones's experience here between the years 1822–26. Unfortunately we have nothing directly from Jones in terms of his thoughts about his life and treatment at Amherst. But we do know that he was from Charleston, South Carolina, with his birth date given as "about" 1808, which would find him as a freshman at Amherst at the tender age of "about" 14 years. This was not altogether unusual at that time, and it appears that during the first four years of the "Collegiate Institution," as Amherst was called until after February 1825, when it received its charter, there were no age stipulations for entering. We first discover this in the Catalogue of October 1825, with the new name for the institution, "Amherst College," now enjoying its hard-won charter since February of that year. Under "Terms of Admissions," the catalogue dealt with "age" among other things. It said that no one was to be admitted "to the Freshman Class until he has completed his fourteenth year nor to any advanced standing without a corresponding increase of age." This was repeated in the catalogue of 1826 and thereafter. It is curious though, that Heman Humphrey, who was president at this time, was later, as ex-president, to exhort the alumni at his commencement address in 1853, not to send their sons to college "*too early.* . . . In rare cases, lads of fourteen and even younger, have taken rank with the first scholars, and graduated with high honors." He recommended sixteen, or seventeen, and even eighteen, as "far better than fourteen."[52] Does this mean that the age stipulation was a dead letter?

Although from a slave state, Jones himself was never a slave, having come from a freed black family, with a father, Jehu Jones, generally characterized as a prosperous businessman, the owner of the leading hotel in Charleston. Jehu Jones must have had a great influence on young Edward. The father was well thought of in his catering establishment, and was viewed as a man of impeccable character. A contemporary who knew him well described him as "active, enterprising, intelligent, honest to the letter,—one whose integrity and responsibility were never doubted"[53]—all good Puritan qualities which, if the son imbibed, would certainly have groomed him perfectly for the Amherst of 1822–1826.

How was Jones treated at the Institution/College? As said earlier, we have not heard from him in this regard but we can begin to garner shreds of evidence here and there and try to arrive at even a tentative conclusion. Of his Freshman Class numbering 40 students, he was the only *known* black—"colored" then—just as he was the only one whose address was South Carolina. Was he also the only one with a southern accent? Most of the others from his class were from Massachusetts, with the exception of two from New York State, five from New Hampshire, three from Connecticut and one from Pennsylvania. When it is remembered that the pious and indigent men to be educated at the Collegiate Institution were to be supplied from New England's countryside, then the geographical homogeneity is understandable. And this is why the question of why the Jones's family from Charleston, South Carolina, chose Amherst for the education of their very young son is so intriguing; but it has not yet been answered. In listing their names, the college catalogues not only gave their home addresses but also their room numbers on campus. We shall therefore follow Jones between 1822 and 1826 to find out if he shared rooms, and with whom. As a freshman in 1822 (Catalogue of October, 1822) we find him in Room 10s (South) sharing with Robert Cutler from Amherst. In his sophomore year, we find him still in the preferred southern rooms, in this case, in Room 26s, sharing with Calvin Babbitt from Hartwick, New York. But Jones's address has now changed to "New York City." Thanks to Professor Hugh Hawkins,[54] we have discovered that this change had its basis in slavery, when in 1822 Denmark Vesey's intended slave uprising in Charleston, Jones's home town, was discovered. Whites were terrified and not only were 35 blacks hanged, but they passed a law making it illegal for any free blacks who were out of the state to return. It is said that Jones's mother was also out of the state, visiting or living in New York; therefore, mother and son were exiled, and as far as we know Edward Jones never returned to Charleston.

In his junior year, Jones is still rooming in the southern building, in this case, Room 9s, and back again to sharing with Robert Cutler from Amherst. In his senior year, with the October catalogue of 1825 for the first time titled, "Amherst College," the College having now received its charter, we find Jones still listing his residence as New York City, sharing Room 25s with Artemas Thompson from Hinsdale. From all this, so far, we have no evidence to suggest any unpleasantness arising from his sharing with his fellow white students—repeating with Robert Cutler from Amherst in his freshman and junior years. An alumnus writing under the heading "Reminiscence" in the *Amherst Student* (of December 4, 1875,

Vol. IX, No. 5), who claimed to have been a contemporary of Jones, said of him, "Notwithstanding the disadvantage of his color (then greater than at present), he was well received by both teachers and pupils,—passing through college without encountering any serious impediments or mortifications." This, of course should be taken for what it is worth, because as a white, how could he know—necessarily—of impediments or mortifications Jones might have encountered?

W. S. Tyler tells us that "soon after the opening of the Institution,"[55] two literary societies were organized, the Alexandrian and the Athenian, to which students were first allotted alphabetically, and later by elective affinity. Jones belonged to the Athenian Society, and George R. Cutting, an alumnus already mentioned, said that "though they [the Athenian Society] had *fewer* men, these were acknowledged to be of *more substantial character*."[56] It is noteworthy that the renowned lexicographer, Noah Webster, was an honorary member of the Athenian Society. Electing "eminent" and "prominent" citizens as honorary members to these Societies was a part of the rivalry that developed between them. "The Athenians deemed it quite an occasion," Cutting observed, "when Noah Webster, L.L.D., . . . attended a regular meeting of their society, and, at its close, delivered an address to the members."[57] Among Jones's roommates, Calvin Babbitt and Artemas Thompson also belonged to the Athenians, but it is curious that there is no listing for Robert Cutler for either Society. We are told that the students fell into these societies "as naturally and spontaneously as all the citizens of a town or of the country fall into one or other of two great parties. And the members of the Societies no more thought of being absent from the weekly meetings than a good citizen would absent himself from the polls. . . ."[58] The Rev. Packard, for instance, class of 1823, regarded "these Societies to have been more beneficial to their members in writing, declamation and debate, than all the College exercises in these departments," an opinion also shared by many other alumni including W. S. Tyler and George Cutting.[59] Later we shall show how these Societies, particularly the Athenian, contributed to the establishment of the library of Amherst College—now Frost Library.

There is every reason to think that young Jones fell naturally into the spirit of these societies which could be considered as having foreshadowed the fraternities at Amherst. Yet, these later fraternities would not have admitted Jones on grounds of race. Indeed only white Protestant Anglo-Saxon males were included, until during President Cole's administration (1946–1960) when he tried to prohibit restrictions based on race, color or creed, and it is possible that Thomas Gibbs was the first black— perhaps the first "other"—to have been admitted to an Amherst fraternity, Phi Kappa Psi in 1948. In admitting Gibbs, the Amherst chapter had defied rules of the national headquarters, and this led to the revocation of the Amherst charter. The incident received national attention and gained Amherst much commendation. The *New York Times*, for instance, said: "In this episode we see the real meaning of a liberal education. An Amherst degree has always been respected. It will be more respected now." Wade has not mentioned the episode with the fraternity but he tells us that the Rev. Thomas W. Gibbs '51 went on to become Dean of the Episcopalian All Saints Cathedral in the Caribbean island of St. Thomas, whence he came.[60]

We have next to nothing of what Jones thought about his contemporaries, students or faculty or what they might have thought about him. We would like to know for instance, what Robert Cutler, with whom he shared rooms on two occasions, had to say about him, and *vice versa*. Its only from the second president of the College, the Rev. Dr. Heman Humphrey, that we have some remarks concerning Jones, apart, that is, from the few general anonymous remarks we quoted from "Reminiscence." Humphrey, who assumed the presidency in 1823 after the death of President Moore, would have known Jones from his sophomore days through to the senior year. At an address to the "Gentlemen Alumni" of Amherst College, delivered in Johnson Chapel at the Commencement of August 1853, the President Emeritus would seem to have been congratulating Jones's classmates and the College, for having treated him "as a brother student." In the course of his address, he proudly referred to the many from among them who were engaged in missionary works in foreign parts, as God's "good soldiers," and within this context he mentioned Jones in a rather odd way. He said, "I could perhaps select some, who deserve the most honorable mention; but I shall name only one, and not him, as if I would place him at the head of the list, but for reason which you will see in a moment"—sounding like a back-handed compliment at best. Then he went on: "Some of you remember *Edward Jones* of the class of 1826. Though his skin was darker than your own, I rejoice to testify here, that you treated him as a brother student; and it was with no ordinary satisfaction, that when you graduated we gave him his diploma with the rest." Humphrey then related that Jones was serving in Sierra Leone in West Africa, "having made a profession of religion," and taken orders in the Episcopal Church and thereafter became a chaplain to one of the British regiments stationed in Sierra Leone[61]—all of which is correct.

There can be no doubt that Humphrey was interested in Jones's career after his graduation, for mixed reasons. When, for instance, in 1830 Jones was "admitted to the Holy Orders of Priests" at Christ Church in Hartford, Connecticut, Humphrey is said to have been in attendance.[62] As a very devout man himself, "a zealous champion of orthodoxy, evangelical religion, Christian missions, and of all the distinctive principles of the founders of Amherst College. . . ."[63] Humphrey must have been proud of his charge, notwithstanding Jones's "conversion" to episcopalianism.

In truth we do not know if Edward Jones "converted" to the episcopal order. The College was built on orthodox Congregationalism but we do not know if Jones was of this persuasion. When Humphrey assumed the office of presidency, the student body consisted of a total of 146, and of these some "ninety-eight were hopefully pious," but it does not appear that Jones was among them. This inference is based on the results of the great Christian revival of 1823, where most of the Amherst students became converted. It was "so pervading," according to Tyler, "that all the irreligious, except one, were said to be under conviction." Was this one exception Edward Jones? We cannot be too certain because we do not know if Tyler is using the word "irreligious" interchangeably with "unconverted." But a few pages later he tells us that the influence of the revival was so strong that it extended even to those who were not reckoned as converts. "Thus Edward Jones, the colored student of the Class of '26, who was counted among the unconverted at the close of the revival, soon after his graduation went out as a missionary to Sierra Leone, and became one of the leading educators of that African State."[64] Therefore, when Humphrey attended the ordination of the Rev. Edward Jones in 1830, he must have been pleased that the unconverted young man of 1823 was not completely lost—despite his slight apostasy. At the commencement address, Humphrey told us that "[f]or a number of years" he had "entirely lost sight of him [Edward Jones] till I met the Rev. Mr. Wilson, of the Gaboon [Gabon] mission, who tells me, that touching at Sierra Leone, on his return to this country, he found Mr. Jones there, heard him preach and was exceedingly interested in what he saw and heard of him. Mr. Wilson says, that he found him one of the most intelligent, respectable and useful men in the colony; an able and popular preacher; secretary of the Episcopal board of missions, and teacher of Hebrew in a collegiate institution, whose curriculum embraces nearly all the branches of a liberal education, which are taught in our American colleges. Who of you, if Edward Jones were here today, would not be proud to grasp his hand and call him brother? It is by such men, chiefly of her own children, that Africa is to be redeemed."[65] Hidden in this last sentence is the other rationale (apart from his sincere interest in Christian evangelical missions abroad), for his interest in Jones's career.

The Rev. Mr. Wilson certainly had a fairly accurate account of the Rev. Edward Jones, although we are not given a time frame. After leaving government service as chaplain, Jones in 1841 became principal of an institution that uncannily resembled the Amherst College he attended: the "Christian Institution," as it was called, was founded by the British Christian Missionary Society (CMS) in 1814—just about the time the Amherst Academy was founded and which was to found the "Collegiate Institution" in 1821. And inasmuch as the Collegiate Institution was to become Amherst College (1825), so was Jones's "Christian Institution" to become the Fourah Bay Institution which evolved into the degree-granting Fourah Bay College by 1848. This is clearly what Wilson referred to as the "collegiate institution." Jones must have felt at home in this institution with its religious earnestness combined with a rigorous regimen of Latin and Greek, Hebrew and Arabic. Altogether the focus was on a classical education with the singular difference that the curriculum included, and *stressed*, West African languages (for historical reasons we cannot pursue here). Like Amherst, Fourah Bay College was also meant for the training of men, primarily as Christian missionaries and teachers.

But when Humphrey ended with the homily that Africa would be "redeemed" by men like Jones, one of "her own children," he was, in fact, stating a philosophy that was near and dear to him. He was convinced that free blacks would not sit well in American society and was thus an active member of the Colonization Society that sought to repatriate all free Afro-Americans back to Africa, not only as a "liberal solution" to the real and potential race problems in America but also to the formal abolition of slavery.[66]

We have yet another President of Amherst who commented on Jones. This was the third President, the Rev. Dr. Edward Hitchcock, in his *Reminiscences of Amherst College*, published in 1863—two years before Jones's death. In reflecting on "College Honors," Hitchcock reiterated the importance of college societies when he placed them with college honors as among "the two most powerful influences" brought to bear on Amherst students then. As we already know, Edward Jones was a member of the Athenian Society, but he was not listed under any of the honors proffered by the College. His listing, with 11 others, went under the heading, "No Appointment," where he was quaintly entered as "Edward Jones, 1826, (Col'd.)." Hitchcock was here impugning the sense of mortification and defeat young men felt at Commencements when they did not receive any honors, considering that "such names as Edward Jones, Aldin Grout William Walker and Henry M. Adams [were] on the list of non-appointees. . . ." These were all missionaries of repute, and, to Hitchcock, their missionary labors would probably lead to "some strange inversions of Faculty decisions." And "one very striking case among these missionary non-appointees, [was] that of Edward Jones."—the only colored student who ever graduated from Amherst. Hitchcock then related that Jones went to Liberia as a missionary of the Episcopal church, but indeed we have no evidence to suggest that Jones went to Liberia although he was expected to have gone there. However, Hitchcock did finally place the Rev. Edward Jones where he belonged—in Sierra Leone, and as President of the Fourah Bay College. Ex-president Hitchcock then recounted with sadness how the English bishops had discussed the question of making Jones a bishop but "the only reason why it is not done is that such a dignity has never been conferred upon a colored man. It is not probable that many of our highest missionary appointees will get ahead of President Jones in rank and dignity."[67]

Jones's admission to Amherst was also atypical in other ways. As we might remind ourselves, the College was established by a Charity Fund for the gratuitous instruction of "indigent young men of promising talents and hopeful piety, who shall manifest a desire to obtain a liberal education with a sole view to the Christian ministry." From the evidence there appear to have been many pious young men and older adults raring to go forth to preach the Word, but could not afford the training for this calling. The Rev. Charles Shepard of the Class of 1825 knew many of this type: "Most of my fellows were mature youths who did not appear to me youths at all, serious in character and manlike in purpose, with an air which seemed to tell of years of yearning for the ministry, and of a brave struggle with the poverty which had kept them from their goal. They seized their late opportunity with eagerness. . . . The Institution was formed for just such pupils."[68] Not so, with Edward Jones. He was young—a mere teenager of "about" 14, and it would be unrealistic to expect that he would have had missionary zeal in his blood at this time. He was from a wealthy family who paid his keep. The term bills consisting of tuition, room lodging, and other small fees were from ten to eleven dollars a term from 1822 to 1824; in addition, payment for board was from one to one and a quarter dollars per week; wood, from one dollar fifty cents to two dollars a cord, while washing cost from twelve to twenty cents per week. Beneficiaries—those struggling with poverty—did not pay term bills but paid other costs if they could. In many cases they could not and some townspeople, particularly housewives, often came to their assistance. It is in this and other contexts that we can even begin to understand the extent to which women have contributed to the development of Amherst College.[69]

But from 1824 inflation began to take its toll in small ways: instead of boarding being, for instance, *from* one dollar *to* one and a quarter dollars per week, it was now the latter, pure and simple, while wood, which was from one dollar fifty cents to two dollars a cord now became one dollar seventy five cents to two dollars a cord. But it was after the College was chartered that the costs rose astronomically, and even the manner of payment became more legalized and formal. Like the age requirement at this time, the state might have influenced these changes. It was now required that the first term's bill be paid by each student upon admission, while a bond of two hundred dollars "for the payment of College bills, must be given within one Term" except by the students who were beneficiaries of charitable associations.

The annual expenses were computed in this manner:

College Bills	$36
Board	$50
Fuel and Light	$05
Washing	$05
Total	$96

An addendum said: "There are several expenses of smaller amount, not included in the above statement, which vary with circumstances, so that no estimate of them can be made."[70]

Thus, in his senior year, Edward Jones, not a beneficiary of charitable associations, nor an "indigent pious youth," had his heftily increased bills paid by his wealthy parents.

Edward Jones went against the grain of popular notions today regarding affirmative actions, financial aid, equal opportunity and all that. And it was just as well for the likes of Jones that the first president of the institution had asked what could safely be called the first affirmative action/equal opportunity question raised at Amherst College. Noting that admission to the college was for the "indigent," before assuming the presidency, the Rev. Zephaniah Swift Moore, in his acceptance letter of June 12, 1821, wanted assurance from the Trustees that non-indigent students would also be eligible for admission.[71] He received it, and the likes of Jones was spared this type of discrimination! The irony is stark.

One must observe here that a full biography of Amherst's first black alumnus is long overdue. His distinguished career in Sierra Leone is particularly little known in any systematic manner. Yet the primary sources are readily available in both Sierra Leone and the impressive repositories in Britain. In the meantime, I find Christopher Fyfe's view of Edward Jones in Sierra Leone most knowledgeable and nuanced. Fyfe, a British historian, now emeritus from the University of Edinburgh, has written great works on Sierra Leone, the authority of which have never been questioned: He recounted that Jones was

> persecuted by a half-crazy governor before transferring from
> government to C.M.S. service. Though relaxed and easygoing

in his everyday manner, he was reserved and sensitive, reacting sharply when roused. White colleagues resented his outspoken opinions. He represented the heritage of protest against racial oppression, otherwise almost absent from the Colony at this time. Such a man opened his students' eyes to a world beyond their little Creole homeland and that of their white teachers in Europe.[72]

It should be of interest to note that Fyfe made this evaluation in a biography that he wrote on one of the Rev. Edward Jones's students, Africanus Horton. As President of Fourah Bay College, Jones taught Horton who was to become a most distinguished scientist and author of West Africa. Horton is said to have accompanied Jones on an expedition in 1853 to investigate the prospects for a Christian mission among the Ibo people to match that already existing among the Yorubas, in which Jones most probably participated. The Ibo mission was eventually founded at Onitsha on the Niger.[73] Jones was thus in line with the veritable mandate of the early Amherst graduates who were expected to be Christian missionaries, planting, in the process, "a church on the burning sands of Africa or in the cheerless wilds of Siberia. . . ." They were to be the "instrument[s] of converting a family, a province, perhaps a kingdom of Pagans and bringing them within the pale of the Christian church!," in the ringing words of Noah Webster, on the occasion of the laying of the first cornerstone of the College.[74]

From the evidence as we know it so far, Edward Jones was the first and only black to have attended Amherst College even long after his death in 1865. Harold Wade is clearly incorrect and confusing when he listed Robert Purvis as another black who attended Amherst and graduated with Jones in the class of 1826. But earlier he had said that "Jones's Amherst colleague, Robert Purvis . . . reportedly entered at about the same time but he did not complete the college course." In truth, the College has no record of Robert Purvis ever attending, and Wade himself obtained this information from secondary sources and not from the records of the College.[75] It is thought that some black men attended the College after the American Civil War, but these have not been traced by Wade, until the class of 1892 when the records are clear. He was certain that "there were blacks at Amherst in the 1870s, but their names are now unknown."[76] Not entirely, for we know the name of Charles H. Moore, for instance, class of 1878, and with further research, as I hope will be done to update Wade's admirable pioneer work, as said earlier, more of these graduates might be discovered.

But the class of 1892 had some interesting black graduates who required at least some passing mention. They were William Henry Lewis, William Sherman Jackson and George Washington Forbes. All three men were to move on to make their marks on society, Jackson being of particular importance to us because he was responsible for what Harold Wade called "the Golden Age of Dunbar High School in Washington."[77] Here he taught from 1912 to 1931 and was pivotal in making a name for the school, as he was influential, according to Wade, in persuading men like Charles Houston, Montague Cobb, William Hastie, Charles Drew, Mercer Cook and many others to attend Amherst. This all-black high school gained such a reputation that Amherst was proud to accept its graduates. Wade tells us that Eugene Wilson, as Dean of Admission, was to visit Dunbar High School routinely for the purpose of recruiting bright blacks for Amherst, and Dunbar "was virtually a black prep school."[78] All three men entered the College older than Edward Jones: Forbes at 24, Jackson at 23 and Lewis, the youngest, at 20 but still six years older than the time of Jones's entry. Wade has not told us much about the family fortunes of Jackson and Forbes, but Lewis would certainly have satisfied the original indigency requirement for admission. He had to work at numerous odd jobs and, with "money earned by working in hotels and restaurants, the industrious Lewis was able to enroll at Amherst College in 1888." At Amherst he continued performing different "chores, including tending to President Julius H. Seelye's horse." This was Lewis's most fortunate encounter for the considerate Seelye was to hand him "one morning" his tuition. And when the surprised Lewis enquired of its source, the President said that "the Lord had sent the money,"[79] making the story again resemble the original orientation of the College—the College Jones knew, not from his own personal financial experience, but from association.

G. W. Forbes, undeservedly not much known, has nevertheless made great contributions to society by fighting for the rights of blacks and other minorities through his journalistic writings. When in 1896 he became the first and only black librarian in the Boston Public Library, he was to assist, in no small way, immigrant Jews in the West End of Boston. This was so noticeable that it generated articles such as, "George Forbes of Boston—a servant of Jew and Gentile" (in *The Crisis* XXXIV, July 1927). Perhaps the best testament to his work in this regard came from the Jewish *Daily Forward* upon the occasion of Forbes's death in 1927. The paper acknowledged that Forbes, "through his knowledge and intelligence and good human heart helped tens and hundreds of intelligent Jews to get on their feet. A great many Jewish doctors, lawyers, engineers and men of other professions have reached their success, or owe a great part of their success, to this Negro."[80] Ted Greene, for his part, has picked out Forbes as one of his favorites of Wade's black alumni of Amherst. He is impressed by the fact that Forbes served his people in the West End of Boston and when they moved out and the Jews arrived, he "sustained his writing and research on the history of his own people while helping another oppressed group to fulfill their own needs for the knowledge he had to offer."[81]

BLACK WOMEN OF THE PIONEER CLASS OF 1980

Of the 129 women who graduated from this class, 18 were black. These are their names in alphabetical order:

Melbia V. Andrews
Lydia I. Blackwood
Laura P. Carrington
Wendy A. (Ross) Drew
Denise M. Francois
Karla R. Fuller
Audrey L. Garrett
Beryl E. Kenney
Tara L. (Fuller) Lamourt
Linder F. Lane
Elaine Levison-Williams
Sheila Y. (Newsome) Maddox
Amina R. Merritt

Susan M. Prattis
Gloriana (Marshall) Sabestian Tecuma
Le Ann Shelton
Berdette E. Thompson
Lynda A. Wright

These women are true pioneers in terms of gender—almost as much as Edward Jones was in terms of race. The black men after 1826 at least had a reference point in Jones, but, with respect to gender, these women had neither white nor any other female "model."

This pioneer class of black women is truly remarkable. From the vantage point of reading their personal statements, I soon discovered a certain grit and determination that came to characterize them all. They knew their worth; they knew they had a place in history and were determined not to allow all the expected and unexpected and seemingly insoluble difficulties prevent them from succeeding. Karla Fuller, for instance, remembers how her pioneer situation at Amherst College helped her in the workplace, especially when she found herself the only Afro-American woman "working at the managerial level. Being one of the first women and one of only a handful of African-American women at Amherst College made any other situation look easy by comparison. My ability to cope independently . . . has come from the experience of being in the first class of women at Amherst." And, most important, these women knew that to succeed they had to work hard. They are, without a doubt, among the type of women that Kim Townsend described as "more than most students—eager to learn. The women I have in mind usually sat in the front row—usually off to the side. From that position they would be less likely to be distracted, less likely to miss anything, and from there they could also keep their eye on me. From there I have often heard voices correcting me—especially in my course on The Literature of the Civil Rights Movement. On a point of fact, a pronunciation, or an interpretation, I have stood corrected—not harshly, not so that I couldn't remain standing, but obviously corrected. On one occasion a woman came from her assigned section of the old ILS [Introduction to Liberal Studies] course on 'Race and Sex' into mine in order to question the validity of the assumptions that she feared—with justification, as I look back—informed the course. As a rule—if less dramatically—all the women I have in mind attended and cared. They were there in class—not just present in class, but engaged. And they were there in my office if class did not make things clear or otherwise live up to their expectations. I think of them as having been here to learn."

Thanks to the intelligent exertions of Harold Wade and others, when the women arrived they found certain institutions and organizations that could help to make them feel "at home." The Black Cultural Center, now also named the Gerald Penny Center, was already established in the Octagon building. By some strange twist of ironic history, the site of the Octagon was that of the original meeting house—"on the highest hill in the town"—of the First Congregational Church, which discriminated against blacks for most of its early history. Up to 1828 the church authorities voted that "no person shall sell or lease his or her pew to any black or mulatto."[82] Even more ironic is the fact we mentioned earlier that the first minister of this church was the prosperous, slave-owning Rev. David Parsons, to be succeeded by his son, the Rev. Dr. David Parsons, the Harvard graduate and merchant in his own right. The son had later managed his father's vast business enterprise and both of them together occupied the pulpit in Amherst for 82 years consecutively. Ted Greene sees the Black Cultural Center as "a dramatic, visible recognition of the felt need to create in Amherst some consciousness and some respected place for the values of Afro-American culture. It was also the place where the black students of Amherst College . . . could preserve an identity of their own within the larger cultural community of the college and the town."[83] And the testimony of most of these black alumnae from different backgrounds proved Greene correct. Repeatedly they stated how the presence of this cultural center helped them to "fit in," giving them a safe anchor from which to proceed to grow and to which they could always return for mutual support.

These women also had the Charles Drew House (formerly Phi Alpha Psi), which was soon to develop into a "Black House"—or "The House" as they fondly called it. Amina Merritt for instance, was closely connected with "The House" which had a profound influence on her. She informed us that she first became acquainted with it as early as 1975 even before entering Amherst College. She was visiting and "was so impressed, because all the brothers seemed to be close, it was like a home. But often it was quiet and when I met people they were interested in me and I learned a lot. I also found that many of the people who lived in The House . . . were attempting to be economics or science/pre-med majors. I say 'attempting to' because it was a topic of discussion at the House among many students whether there was a conspiracy to keep us out of the sciences [and] whether we should just give up. . . ." But it appears that Charles Drew House then had a number of earnest and exemplary young men who became good role-models for Anima. They worked hard and were determined to succeed despite the discriminations they perceived. "A perfect example of a Charles Drew resident who persevered in these areas," Amina observed, "is Keith Rawlings, who was featured in *Amherst* magazine this quarter . . . [and] was one of those gentlemen in the tradition of Charles Drew who studied hard and became an important person in his community." Amina saw Drew House as "the reason other blacks could make it through Amherst," as it also had a cultural component, one that sought to preserve and celebrate black culture. It seems most fitting that Amina was to become the first woman president of Charles Drew House, whose name was *officially* dedicated through her efforts, as will be seen under her biographical profile.

The artistic Sonya Clarke '89 indeed used Charles Drew House to good purpose for her creative and cultural activities. She organized a Fashion Show called "Adornment of African People," as well as the communal construction of a magnificent "pieced quilt," with the cooperation of the women of the Black Students Union—"a celebration of the creativity of black women"—she named it, and these are just a few among other interesting creative endeavors. For more on Sonya Clarke, see her biographical outline under the class of '89.

The black men of the '60s were also responsible for the establishment of the Black Studies Department at the College. This Department was meant to concentrate critically on black history and culture from Africa to its Diaspora, and it seems most fitting that one of the first undergraduate Senior theses coming from this Department was on Edward Jones: "The Life and Times of Edward Jones: Sower of the African Diaspora," by Stephen Herbert Keith '73, for which he received a *magna cum laude*, under the supervision of Professor Asa Davis. Back then some of the brightest of black students would major in the Black Studies Department—from choice. These black women also found the Afro-American Society well established—an organization Wade and his group used so positively and intelligently to effect positive changes. The most visible example of this, as noted earlier, could be seen in the increased enrollment of black men and other ethnic groups in the '60s, but particularly in the 1970s.

Thus the Amherst College that these black women of the Class of '80 entered was vastly different from that of Edward Jones. There was now diversity, not only in terms of gender but also of race and religion. They came into a milieu generated by the '60s where it was fashionable to stress one's difference or one's ethnicity. Harold Wade acknowledges the configurations from the time when blacks and other ethnic groups strove to be what he calls "WASP-types," but, to him "the 1960s saw the arrival of ethnic-type blacks."[84] The conversion made itself outwardly apparent in terms of dress—the donning of African styles and other sartorial modes, stressing also African fabrics and elaborate "Afro" hair styles. (We cannot, even for a moment, imagine Edward Jones with an "Afro" hair style!) Wade tells us how his generation of students came under the influence of black nationalism and the Black Power Movement, with its slogan of "Black is Beautiful" which was really intended to shore up the confidence of an oppressed people. Black culture, often suppressed by the black bourgeoisie, was now openly embraced. With his usual sardonic wit, Wade explains how these "'converted Negroes' who had quietly played their soul music beyond hearing range of whites . . . now found themselves proud *exponents* of their culture, which many white students unconsciously adopted as their own." This is certainly in contrast to blacks before the '60s who took pride in their ability to imitate "Wasp ways and deny their own heritage." But what was more, the College authorities of that earlier time encouraged this, according to Wade. They "took pride" in the WASP-ness of "their Negroes."[85] But all this was to change with the '60s.

There was also diversity in terms of curricular offerings that would have made our chief referent, Edward Jones, probably quite bemused. His catalogue consisted originally of "a single sheet, about 12 by 14 inches in size, and printed only on one side, like a hand-bill,"[86] and on this, names and titles of faculty, president and students were printed. Tyler tells us that these early students were very dissatisfied with this skimpy affair and the same month of the same year (March 1822) reissued the same catalogue in the form of a pamphlet of eight pages, but added three important pieces of information which would certainly be useful to prospective students. Added were, first, the requirements for admission to the freshman's class, second, an outline of the course of study, and third, a statement of the number of books in the library and the literary societies. It is clear that they did not follow through with this last addition, probably because it was simply not easy to keep a regular count on books in a new developing library. In March of 1822, 900 volumes were listed as belonging to the "Institution," while the Society libraries, together, possessed 400 volumes. From these catalogues with requirements for admission, for the first, second, third and fourth years, it will be noted that the stress was on a classical education. Class instructions consisted largely of recitations from Greek texts, and numerous exercises in speaking and composition, and it is no wonder that the Societies were so useful in improving these skills. Every course was required for each student and even the particular book for each course was preordained as the catalogues will reveal. The studied restrictiveness of this education of Jones's times "was," in Ted Greene's words, "to discipline the faculties of the mind, to inculcate the great truth already revealed, and, if possible, to awaken in the student a sense of Christian grace and of Christian vocation."[87] Or, to put it another way, it was not meant to open the mind too wide but to drill it deep with discipline and piety.

It is not too surprising, therefore, that not much attention was paid to libraries at this time. "The college library" says George Cutting, "was then [1820s] very small, and ill-adapted to the growing wants of the students; indeed it was all contained in a single case 6 feet wide, placed in the north entry of South College."[88] W. S. Tyler also said that, "Our library did not surpass the scholarly range of a country clergyman in fair circumstances. Apparatus and collections were unknown in our first year, and they had made but feeble beginnings before our graduations."[89] Indeed it was the Societies, particularly the Athenian, through creative and intelligent efforts, that first paid serious attention to the development of library resources at the College. To Cutting, the main object of these Societies was the "general improvement in literature and oratory, [which] could not be attained without access to a different class of books,"[90] that is, apart from those rigidly stipulated and required for the different courses. And, despite the indigence of most of the students they, nevertheless, through donations and solicitations from others, jointly began a new library. Later, with intense rivalry between the two Societies the libraries became separated with the Athenians in the lead by 1828 with 1,172 volumes, and in 1832 the Athenians paid the well-traveled Professor Hovey $450 for books he purchased for them in London and Paris.[91] Whatever the number of volumes of these libraries, they soon formed a part of the main college library, although "a large minority" of the Alexandrians were so opposed to this that a splinter group broke off and formed another society while "the Athenian Society, with few exceptions assented."[92] We can assume that Edward Jones, like other Athenians, contributed to the accession of this library. Thus, through his contribution to the original affiliated library of the two Societies, and later to the Athenian singly, Edward Jones can be said to have been a participant in the original foundation of our great Frost Library today. And a library is a prerequisite for a liberal arts institution into which the College had been transformed by the 1960s, which in turn helped to open up the curriculum further to include disciplines and area studies not pursued before.

The black alumnae of our recent past could thus take courses from a wide spectrum of offerings throughout the College, having at their disposal the marvelous Frost Library with its over 800,000 volumes at present. They could choose or even *create* their own majors as at least one of them, Susan Prattis, had done. The very concept of a major—the ability to choose a field of study on which to concentrate—also reflected the College's consciousness of the importance of the right intellectual balance between breadth and depth, essential for the liberal arts. These pioneer black women majored altogether in about 12 different disciplines, some in two (double majors). The majors included the disciplines of Asian Languages and Civilizations, Black Studies, Drama, Economics, English, Greek, History, Political Science, Sociology, Spanish, Psychology, Music, and the Interdisciplinary major combining Biology and Psychology, and a minor in Third World Studies, constructed by Susan Prattis.

Generally speaking, majors are often indicators of the career goals of students. But at a liberal arts college they are not perfect career indicators since this type of college does not normally have departments focused on the professions. In his work on Amherst's black male alumni, Wade has found that most of them pursued careers in law and medicine, producing in the process some very distinguished legal and medical minds. In examining the careers of the black women who responded, one can also see a strong orientation toward careers in law and medicine. But this pattern is not confined only to Amherst's graduates. A recent survey across the country shows that black graduates, both men and women, are "more career oriented and pragmatic in their educational objectives than are whites. . . . Almost no blacks do graduate work in the humanities, foreign languages, or the physical and life sciences. Yet every year over 8,000 blacks are enrolled in law school and 4,000 African Americans are enrolled in medical schools."[93]

But, like all generalizations, much is left out of the wide sweep. We have, for instance, from the pioneer class of '80, two actresses, Laura Carrington and Tara Fuller (Mrs. Lamourt), who began as an actress but is now an art teacher in the school system. We also have one, Susan Prattis, already noted, in the Veterinarian sciences; and there are a few others who did not fit the pattern.

Notes

INTRODUCTION

1. Harold Wade, Jr., *Black Men of Amherst* (Amherst: Amherst College Press, 1976), p. 1.
2. *The Journal of Blacks In Higher Education* (JBHE): See Spring, 1994, No. 3; Winter, 1994/1995, No. 6; Spring, 1995, No. 7; and Summer, 1995, among others.
3. Beverly Lindsay, "African American Women and Brown: A Lingering Twilight or Emerging Dawn?" in *Journal of Negro Education*, Vol. 63, No. 3 (1994), pp. 430–442.

PART I

1. Wade, p. xxii.
2. Ibid., pp. 85–86.
3. Ibid., pp. 78–79.
4. Ibid., pp. xvi–xvii.
5. Theodore P. Greene, "The Gown Overwhelms the Town," in *Essays On Amherst's History* (Amherst, Mass.: The Vista Press), p. 303.

6. Ibid., p. 302.

7. Wade, pp. 86–87.

8. Ibid., p. xxi. Wade felt that Amherst helped to inculcate confidence in the Afro-American, unlike Harvard and some other white institutions that "tended to destroy the confidence and kill the motivation of promising blacks." See p. 98.

9. Greene, "Visiting Committee on Coeducation," p. II E/9.

10. Greene, *Essays*, pp. 328–329.

11. See "The Education of Women at Princeton: A Special Report" in *The Princeton Alumni Weekly*, Vol. LXIX, No. 1, September 24, 1968, where the entire Report is published. Because "of the urgency of the issue of coeducation—the most important question the University as a community has faced for many decades," this issue of the Journal carried nothing else.

12. The Gardner Patterson Report, p. 52.

13. Greene, *Essays*, pp. 325–332.

14. Ibid.

15. Ibid.

16. For these debates, I have drawn heavily from W. S. Tyler, *History of Amherst College During Its First Half Century* (Springfield, Mass.: Clark W. Bryan and Company, 1873) and L. Clark Seelye, *The Early History of Smith College, 1871–1910* (Boston: Houghton Mifflin Company, 1923). The quotation is taken from Seelye, p. 9.

17. Ibid., pp. 8–9.

18. Seelye has not mentioned the amount Bullock offered to the Trustees, but I am grateful to Daria D'Arienzo, Archivist of the College, who sent me a short document dated July 1871, titled, "Bullock Scholarship," which said: "A letter was read from Governor Bullock, presenting $1,500 to endow a scholarship" without mentioning gender here. A clarification of this would certainly be welcome.

19. Seelye, p. 10.

20. Ibid.

21. Ibid.

22. Tyler, p. 38.

23. Seelye, p. 14.

24. Tyler, p. 433.

25. Seelye, p. 1.

26. Tyler, p. 536.

27. Seelye, pp. 9–10.

28. Letter of John H. Greene to Professor L. C. Seelye, Lowell, Mass., May 7, 1873; also, Seelye, p. 17.

29. Seelye, Ibid.

30. Ibid., pp. 12 and 16.

31. George R. Cutting, *Student Life at Amherst College . . .* (Amherst, Mass.: Hatch and Williams, 1871), pp. 107–110.

32. Ibid.

33. "Final Report of the Amherst Visiting Committee on Coeducation," June, 1974, chaired by Theodore P. Greene, in "The Casebook on Coeducation at Amherst College," p. II E/6.

34. Seelye, p. 48.

35. Ibid., pp. 29–30.

36. Ibid., pp. 47 and 51.

37. Ibid., p. 51.

38. Ibid., p. 29.

39. Ibid., p. 50.

40. Ibid., p. 48.

41. Greene, "Amherst's Decision for Coeducation"—a speech on the tenth anniversary of Women at Amherst, April 12, 1986.

42. The Special Report of "The Education of Women at Princeton," pp. 7 and 52–3, particularly.

43. President John William Ward, Introduction to the "Casebook."

PART II

44. For a good overview of the First Congregational Church and some of the main personalities who served this Church, see *250 Years at First Church in Amherst, 1739–1989*, with an Introduction by Jeanette Good, Amherst, Mass., 1990.

45. See James Avery Smith, "Age, Estate, and Quality, The First Forty Years of the Church," in *250 Years . . .* , pp. 3–30. With very few exceptions—Avery Smith's article, for instance—the tendency is to gloss over slaveholding in Amherst, and when mentioned at all, it is treated as if unusual and insignificant. One source referred to the Rev. David Parsons (the father) as having "ownership of a slave, the giant Pomp [Pompey]" when we know that he owned Pompey's family consisting of a wife and at least a son, and other slaves whose numbers are unclear. Nevertheless, this same source rightly said that slaveholding was "not unique" for some of Parsons's parishioners, naming Zechariah Field, Richard Chauncey and the Kelloggs as among them. See Hugh F. Bell and Andrew Raymond, "Early Amherst" in *Essays on Amherst's History*, p. 12.

46. Avery Smith, "Age, Estate and Quality," p. 21.

47. Tyler, pp. 56–57; 104–107; 652.

48. Avery Smith, p. 24.

49. Ibid., p. 21.

50. Wade, p. 100, n. 11.

51. Ibid., pp. 1 and 98.

52. "An Address Before the Alumni of Amherst College by Dr. Humphrey, Delivered in the Chapel at the Commencement, August 1853," pp. 14–15 (to be referred to hereafter as "Humphrey's Address").

53. For some information on Edward Jones's life especially in America, see, for example, *Amherst Student*, "A Reminiscence," December 4, 1875; Stephen N. Keith, "The Life and

Times of Edward Jones; Sower of the African Diaspora," B.A. Honors Thesis, Black Studies (Professor Asa Davis, Supervisor), Amherst College, 1973; Hugh Hawkins, "Edward Jones, Marginal Man," *Amherst,* Spring 1982, and for a good synthesis skillfully pulled together from many secondary sources, see Michael Crowder, "From Amherst to Fourah Bay: Principal Edward Jones," paper presented at the Bicentenary of Sierra Leone Symposium, Fourah Bay College, University of Sierra Leone: "Two Hundred Years of Intercultural Evolution and Perspectives for the Future," May, 1987. For the quotation on Jehu Jones's character, see Ibid., p. 3 and n. 4.

54. Hugh Hawkins, "Edward Jones," p. 8.

55. Tyler, p. 79.

56. Cutting, p. 17; Cutting was here quoting a "prominent" Athenian alumnus, who might well have been biased.

57. Ibid., p. 16.

58. Tyler, p. 628.

59. Ibid., pp. 628–629; also Cutting, *passim.*

60. Wade, p. 81.

61. Humphrey's Address (1853), pp. 4–5.

62. Crowder, p. 18.

63. Tyler, p. 127.

64. Ibid., pp. 84–87.

65. Humphrey's Address, pp. 4–5.

66. For a most well-researched and intelligent analysis of Humphrey's attitude to Afro-Americans and the question of slavery, see Robert J. Brigham, "Amherst College: A Pious Institution's Reaction to Slavery, 1821–1841," B.A. Honors Thesis, Department of American Studies (Professor Theodore P. Greene, Supervisor), Amherst College, 1985, *passim.*

67. See Edward Hitchcock, *Reminiscences of Amherst College* (Northampton, Mass.: Bridgman and Childs, 1863), pp. 326–331.

68. Tyler, p. 80.

69. As stated earlier, this author has written a short article on this, "Participation of Women in the Establishment and Development of Amherst College," forthcoming.

70. See, particularly, Catalogue of October 1825, Amherst College.

71. Tyler, pp. 69–70.

72. Christopher Fyfe, *Africanus Horton: West African Scientist and Patriot* (New York: Oxford University Press, 1972), p. 25.

73. Ibid., pp. 26–27.

74. Tyler, p. 67.

75. Wade, pp. 5 and Appendix I, p. 111. But Robert Purvis is indeed an interesting Afro-American. As a member of the Philadelphia "Black Elite," and son-in-law of the wealthy and influential black businessman, James Forten, he was one of the founders of the American Anti-Slavery Society and he and his group were adamantly against the Colonization Society which, as we saw, Heman Humphrey espoused. For an ac-

count of Purvis, see Crowder, p. 5 and n. 10. See also Julie Winch, *Philadelphia's Black Elite: Activism, Accommodation, and the Struggle for Autonomy, 1787–1848* (Philadelphia: Temple University Press, 1988), *passim,* where Winch has made no mention of Purvis's attending Amherst, and in a conversation with her, August 1996, she maintained that she was certain Purvis did not attend Amherst College.

76. Wade, p. 111, Appendix I.

77. Ibid., p. 23.

78. Ibid., p. 24.

79. Ibid., p. 15.

80. Ibid., pp. 22–23.

81. Greene, "Remarks on Publication Date of Harold Wade's, *Black Men of Amherst,*" delivered in the Gerald Penny Cultural Center, Amherst College, May 7, 1976, p. 6.

82. Jeanette A. Gold, *250 Years . . . ,* Introduction, n.p.

83. Greene, *Essays,* pp. 329–330.

84. Wade, p. 16.

85. Ibid., and pp. 82–83. In his writings on Amherst, Ted Greene points out, echoing Wade, that members of other ethnic groups were also rejecting Amherst's propensity to "mold." He mentioned Peter Schrag, class of 1953, who wrote a book in 1970 with the telling title of *The Decline of the Wasp.* In it Schrag said: "I was born a German Jew, moved to Luxembourg when I was four, to Belgium when I was not quite ten. . . . Growing up in Queens in the forties I regarded myself simply as a New York Jew, thereafter, going to Amherst College, I tried (with less success than I imagined at the time) to become a WASP, an attempt I did not give up until, years later, I began to suspect that there were, for me, other and better ways of being an American." See Greene in *Essays,* p. 304.

86. Tyler, p. 76.

87. Greene, "Piety and Play in Amherst's History," in *Five College's Five Histories,* p. 10.

88. Cutting, p. 14.

89. Tyler, p. 81.

90. Cutting, pp. 14–15.

91. Ibid., p. 21.

92. Ibid., pp. 18–19.

93. See, for example, *JBHE,* Winter, 1994/1995, No. 6, p. 27.

BIOGRAPHICAL SKETCHES

Class of '80

∽

L. Isabelle Blackwood-Ellis majored in Psychology and it is clear that she had, while in college, no ambiguity about her career goals. She articulates them now as wishing to "function as a clinical psychologist doing individual, family and group therapy, psychodiagnostic evaluations, mental health consultation and training." Not surprisingly, after Amherst, she went straight to the pursuit of her goals, enrolling with the University of Virginia in the School of Clinical Child Psychology Department, and within a year (1981) she gained the Master of Education in child psychology. But she proceeded further, and by 1985 she was awarded the Ph.D. in the same subject with a minor in Special Education at the same University of Virginia.

Armed with her doctorate, she became a Clinical Psychologist at the St. Elizabeth Hospital in Washington, D.C., where her responsibilities were many and varied. They included: "individual psychotherapy with children, adolescents, and parents; family therapy; group therapy with latency age children and adolescents; full battery psychodiagnostic evaluations; intake screening and admission services; case management services; consultation services to schools in the form of crisis intervention, case oriented consultation, and presentations; consultation with appropriate agencies around case management issues; consultation to a foster care prevention program; supervision of staff social worker; presentations to community agencies; and participation in seminars, conferences, and workshops."

She remained in this position until 1986, and then between this date and 1989, she held the same title, Clinical Psychologist, at the Children's National Medical Center, also in Washington, D.C. As would be expected, her duties dealt almost wholly with children here. She was "on call" to deal with crises relating to physically and sexually abused children, rendering individual psychotherapy as well as to families and groups; she was also engaged in full battery psychodiagnostic evaluations, consultations within the hospitals and outside agencies, case management, liaison between the inpatient psychiatry unit and the Division of Child Protection. In addition, she was also involved in training and supervision of clinical psychology interns in APA-approved clinical internships; also, she audited clinical records and again participated in conferences and workshops.

Indeed, from 1989 to the present, she held many appointments, some as Clinical Supervisor and some as Psychologist. Her first position as Clinical Supervisor was with the Health Care for the Homeless Project in Washington, D.C., and at the Children's National Medical Center in this same city. She worked as a Psychologist at the Community Health Care, Inc., again in Washington, D.C. In most of these situations, her duties were replicated to a degree, but as a Clinical Supervisor for the Health Care of the Homeless Project, she was also engaged in the clinical supervision of Ph.D.-level psychologists in the areas of psychological evaluations, psychotherapy, and case management.

In addition, Isabelle is also involved in consultations. During 1988 and 1989, she was Consulting Psychodiagnostician to the ARCH Program, Washington, D.C. Here her duties involved psychological testing of homeless adults with a view to making recommendations for vocational counseling and placement, and here again she supervised psychologists who were working toward the Ph.D. degree. She also did consultancy work with the Fairfax County Public School at Falls Church in Virginia, and at the District of Columbia Public Schools in Washington, D.C. From 1991 to the present, she has been the Consulting Psychologist at the City Lights School in Washington, D.C., where her responsibilities include clinical case consultation with clinical staff of alternative school for adolescents. Her full-time position at present is that of Clinical Psychologist at the Psychological and Educational Associates, Inc., in Washington, D.C. Here her responsibilities are varied, including adults, adolescents and children, in individual, group or family treatments in psychotherapy. She is also engaged in evaluations, consultations, supervision and training.

In her participation in seminars, conferences and workshops, she presented papers on different occasions: the topics of these papers include, "Sexual and Physical Abuse," "Coping with Death," "Cultural Sensitivity," and "Self-Esteem," among others. She has also written an article, "Children's Neighborhood: An Alternative Approach to Community Intervention," published in *Community Psychologists*, in 1988.

Licensed to practice psychology in the State of Maryland and the District of Columbia, she is also a member of different professional associations. These include the American Psychological Association, the Association of Black Psychologists and the Maryland Psychological Association. In an outreach activity, she is a member of the Screening Committee for the Pro Bono Psychological Services for Homeless Children and Families.

ᘓᖣ

Laura Patricia Carrington majored in Psychology and Drama and has since had a very successful career in acting. Her promoter introduces her as "the newest kind of star in the entertainment galaxy, a video star." Yet her upbringing did not presage an acting career. She herself said that it was "a conservative, traditional upbringing where home skills like cooking and sewing were stressed as well as interest in the arts." But her parents, originally from the Caribbean (Guyana), might have wished her to follow in the footsteps of her father, who qualified for his medical degree while Laura was growing up. When she was admitted to Amherst, therefore, even she thought that she was going to be a "pre-med" student;

but this idea lasted only "half a semester and then the magic of the theater got to me and I turned back to the plays," she reminisces. In saying that she turned back to the plays, she is merely remarking on her favorite activities at her high school. Here "Laura began starring in theatrical productions, including 'Fiddler on the Roof,' and the annual competitive 'Sings' held by each class." She admitted that she "was always outgoing; I was a member of every club you could imagine—I was even the student government vice president, one year."

During her four years at Amherst she went "back to the plays" with a vengeance. She even played in some prominent and classical parts, including, "The Tempest," "The Merchant of Venice,"and "Medea," as well as modern stuff such as, "For Colored Girls Who Have Considered Suicide When the Rainbow Is Enough," "and lots of musical and college spoofs."

While still at Amherst, Laura received an invitation to model for the college issue of the *Mademoiselle* magazine. This led to several assignments for *Mademoiselle* and similar work for *Essence* magazine. "I'd always wanted to model so this was a dream come true." Soon Laura was seen in different commercials, including Dimension Shampoo, Sugar Free Canada Dry, several CBS video games and a hair-care treatment.

After graduating from Amherst, Laura worked for a year as a teaching assistant at the University of Massachusetts at Amherst and directed two plays and "The Beggar's Opera" for Amherst College. Then came her much acclaimed video successes which included, "Clarence Clemons," "A Woman's Got the Power," "My Life Is Good," and "Hello Lionel Richie," for which she won the American Music Award for Best Video, among others. She herself seemed amazed by her success in video: "Four years ago," she says, "there was no such animal as a music video but suddenly it can be a very important stepping stone in a performance career." She felt that this medium not only helped her as an actress but it also, in no time "created a groundswell of interest in me that I'm thankful for and happily surprised about. To my mind, its a superb new conduit for talent...." And so it has been for Laura for she has gone on to acting in television and films. It is said that Laura has "won the affection of millions of television viewers . . . (and she) has received virtually thousands of fan letters in response to her video appearances. . . ." Some of her TV shows include "Shanandoah," "All My Children," "General Hospital," "Max Headroom," and "One Life to Live."

There are some powerful excerpts on Laura from different sources:

> Laura Carrington clearly reflects the spirit of an individualist and a woman of independent means.

> A no-nonsense type of person whose attitude remains professional and fun.

> Good taste is always an asset. And Laura Carrington is a woman who gives new meaning to the term natural. She represents self-reliance and strength combined with a romantic version of life. She feels good about her life and we feel good about her.

But Laura also has a private family life. She is married to New York photographer, Anthony Barbosa, with whom she has three children; Danica Chizu-Alita the first, who is about nine years old and the second is about three years old, while the last one is just about a year old. Laura is now busily engaged in raising her children at home. I spoke to her a few weeks ago (May 6, 1997), and, although she is enjoying motherhood, one senses a degree of restiveness—as if she is looking forward to returning to work.

Laura is very talented with numerous interests and skills, including Hula, Fencing, Tai Chi, Horseback Riding, Archery, Ice and Roller Skating, Piano and Flute playing, Indian Beadwork, Sumie (Japanese brush painting), Miming, Juggling, Badminton and Volleyball.

How does she look back on Amherst College? She tells me she loved it. It taught her so much. It was a "wonderful coming out experience" and a nurturing one. Her only regret is that she had not taken sufficient advantage of all the opportunities the College offered.

ॐ

Denise Michelle Francois majored in Political Science and always knew that she wanted to pursue a career in the legal profession, thus making her very much in line with Harold Wade's male alumni who gravitated toward either law or medicine. I was Denise's advisor before she declared her major in Political Science, and even after this she kept in close contact with me. I remember well advising her to take courses from across the wide spectrum of College offerings, particularly in the sciences and philosophy and not just "pre-law" courses. Some of these courses were quiet unfamiliar to her but invariably she accepted the challenge and was much the better for each experience. This was not difficult to achieve because Denise was an intelligent and hard-working student, capable of getting along with any ethnic group either within a peer-group situation or within a student/teacher relationship.

Even before graduation, Denise had acquired useful work experiences, especially that during her senior year when she worked as an intern at the U.S. House of Representatives. In this position, her functions included the drafting of reports, the writing of memoranda, and even the responsibility of writing speeches for some lawmakers.

After graduating in 1980, Denise deferred going to law school for a year and worked as an investigator for the Virgin Islands Department of Human Services. Here she was engaged in what she understandably called the "depressing job," of tracking down fathers who had relinquished paternity and child support for their children. Small wonder, she left after six months before serving in the Virgin Islands Department of Commerce. This position she found more satisfying, working as she did with broad issues of development, including policy planning and research for the Virgin Islands. After another six months here, she knew she was ready for law school, and enrolled at the University of San Diego from which she graduated with the J.D. degree in May of 1984. Before returning to the Virgin Islands, she worked for a law firm in San Diego that specialized in construction defect litigation, and assisted one of the partners in research for a book on this topic. Upon returning home to St.

Thomas (one of the U.S. Virgin Islands) she worked in a private law firm and soon became a partner with the new name "Hodge & Francois." This firm "has a general practice with emphasis in litigation, land use and real estate," Denise tells us.

Denise is a member of many associations and professional organizations and this is in keeping with her activist personality and her strong sense of social commitment. Among her professional organizations, she is a member of both the State Bar of California and the Virgin Islands Bar Association, becoming president of the latter since January of 1996. As President, she also serves on the Judicial Council of the Virgin Islands. She is also a member of the United States Court of Appeals for the Third Circuit, the Association of Trial Lawyers of America and the American Bar Association.

꒚

Karla Rae Fuller came from Chicago and entered Amherst with her twin sister Tara, and soon they were to be known on campus as "The Twins." Both went to an all-black inner city high school in Chicago and the success story of these two Amherst College alumnae should serve as an inspiration to many.

Karla's career goals took a dramatic turn in her junior year at Amherst, as we mentioned earlier, when she enrolled in a course on "Japanese Theatre and Film" without quite knowing what to expect. Prior to this, she had a somewhat half-hearted notion of pursuing a career in either journalism or law, but having taken this course, the section on Japanese films, particularly, changed her life "forever" as she recounts it: she knew she wanted to study films seriously and to visit Japan. The first objective she considered not too difficult to achieve as there were reputable graduate schools in this country that offered courses in film making. But to go to Japan! And the way it came about that she did go to Japan, becoming the first woman and black to have been awarded the highly competitive Amherst-Doshisha Fellowship for a year, is a story that the reader should hear from her own voice below. Following her bliss, Karla majored in History, concentrating on Japanese history, and, in her senior year, wrote a thesis: "From Defeat to Protest: Reflections of the Postwar Japanese Cinema 1945-1960." During this time, she applied to and was accepted by Columbia University's School of the Arts—Film Division, but this she deferred until after her return from Japan. The opportunity to go to Japan, she tells us, came in her senior year:

> It came in a notice in every mailbox. A small red card announced the annual Amherst-Doshisha Fellowship which offered a funded year of teaching and travel in Kyoto, Japan. I was stunned that something so perfectly fitting my desires was possibly open to me. My twin sister Tara (also a student at Amherst) wistfully showed me the notice, sensing that it was just what I had been hoping for. She knew I would try for it and if I was awarded the fellowship, I would be going far away.
>
> Little did I anticipate how complex the process would be. I applied along with seven others for the fellowship (I was amazed that more people didn't apply, but that says a lot about my focus), including only one other woman (Nancy Seid?). I was confident about my application, clearly my love and excitement about the Japanese culture would be perceived. The group interview with several faculty members and the dean of the faculty was tough, but went very well. I could feel that they knew I not only wanted the position, but could also handle potentially challenging situations particularly regarding my gender. After waiting and hoping, I was told that the selection was down to two students, myself and David Gardner, and that I would have to wait longer until a final decision was made by the committee.
>
> Throughout the spring semester of 1980, I wondered why the decision was taking so long. I had also applied to graduate school and was accepted by Columbia University, but since I didn't know what my status would be, I could not respond to them. It was not until May of 1980 that I was told that I had won the fellowship to Japan, and also that I would be spending the summer at the Middlebury intensive language program studying Japanese for nine weeks. I deferred for a year at

Columbia and excitedly began the process of studying. The summer was difficult and wonderful. I never worked so hard studying a language particularly since the policy at the program is no English after two weeks. I did wonder why the process at Amherst had taken so long. I wondered since the competition had been so close, why they decided to pick me. It was only later that I learned that I had not been part of a tie with David Gardner, but that I was the first choice. The committee had decided to do this in order to protect me, the first female applicant, from potential rejection from the Japanese end of the selection process. Their thinking was, if there was a tie, I would not feel personally singled out because of my gender. However, in the end, I was selected and I was thrilled.

Part of the challenge of the fellowship, it was put to me, would be living as the only woman in male dormitory housing. I had no problem with this, as I had spent the first two years of undergraduate life as part of a distinctly small group of women. However, when I arrived at Amherst House at 12:30 A.M., the guys in the house were waiting to see the new female fellow. I was tired but happy to finally arrive. Professor Kitagaki of Doshisha University accompanied me to the residence. However, when the students opened the door of the house, their looks of shock were unmistakable. I couldn't understand why, when they knew, I assumed, exactly what kind of person to be expecting. Later, talking with the students, they told me that they knew I would be female but were not told that I would be an African-American. I asked about this oversight later and was told that they had an uphill fight to have the first female fellow with the Japanese and didn't want to add more to the controversy which might have hurt my chances.

Despite a complicated start, the year was one of the most memorable of my life. I taught the Doshisha University students English and had the opportunity to travel throughout Japan (i.e., Hokkaido, Tokyo, Hiroshima) and visit the Peoples Republic of China. In my experience, I felt nothing but warmth and friendliness from the Japanese people I met. Of course, there was a lot of staring at my five-foot-eight-inch frame. Afro-American, female, and tall, I attracted a lot of attention in the small city of Kyoto. This was not Tokyo, an international city accustomed to many different foreign visitors, but Kyoto, a most charming old capital of Japan, filled with beautiful temples which were thankfully not bombed during the war. It was an amazing stay. I can say truly that it changed my life.

Upon returning from Japan and after her graduation from Amherst, Karla then went to Columbia where she wrote a Master's thesis on "Perceptions of Poitier"—an image study of the actor—for which she was awarded the M.F.A. in 1983, and now she is registered at Northwestern University (Department of Radio/TV/Films) where she is working toward a Ph.D. in Film History, Ethnic Representation and Cultural Performance Studies. Roughly, her dissertation topic deals with Asian representations in Hollywood films, and we look forward to its early completion.

Karla's interest in film-making is not only for aesthetic, dramatic or professional satisfaction—which, alone, would have been quite in order. But from the time of her junior year at Amherst, when she saw those Japanese films made in Japan that depicted Japanese people in a multidimensional manner rather than in the stereotypical way in which the subject is treated by Hollywood, she became even more sensitized to the notion of imagery. Its power to shape or to reinforce ideas or ideologies for good or ill is immeasurable. And perhaps no other group in this country has suffered more from negative media imagery than Afro-Americans. Karla is very much aware of this and it is for this reason that she was so shocked to find that even she could have been taken in by stereotypical media imagery of Asian peoples before she saw "authentic" Japanese films and before she went to Japan. "I had unconsciously formed a set of expectations that were patently distorted without any real human contacts to mitigate them. And suddenly I began to have more sympathy for anyone whose only exposure to a different racial group or different culture has been filtered through a specific ideological lens. If this could happen to me, this could happen to anyone. I hope through my teaching to help all students become aware of the power of media images to shape ideas, expectations and perceptions." It is no wonder, she tells us, that before every lecture or class, she would inform the audience or students, that: "It all started in a course at Amherst College."

Karla's work experience since she graduated from Amherst is impressive. After her Master's Degree from Columbia, between 1985 and 1986, she evaluated screenplays for Home Video Acquisition, in Stanford, Conn., then she became Script Evaluation Manager at Vestron Video before becoming Associate Director, Feature Film Evaluation at Vestron, Inc., where she supervised the staff, and by 1987 she was Director of this outfit, with much greater responsibilities. Between 1987 and 1989 she became a freelance script reader for different companies such as New Line Cinema, Cinecom International Films and Miramax Films, and in this capacity she evaluated feature film scripts for theaters. She even gained experience in sales and marketing when she was Assistant to the Senior Vice President, Sales and Marketing with MTV Network, Inc. In addition, she worked with PBS as Production Assistant in the series *Brown Sugar*, and since 1993 she has been doing part-time teaching at Northwestern University along with writing her dissertation. She has also given many lectures to different Universities including Columbia and Northwestern mainly on ethnic images in films and the media generally. She has attended professional conferences and presented papers, has written film scripts and is now beginning to publish scholarly articles.

We have no doubt that we will be hearing much more about Karla Fuller who has already proven herself capable of dealing with difficult, sensitive and challenging situations. At Amherst even in the face of the most painful situations, as her twin sister, Tara, explained below, they both did not just "react" negatively but actively participated and contributed to the improvement of the life of the College community. Karla, for example, is proud to have been a co-founder of the Sabrinas singing group, the female counterpart to the Zumbyes.

In speaking with Karla, and from reading of her achievements, it is clear that one is in the presence of a disciplined woman with great intellectual poise. She knows herself—the safest basis of real self confidence. But let her speak for herself: "I think I developed a sense of self that cannot be shaken by anyone or most anything. My surroundings are relative, my sense of identity is not." Touché!

ॐ

Tara Fuller (now Mrs. Lamourt), twin sister of Karla, entered Amherst
at the same time and graduated in the pioneer Class of '80. More forthcoming about her experience at Amherst than her sister, this is what Tara
has to say about it:

> When I first came to Amherst in the fall of 1976 I was very
> naive about New England (I am originally from Chicago—
> born and raised) and an elitist college environment. I also
> came from a predominantly black neighborhood and an inner
> city high school. Wow! What a culture shock I found myself in
> having little in common with some of the other black students
> who had attended prep schools and were fairly economically
> well-to-do. Also I came in with my twin sister Karla which
> [was] also quite unusual. I also found we had difficulty fitting
> in with many of the African Americans on campus because we
> didn't take a militant stance on many issues and were very
> much in denial or were unaware of the racism that existed on
> campus. We also were very anxious to fit in and be accepted by
> the mainstream college community. It was tough. By sopho-
> more year and junior year my personal goal was to adopt and
> assimilate to all of the elitist norms I saw around me. It was a
> difficult time as the naive gloss of Amherst was beginning to
> wear thin and the excitement of making history freshman year
> was discouraged by the exposure to racist remarks and ac-
> tions/exclusions by professors, staff and students. Because of
> my background, my first frontline exposure to racism began at
> Amherst—but by senior year I was very disenchanted.

Yet Tara was to contribute a great deal to the life of the college community, and was to make "history" in many ways. She was the first black
woman to have been elected to the student assembly and also to have been
a reporter for *The Amherst Student*, all this in her sophomore year. Her as-

signment, predictably, for *The Amherst Student*, was to report on "Racism on Campus." Obviously possessing leadership qualities, in her junior year she was elected advisor to a dormitory, making her the first female and black to have served in this capacity. Like her sister, she became a co-founder of a singing group, called, in this case, the "Cacophony," a madrigal for both genders.

Tara's major was Psychology and like Laura Carrington, her classmate, she was also very interested in acting. She worked closely with the late Professor Boughton, then Director of the Kirby Memorial Theater, and soon Tara was to be the first black woman to have performed in the Weston Theater Playhouse. During the summer of 1978, she did "plays all summer long" as she expresses it. Obviously she did not follow through with her acting but has done many other things since graduating from Amherst. Upon leaving, she took up a position as instructor for autistic children in a psycho-educational setting at the Teacher-Therapist, Developmental Institute, Michael Reese Hospital, Chicago, from September 1980 to August of 1981. In this situation she was kept very busy, creating and conducting activities for these children, aged 3–6, with special needs, at the same time keeping a detailed journal on their achievements. And through the parent-teacher meetings, which she organized, she could keep the parents abreast with the progress of the children.

She left this position to enter the University of Chicago where she gained the Master of Arts degree in 1983. At this point it is clear that Tara was not altogether certain about her career goals. Between 1984 and 1986 she took a position as a Commercial Banking Representative at the ABN/LaSalle National Bank, Chicago, where she participated in the bank's management and credit training programs. In addition, she was a part of the financial analyst team for Fortune 1000 companies. Then she moved to another bank in Chicago, in this case, the Harris Trust and Savings Bank, serving as the credit officer for the Foreign Exchange sector, government securities and the Harris Futures Trading Groups.

But it is clear that Tara had her sights set elsewhere, and her banking excursion was just a means to an end. She obviously had become interested in teaching. Perhaps her first appointment in this field after graduating from Amherst had suggested this career to her and, while still involved in the banking and other money-related organizations, she attended the

School of the Art Institute of Chicago between 1986 and 1988 where she studied painting and drawing. During this time, she worked as Administrative Assistant at the Sahara Coal Company as assistant to the CEO of a $35-million coal corporation from June of 1987 to November 1988, and upon leaving the Chicago Art Institute, she worked as a temporary Administrative Assistant in New York City for a few months in 1989 before going to Shearson Lehman Brothers in this city between January 1990 to September 1991. Here she was Assistant to the Senior Executive Vice President who co-managed an $85-million mutual fund portfolio. While in New York City, she attended The School of Visual Arts, from where she gained a Certificate in Art Education in 1991. In the meantime, she became an Art Instructor at a Red Cross Shelter in this city. Once again we find her teaching young children, in this case ages 5–8, with special educational needs. She also helped the homeless to develop art skills. Her art instruction included murals, self-portraits, decorative box construction, pastel work, printmaking, paper bag mask-making and the making of puppets. During this same period, September 1990 to May 1991, as if she was not sufficiently occupied, she was also a teacher at the Saturday Art Program in New York City's School of Visual Arts.

Tara now seems to have settled down and since September 1, 1991 to the present, she has been an Art Teacher at the St. Benedict's Preparatory School, Newark, New Jersey. She conducts art classes for the 7th and 8th grades as well as advanced classes to junior and senior high school students.

She has recently been married and is looking forward toward establishing a family.

Since leaving Amherst in the pioneer class of '80, Tara has now acquired, in addition to her B.A., Amherst College, an M.S., University of Chicago (1983), Certificate in Art Education, School of Visual Arts, New York City, 1991, as well as the professional skills in painting and drawing she acquired from attending The School of the Art Institute of Chicago (1986–1988).

ॐ

Amina R. Merritt is a pioneer in every good sense of the term. She was very much aware of the place of history of her class, both in terms of race and gender. She articulated this when she remarked that they were entering

> a traditionally white male institution where we were attempt-
> ing to redefine not only institutional gender issues but also
> race, gender and class issues within our own black commu-
> nity. Although Amherst had already experienced *Black Men of
> Amherst*, it had not had to contend with black women on any
> large scale. . . .
>
> The women at Smith and Mount Holyoke had not yet had
> to deal with women at Amherst. The black men at Amherst
> may have thought we were coming for husbands. But women
> of my class were for the most part tough urban sisters with
> fascinating intelligence. Women at that time were dealing with
> the effects of the so-called "sexual revolution." We had so
> many negative images to destroy and redefine for white men,
> white women, black men and ourselves. We also had to deal
> with the physical problems of being at a place constructed for
> males only—the gym, urinals in the bathrooms, and dark pas-
> sages on campus. These struggles were in addition to the chal-
> lenge of proving our intellectual abilities at the school. I think
> we certainly rose to the challenge. We were truly pioneers.

On other levels, Amina was to demonstrate her pioneer spirit. She was, for example, among the first to have responded to Mrs. Janice Denton's letter upon the occasion of her photographic exhibition of Black Women of Amherst College in the Frost Library during the spring of 1995. Equally, she was in the forefront in replying to my communications about the book on this same subject and we have kept in touch throughout. It is quite interesting to note also that as I speak to many of these black alum-nae on the telephone, how most of them responded favorably when Amina's name was mentioned: "Oh! Amina, she was so supportive," was a typical reply.

Amina was no stranger to Amherst before she entered the College as a "freshman" in 1976. She is from Springfield, Massachusetts, and will tell you that:

> When I think back, I feel like a spoiled daughter of Amherst. I probably, collectively spent more time at Amherst than any other African-American woman in my class. Beginning in 1971, my mother used to drive me, my brother, my cousins, and other junior high school students to UMass for a Saturday dance class with Danny Scarborough. When we would pass the Octagon (before it became Gerald Penny), I was fascinated, but none of us including Mom knew what it or Amherst was. It looked so untouchable. It was not until the summer of 1973 when I came to the Springfield-Amherst Summer Academy (SASA) that I found out what Amherst and the Octagon are. I was lucky to learn Amherst first as a teenager in quiet summers. I think I may have been one of few who knew of, saw and used Amherst's computer in 1973. By the time I came to Amherst as a student in 1976, me and my Springfield homies had covered all the physical grounds, and I, as a SASA employee, had interfaced with many administrative offices and employees. I felt very comfortable at Amherst and needed no freshman orientation.

Indeed she would need no orientation considering her meaningful participation with the Springfield-Amherst Summer Academy (SASA), which she was to repeat as a student during summers of 1977 and 1978.

Amina must be easily one of the most active and creative students to have entered Amherst during the '80s and her contribution to the college community must certainly be acknowledged. She was responsible, for instance, for the formal renaming of what was originally the Phi Kappa Psi fraternity into the Charles Drew House, and she was one of the first of two women to have moved into this House, without realizing that the act would have drawn negative comments. "I was shocked," she recounted, "when I later realized that what I thought was pioneering, others thought was sexually suspect ('living with all those men')."

The first woman to have been president of Drew House, she was also a part of the Charles Drew Memorial Award Foundation. This was established by Donald Parks, M.D., of Philadelphia to celebrate the memory of Dr. Charles Drew, class of 1926, the noted surgeon who became famous for his pioneer work on the preservation of blood plasma. The manner in which Amina met Dr. Parks is most intriguing. She tells us that Christopher Hannum, class of '79, who lived in "The House," met Dr. Parks in Philadelphia and told him of her desire to name the house, for-

mally after Dr. Charles Drew. This obviously delighted Parks, who contacted Amina and in no time he made a trip to Amherst to see the students who were involved. "We had dinner with him and he shared Zambvuca and coffee beans with us in our elegant living room. At the time he was a scientist at a Philadelphia pharmaceutical corporation and we were impressed. He was on campus a few hours before the President of the College, Bill Ward [in truth, it was President Julian Gibbs], found out he was here and what our purpose was, so we were all invited to the President's office. I rounded up my officers and others from the house (we were all scroungy in the midst of finals), and we changed from our jeans and went to the office. Dr. Parks presented me with a medal and a bust of Dr. Drew. The College photographer took photos and we appeared in the Summer 1980 edition of the *Amherst* magazine," as herein entered:

Charles Drew '27 is honored at Amherst and in Washington. The memory of a distinguished Amherst graduate, Charles Drew '27, was honored recently when the Charles Drew Award Committee of Philadelphia presented a memorial bust of Drew to Amina Merritt '80. Merritt accepted the award on behalf of the Charles Drew Memorial House (formerly Phi Alpha Psi) in a ceremony in the office of President Gibbs. Dur-

ing the occasion, each resident of the house was given a com-
memorative Charles Drew medal.

Drew, an outstanding surgeon, is best remembered for his
work in the field of blood research. He did pioneering research in the science of blood banks and the use of blood
plasma, and in 1940 he supervised collection of blood plasma
for the "Blood for Britain" program during the early part of
World War II. He was later appointed director of the first
American Red Cross Blood Bank. At the time, ironically, he
was ineligible himself to donate blood to the Red Cross. The
organization first refused to accept blacks as donors and later
segregated blood according to the donor's race. He resigned
the Red Cross post after five months, largely because of such
policies, and joined the faculty of Howard University. His life
was cut short in an automobile accident in 1950.

The bust and a portrait of Drew were placed on display in
the Charles Drew Memorial House.

A similar bust was presented at the White House a year ago
and was later installed at the National Institutes of Health.
Vice President Walter Mondale accepted the bronze likeness
on behalf of the government. Drew's widow, Lenore, and his
daughter, Washington, D.C. City Council member Charlene
Drew Jarvis, attended the White House ceremony, at which
Mondale called Drew, "one of the most remarkable medical
men in the history of our country." He noted that Drew also
"was a profound and dedicated human being, dedicated to the
cause of justice."

Fall 1980 *Amherst*

Amina was also one of the first black females to have worked with "admissions" at Amherst. Like Harold Wade and his group, she also saw the
importance of the role of the Admission Office in creating any meaningful diversity as articulated by the College. She thought that Amherst has a
long way to go in integrating a sense of diversity at the institution and in
alumni associations. "For that reason I worked on admissions at Amherst, at USC (University of Southern California) Law Center, and as a

member of the Board of Directors for the Amherst Alumni Association of Southern California."

Amina must have been the first black woman also to have been Assistant Director of Counseling to the Springfield-Amherst Summer Academy (SASA), which, as noted earlier, she had first attended in 1973 before becoming a student of the College. As Assistant Director during the summers of 1977 and 1978, she assisted in implementing on-campus summer programs for 150 urban high school youths; she supervised some 40 counselors and 75 students; organized class schedules, field trips, tutorials and recreational activities; she made reports to officials including the president of this College, and to the City Council with a view to the re-funding of the program; she assisted in the preparation of budgets, program proposals and evaluations; she supervised dorm activities, managed Fall follow-up tutorial programs, and even managed to have assisted in teaching remedial English as well as typing/shorthand and dance. In addition to all these numerous activities she also found some time to assist the Black Studies Department during the spring of her final year, as its Executive Secretary.

It is quite a wonder that this very public-spirited student graduated from the College in good time with a decent degree. She majored in History and wrote a thesis, "In Light of Darkness: A History of the Mulatto in the United States," for which, she spent a semester at Columbia University (Barnard College) for research purposes. Amina said that her topic was inspired by one of my books, and some of my courses, but I was not her advisor. In her letter to me of March 30, 1996, she expressed "regrets that you were on sabbatical, and I missed your tutelage during my senior year at Amherst. I have no doubt that you would have encouraged me to write an excellent thesis and probably would have launched my history teaching career. Alas, I wallow in the scum of L.A. Law! Along with many other lawyers, politicians, actors and 'entrepreneurs.' However, I have made drastic changes in my life."

Indeed, although Amina went into the legal profession, it is clear she has a nostalgia for history. In a more recent letter to me (September 23, 1996) she said that she discovered some history of her own family in New England "that is astonishing," and she would like to do a project on it. So serious is she about this that she wrote "a grant proposal to the NEH two years ago to include the study of my family in Connecticut (Black and Native American) but it was rejected." Nevertheless, she is seeing it as a "project for retirement."

Upon graduating from Amherst in 1980, Amina took an appointment as a Paralegal Assistant in the law office of Arthur Wasserman in Encino, California—a long way away from her Massachusetts home. In this law firm, she prepared documents for personal injury practice with emphasis on aviation and workers' compensation. She also assisted in the then relatively new computerization of the office, and also reorganized the filing system.

Apparently, after leaving the Wasserman firm in the fall of 1981, she entered the University of Southern California Law Center in Los Angeles, and obtained the J.D. degree in 1984. At this point she was the recipient of the Merit Scholar Award, and the Beverly Hills Bar Association Scholarship. Before receiving her law degree, she worked as a Research Assistant for the Lockheed Corporation in Burbank California, and as a Law Clerk with "Anderson, McPharlin and Conners." In this position she was assigned to the banking department where she prepared litigation files, including research and discovery, in addition to other issues related to the banking industry.

With her J.D. degree in hand, she took a position with the County of Los Angeles (Office of County Counsel) as Senior Law Clerk, where she was attached to the Dependency Unit. Her responsibilities included cases involving child abuse and neglect; general litigations, and she also handled government tort claims, and assisted in research preparation of legal opinions regarding different legislations and drafted regulatory and statutory amendments.

Her next appointment was with the private firm, Collins, Collins, Muir & Traver in Pasadena, first as Supervising Law Clerk from February 1985 to November 1992 and then as Associate Attorney from December 1992 to February 1996. Her duties and responsibilities with this firm were enormous. But let us listen to her as she tells it:

> I was an associate at the Pasadena law firm of Collins, Collins,
> Muir & Traver, working 12–15–18 hours per day as a litigator.
> ... Scrambling to make 8:00 a.m. court appearances, 10:00 de-

positions, 4:00 client meetings and a mountain of office work. Nights to write briefs and summarize depositions. When did I eat, sleep, or get to my personal life? In between traveling L.A. County, which stretches from Lancaster (N) to Orange County (S) and from San Bernardino (E) to the Pacific Ocean (W). Frankly, it seemed I had no life. There are about 28 Superior Court branches in L.A. County, and I appeared in almost all of them. I averaged about 100 miles per day on a busy week, just for work. Not to mention my chairship of the Committee on Elimination of Bias in the Legal Profession and work as an Executive Committee Member for the Barristers of the Los Angeles County Bar Association. I am also an usher at First A.M.E. Church, L.A. I am a student mentor for two law, two high school, and one elementary school student. I am a volunteer lawyer at the First A.M.E. Legal Clinic and West Angeles Church of God In Christ Law Day Clinics.

Of course, after all this, a husband and children are those distant illusions that sometimes float through my dreams like a distant ship sauntering across the horizon. Ah . . . someday, someday. Is this the price of women's lib?? Who needs it?

The "drastic changes" in her life, mentioned earlier, meant she had just resigned from this position, the firm of Collins, Collins, Muir and Traver, and although she thought that it was "long overdue" nevertheless, she had mixed feelings about it. After 11 years "and no raise for years, I parted company on 2-23-96. . . . I think I had just about bumped my head on the proverbial glass ceiling . . . I do admit that I gave up a lot by leaving my firm—things both negative and positive."

In this firm Amina was involved in "some very high-profile and important cases in which I represented the defendant, County of Los Angeles and its employees. In one, I represented Gil Garcetti, the district Attorney, his Chief Assistant and his third in command. Garcetti's administration has gained notoriety in the much publicized cases of *People v. O. J. Simpson* and *People v. Eric and Lyle Menendez. . . .*" But she has also worked on other cases involving claims of gender bias, sexual and racial discrimination, and violations of First Amendment rights. Known for her deep commitment to helping the underprivileged in society, Amina bemoans the fact that at times "in litigation, I found myself on the 'wrong side' ideologically . . . considering who I am, historically, politically and socially." She was glad, however, to have been on the "right side" in some of her cases.

Despite her very high-pressured, complex job situation, Amina yet finds time for a great number of community and outreach activities. And for this community spirit, she has given Amherst College the credit: "Amherst did teach me how important it is to give back to the community and to try to make a difference to youth coming after me." Those of us who know Amina well, know perfectly that a sense of caring for others is natural to her; Amherst certainly might have merely helped to reinforce this noble trait in her. Among her activities, she is intimately involved with her church, the First A.M.E. Church, L.A.: for this church, she is an usher and is the Recording Secretary of the Usher Board, and is even thinking of beginning an oral history project of some of the Usher Board members at this church, who have been ushering for 50 or more years. She is also a volunteer lawyer for her church, as well as for the West Angeles Church of God In Christ in its Law Day Clinics. She also gave her services to the Urban Youth Lock-IN Project where she planned and implemented matters concerning juvenile justice, but above all, in dealing with these youths, she focuses on values and self-esteem. She also trained various youth organizations and churches to develop youth programs. Equally, she acted as mentor to teenage girls, to law students, and to highschool and elementary school children. As a member of the Board of Directors for the Amherst Alumni Association of Southern California, she sees this position as an opportunity to assist in "integrating a sense of diversity" at Amherst College.

It should also be mentioned that Amina has been consistently distressed by discrimination against blacks in the legal profession, and soon became chair of The Barrister's Committee on the Elimination of Bias in the Legal Profession. But perhaps she is even more dismayed by what she calls "an apparent conspiracy of silence among minority attorneys at major firms that prevents the expression of dissent about institutional bias—for fear of injury to career or reputation, or other forms of backlash." She expresses this in a well written, very balanced and well argued article in the January (1996) issue of *The Los Angeles Lawyer* (pp. 15–16).

In enclosing a copy of this short article to me, she mentioned that it was originally a nine-page "expose" of L.A. Law, and then went on to say, wryly, that her senior partner commented on it to her in a memo in this way: "Good article, nice picture [obviously of Amina who is pictured in the article]; good publicity."

Amina has several professional affiliations: she is a member of the Association of Southern California Defense Counsel, of the Black Women Lawyers' Association of Los Angeles, the California Women Lawyers, the California State Bar, the Los Angeles County Bar Association, the national Honor Society, the Pasadena Bar Association, Phi Alpha Delta law Fraternity International and a Patron Member of the Tournament of Roses.

It is no wonder that this very conscientious young woman has recognized that she had no private life. At a transitional stage at this point in her career, Amina was in a reflective mood. But we know that she will soon be on her feet again moving forward.

Amina is a true pioneer of the Class of '80 as she is a true daughter of Amherst College. Her love of the institution is as great as that of Harold Wade's despite his occasional criticism. She strongly felt, like so many of these women I am writing about, that "Amherst has had a profound effect on my life. I don't think I came to realize this until after leaving Amherst," prompting one to say that it appears that Amherst in retrospect is better than Amherst *au courant* since so many of these alumnae have expressed a similar opinion.

༉

Susan M. Prattis was among those who indicated to me that I use the material she sent to Mrs. Denton. We have already identified this very independent young woman who designed her own major. She saw this as important because of the nature of her many-sided interests: she was keenly interested in the veterinary sciences, and regarded this in terms of her career goals, but she also "had a strong interest in the history, literature and art of the Diaspora"—presumably the African Diaspora. And it was with a view to addressing these divergent interests that she designed an interdisciplinary major in Biopsychology and what she calls "a minor in Third World Studies." To this end, she intelligently availed herself of the relevant offerings of the other colleges in the Valley, and all this turned out to have been a very profitable experience for her, both professionally and socially. "Through my interdisciplinary major," she reminisced, "I became exposed to supervised independent research, albeit late in my college courses; indeed, when preparing for my comprehensive doctoral examination eleven years later, I was reminded of this process. As a side benefit I met several wonderful women at the other institutions, with several of whom I have maintained . . . contact."

As would be expected, upon graduation, she soon entered graduate school to pursue her goals in veterinary medicine. From the University of Pennsylvania School of Veterinary Medicine, she was awarded the VMD (Veterinary Medical Doctor) in 1985, and then, after some interim work, she enrolled at the North Carolina State University at the College of Veterinary Medicine, where she was awarded the Ph.D. in 1992. From this institution she was honored with the Dean's Scholastic Achievement Award and the North Carolina State University Outstanding Research Award, between 1990 and 1993. Among her other awards are the American Society for Cell Biology Travel Award and the Minority Supplemental Award Fellow, and in the summer of 1990, she had a valuable experience abroad, when she was a Visiting International Scholar at the Charing Cross and Westminister Medical School at the University of London, England.

Her work experience is varied, involving teaching (Department of Pathology at the University of Chicago, Illinois), research, clinical and laboratory management. She has also done consultancy work for various veterinarian clinics, or laboratories, or "animal colonies."

Susan has given many presentations in her field to different institutions of higher education: these include Fisk University and the Rockefeller University of New York City. In addition, she has made her mark in the scholarly world by her publications in scholarly journals. In combination with others in her field she has coauthored articles in *Journal of Comparative Pathology, Experimental Cell Science, Journal of Cell Biology, Experimental Neurology and Neuropathology, Journal of Cellular Biochemistry*, among others.

Her professional affiliations include memberships in the American Association for the Advancement of Sciences (AAAS), the American Veterinary Medical Association (AVMA), the Association of Women Veterinarians (AWA), the American Society of Laboratory Animal Practiners (ASLAP) and the American Association for Laboratory Animal Science (AALAS).

Susan is a true representative of the spirit of the class of '80 with her strong awareness of her place in the history of the College and her commitment to succeed. She chose Amherst College, she tells us, partly "because I was intrigued by the prospect of being among the first women to attend this venera-

ble, male institution." She found the experience challenging on different levels, but perhaps, most important of all, because of the "definitely chilly reception in some of the science classes"—a point of view that was expressed, as noted before, equally by the black male alumni. And, like some of these early alumni, this chilliness did not damp the spirit of Susan, but, rather, it gave her an added impetus to succeed. She said, "I worked harder than ever I had to that point, and became extremely disciplined." She was somewhat disappointed that some, especially the graduating seniors, did not share her enthusiasm for coeducation at the College.

In taking courses from other colleges in the Valley, she soon discovered that the single-sex women's colleges were more science-friendly to women in general. They "did a better job of supporting aspiring health professionals and scientists [than] did Amherst *at that time*, due to their expectations that 1) it was appropriate for women to be present in these types of classes, and 2) they would be successful in them. Presumably, this is no longer the case now that Amherst['s] coeducation has been in place for 20 years." Unfortunately, from the complaints we have from women generally, the deck is not yet completely cleared.

Altogether, though, Susan felt that her "Amherst experience was valuable. It was my first experience in the determination required, and enjoyment and satisfaction that resulted, from the efforts of black women to participate in processes, and areas of interest, in which they have not traditionally been found. For me at Amherst, those areas included sports (field hockey), the classical arts (Amherst choir), communications (Amherst radio) and the sciences." It also worked for her "because I learned to think clearly, and concisely, and to write well, and it strengthened my ability to set, and pursue, self-directed goals. Many of my experiences subsequent to achieving my Bachelor's degree at Amherst have subsequently confirmed the advantage that this approach has conferred upon me."

ᘒ

Le Ann Shelton majored in Classical Greek history and after graduation, went to the Columbia University School of Law, New York City, where she obtained the JD degree in 1983 and was admitted to the Bar a year later. Her first legal appointment was with the firm of Liebman, Adolf and Charme, in New York City. As an associate at this firm she specialized in real estate and litigation, where she gained extensive experience in city zoning, land use as well as in analyzing building codes. The litigation she was engaged in, on the other hand, included preparation of trial briefs and memoranda of law regarding private development and government regulations for State and Federal court cases.

After leaving the Liebman, Adolf and Charme firm, Le Ann then took on a new appointment that might well be considered as having foreshadowed her future career. During the summer of 1988, she worked with the Office of Urban Design, Department of Transportation in New York City. As an intern for this position, she prepared drawings, designs and models, all this with a view to assisting particularly in the paving system of the Sixth Avenue Capital Improvement Plan. But during this time she enrolled at the Columbia University School of Architecture, Planning and Preservation, for the M.A. in Architecture which she obtained in March of 1990.

During the summer of 1989, before graduating from Columbia, she was awarded the Kinne Traveling Fellowship which took her to Rome where she studied Renaissance architecture and urban design, and then to Switzerland where she became acquainted with this country's contemporary Ticinese architecture. This must have been a very rewarding experience for Le Ann, and for her new career in architecture.

Her first appointment as an architect was in September of 1990 with the firm Doman & Associates, Architects in New York City. In this position she was engaged in designing and production for new constructions, "high-end" residential renovation, landmark preservation and government-sponsored rehabilitation projects. Her summer experience as an intern at the Office of Urban Design must have come to her assistance when she was also engaged in construction drawings. She was also involved in making judgments about cost estimates and the scope and nature of different proposals for constructions. In addition, she was successful in preparing grant applications for some of New York City's landmark churches.

In June of 1991 Le Ann took a new position with H.T. Graves & Associates, Architects, in Greenwich, Connecticut. She continued with designing, in this case for private residential projects. Here again, she participated in construction drawings, in addition to conducting field surveys for new construction and renovation projects. She remained in this position until September of 1991.

March 1992 saw Le Ann back in New York City, working with the firm, Haines, Lundberg, Waehler. In this position, once again, she was involved in urban design and planning but with a host of new functions: some of these numerous projects included film production studios, corporate campuses, zoological parks and different city planning studies. She participated in the New York City Waterfront Zoning Study , the Brooklyn Navy Yard and the Olympus-LIDC Redevelopment Plans. Among the many responsibilities involved in these numerous activities were the writing of multi-volume reports incorporating both the written word and graphics. She also provided legal land-use analyses for large-scale public and private development projects. Le Ann remained in this position until June of 1993 and by July of this year she was in another situation.

At the Stv/Silver & Ziskind firm in New York City, where she is working up to the present, (July 1996), Le Ann's activities are even more numerous. These include planning for large-scale institutional projects, such as the

Rikers' Island Correctional Facilities, North Brother Island and a Water-borne Transportation Feasibility studies. In addition, she provided land-use planning, zoning analyses and environmentally related evaluations, and again she is made to devise and produce texts and graphics for multi-volume project reports and "presentation documents."

But her work also enables her to interact with different people, through extensive client contacts as well as through her involvement with the co-ordination of consultants at different levels. Currently she is acting as Administrative Representative for the Commonwealth of Puerto Rico and Administration of Correction in a $200-million construction project.

Since graduating in 1980, then, apart from her accumulated work experience, Le Ann has acquired the J.D. degree from the Columbia University School of Law, but has changed her career to Architecture and gained the M.A. degree in this field.

We did not receive a personal statement and photograph, but we hope she will supply more material in an updated edition of this work.

Class of '81

స

Wendy L. Blair finally responded in October 1996 to my numerous proddings. She majored in Political Science and English, and went on a Study Abroad program to the Centro Por Estudios Universitarios Colombo-Americano in South America apparently during her junior year. Within two years of her graduation from Amherst, she was awarded the degree, M.P.A. (Master of Public Administration) from the New York University Graduate School of Public Administration. Wendy seemed very clear about her career goals: she wanted to be involved in real estate and property development. To this end, she also attended (apparently while at law school) the New York University Real Estate Institute and completed course work in the areas of finance, leasing, appraisal, market research and computer applications. In a personal statement she describes herself in the third person as one who

> has been involved in real estate development for over 15 years.
> She began her career in New York City with the Dept. of Hous-

ing Preservation & Development where she identified development opportunities and worked with the development community on both housing and mixed-use developments.

While in New York City, she also worked for the New York Metropolitan Transportation Authority (MTA) where she was responsible for the development of surplus properties including the redevelopment of the East Site Airlines Terminal into 850 residential condominiums. At the MTA, she was also project manager for the Coliseum redevelopment project, a mixed-use development of approximately 1,900,000 square feet of offices, 300,000 square feet of retail space, a 325-room hotel and 350 condominium apartments.

Formerly a Development Director at Struever Bros., Eccles & Rouse, she was responsible for developing affordable housing including both multi-family rental and for-sale housing. As a development consultant to SBER, she is currently completing the Woodlands at Coldspring, an 102-home planned unit development, and closing on the financing for Oliver Plaza, a low income tax credit syndication with five different funding sources.

Her civic activities included membership on the Board of Managers at the Druid Hill YMCA and on the Board of Directors for People Aiding Travelers and the Homeless (PATH), since 1993, apparently in Baltimore, Maryland.

&

Julie Lauryn Jarrett (Keith)   It is with extreme sadness that we report the untimely death of Julie from this class. Her brother, Dr. Stephen N. Keith '75, has already been mentioned in connection with his senior thesis on Edward Jones. I was somewhat wary in asking Stephen if he would write a piece on his sister, but characteristically, he nobly agreed immediately. Indeed, in writing to me he said that he "was very pleased to be able to provide the following biographical information on my sister."

It is a dignified yet moving piece which will be reproduced verbatim:

> Julie Lauryn Jarrett (Keith) graduated from Amherst College on May 31, 1981, having majored in sociology. At the age of 22, she was extremely proud of her achievement, which was shared by the members of family. This event also marked the beginning of her life as an independent adult.
>
> Julie was born on May 5, 1959, to Elizabeth and Laurel Keith. She grew up on the south side of Chicago. Starting school at the University of Chicago Laboratory School, she followed her brother Stephen through the U. of C. High School and then on to Amherst. Along the way she enjoyed a happy childhood and adolescence, and dabbled in modeling. She was always very popular among her friends and peers. Not a "perfect angel," she could at times exhibit great stubbornness.
>
> As a student at Amherst, Jule did not encounter any academic difficulty and she particularly enjoyed meeting new friends at colleges throughout New England.
>
> Following her graduation from Amherst Julie accepted a position with IBM, first as a Systems Engineer and later a Marketing Representative, and relocated to the St. Louis area. In 1983, she relocated again back to the Chicago area. Throughout this time, Julie enjoyed her independence but remained close to her family. In fact, family members were always her most important priority.
>
> She had known her future husband since childhood, and in 1987 Julie and Thomas Jarrett were married in Chicago. At the time she was still working for IBM and Thomas was and still is working with the ABC television affiliate in Chicago. Their first and only child Tracy was born in 1989. Following the birth of her daughter, Julie proved to be an excellent mother; Tracy became her top priority.
>
> Julie's tenure with IBM came to end in 1990; she was an early victim of corporate "downsizing." She quickly found a position with the City of Chicago, working in the Department of Public Health and later in the Office of the Mayor.

Also in 1990, Julie began experiencing frequent infectious illnesses. And in 1991, she was hospitalized with pneumonia and diagnosed as having acquired immune deficiency syndrome (AIDS). Following her recovery from her acute illness, she returned to work full-time. She also committed herself to enjoying every minute possible with her daughter Tracy, and other members of her close family.

Julie enjoyed good health generally until early 1993, at which time she began to lose weight and stamina. She was able to continue working for the City of Chicago until late 1993. Despite the best of care, her health continued to deteriorate through the early half of 1994. Hospitalized in June 1994 with another episode of pneumonia along with complications from medications she was taking, Julie was no longer able to fight against the progressive course of her disease. Rather than continue her suffering, she chose to discontinue all treatment, came home, and died suddenly on July 17, 1994, sleeping quietly next to her mother.

Julie may not be remembered for any historic achievements—her most important priority was always her daughter Tracy, and she was committed to being a good mother—but she did succeed in leading a happy life. As an African-American woman, she was a part of the wave of individuals that sought success as professional women, wives and mothers— she wanted to do it all. She should be remembered as a good daughter, sister, wife, mother and friend. She should also be remembered as an example of how AIDS does not strike just "misfits" and the downtrodden.

Julie Jarrett benefitted greatly from the good fortune of her family and built upon that through her energy and hardwork. She enjoyed life. She loved her daughter and the members of her family. She will be remembered not so much for any one achievement, but for her smile, her warmth, and her love.

Stephen N. Keith '75, M.D., MSPH

〜

Gina Marie Stevens   After a telephone conversation with Gina during the early part of the summer of 1996, she finally decided to send me her *c.v.* and very helpfully promised to get "others from 1981 to reply." She also promised to send me the personal statement I had requested, but, unfortunately, I still have not received that. Gina majored in Anthropology and Black Studies, and her first appointment after graduation, was with Retailer Financial Department as a Business Analyst for a short time before becoming a Tax Specialist with Income and Franchise Taxes between 1982 and 1983. In this position, apparently in New York City, she filed returns for General Electric Credit Corporation for both the city and the state of New York. In the process, she converted manual returns to an automated system.

Between 1983 and 1984 she moved on to become an Investment Analyst with General Electric Trust Accounting Operation. She was responsible for equity purchases, sales and dividends for pension funds amounting to some twelve billion dollars. Having left this position, she became an Internal Controls Auditor with Southeast Service Center in Atlanta, Georgia. She spent just a short time here dealing with accounting and auditing before taking a position with Corporate Finance Services as a Senior Field Analyst. She held this position between 1984 and 1985 and was involved with different activities, as described by her: she "supervised due diligence reviews for $25 million plus leveraged buy-out transactions. Evaluated validity of collateral, established loan formulas, supervised junior auditors, and wrote audit reports, 90-percent travel."

Apparently she has now moved to Stamford, Connecticut, where she was again with General Electric Credit Corporation. In this case she was Senior Financial Analyst, at the Computer and Telecommunications Services department during 1985 and 1987. Her responsibilities involved, in her own words: "Reporting, analysis and budget preparation for $30-million multisite IBM mainframe operation. Equipment lease-buy analysis and administration of billing system for corporate computer users. Monthly closing of books [and] telephone billing for corporation."

At this point in her career, after having received high recognition from the General Electric Credit Corporation— Certificate of Excellence, 1984, Management Award, 1985, and Service Award, 1986—Gina turned her attention to the legal profession. With this in mind, she enrolled at the Albany Law School of Union University, Albany, New York, and was awarded the J.D. degree in 1990. During this period, she took on certain summer appointments: she was Graduate Assistant at the New York State Public Authorities Control Board (PACB) for the summer of 1988. Here she reviewed bond resolutions issued by different public authorities; prepared memoranda on State Finance relating to law limitations on voting activities. For the following summer of 1989, she was a Legal Intern with Cable Television Association of New York, Inc., in Albany, and just before her J.D. degree she was again a Legal Intern with the Governor's Task Force on Rape and Sexual Assault, also in Albany.

With her law degree, since 1990 she has been Legislative Attorney at the American Law Division (Congressional Research Service) at the Library of Congress in Washington, D.C., and this appears to be a most important position. The official brochure states that:

> ***The staff of the American Law Division (ALD) functions as legal advisor to committees, Members of Congress and their staffs.*** ALD provides Congress objective, nonpartisan legal analyses in a responsive and timely manner. One of seven research divisions in CRS, ALD has direct access to the extensive legal resources of the Library of Congress and has established expertise in fields such as constitutional law, election law, tax law, international law, congressional ethics, civil rights, environmental law, criminal law, administrative law, and congres-

sional practices and procedures. Drawn from diverse backgrounds, the staff includes former law professors, trial lawyers, government attorneys, and judicial clerks, many of whom have lectured extensively in their fields and published scholarly works. In 1994 the American Bar Association selected ALD as the recipient of the *Hodson Award,* given 'in recognition of sustained extraordinary service and achievement in the field of public law.'

Staff attorneys are available for confidential in-person or telephone consultation on all legal issues that arise in the legislative process. A typical consultation might include a discussion of the constitutional implications of proposed legislation, its impact on existing laws and regulations, and an analysis of whether the language achieves the desired legislative result. Although Division attorneys defer actual legislative drafting to the Office of Legislative Counsel, they are often asked to comment on legal issues raised by specific legislative proposals.

Gina is thus called upon to prepare written legal analyses and reports for individual members of Congress or for committees, and the official brochure states that such reports should be impartial and in-depth analyses. These reports could be related to the development, interpretation or implementation of public policy on matters as varied as genetic privacy, information privacy, cryptography, child-welfare, domestic relations, and AIDS. She is also involved in extensive consultations and oral briefings provided to congressional members, committees and congressional staff. Equally, she made presentations at seminars on a variety of topics for the Congressional Research Service, the public policy institutes, and for the Federal continuing legal education series; she assisted in congressional hearings by recommending witnesses and drafting questions, as well as in the evaluation and drafting of legislation.

Her career now seems well established and she is becoming known enough to have been invited to the University of Maryland School of Law as a Guest Lecturer in 1992. One of her congressional reports, "Interstate Marriage Recognition: And the Defense of Marriage Act," published by

The Library of Congress, is a substantial piece, of which Gina should be proud. In the process, she has also acquired extensive personal computer knowledge, being familiar with financial word processing, database and graphics software, and is proficient in the use of Westlaw and Lexis.

I regret that Gina did not find the time to have sent me the promised personal statement, which, I am sure, would have been rewarding.

Class of '82

〜

Bonnie Denise Jenkins, or "Lady" as she was affectionately called on campus by just about everyone of us, including President Julian Gibbs, majored in Black Studies and Psychology. Bonnie was highly respected and very popular both with her peer group as well as with faculty and top administrators here, and it came as no surprise to us when she made entry into the Amherst Students' *Who's Who* among students. Bonnie remembers the small as well as the big things at Amherst. She has nothing, she tells me, "but fond memories of my time at the College. I remember eating in Valentine Hall, walking into town, taking the Five-College bus to Smith College and the University of Massachusetts.... I remember living in the Charles Drew House and the wonderful parties we used to have there. I recall playing basketball in the gym and eating hamburgers at the snack bar."

Bonnie has chalked up many "firsts" for herself on this campus. She was the first woman to have been elected chairperson of the Black Student Union (BSU). "I remember the day I was elected.... I was so happy and

yet, also somewhat nervous of the year ahead. I recall, while Chairperson, staying up all night discussing the funding of the BSU with the Student Council." And it was, indeed, a serious series of discussions because the discourse was over disagreements pertaining to budgetary funding and distribution. How to share fairly the relatively limited funds with *all* the other student organizations? The disagreements were initially very sharp but by the second day of her chairmanship the whole issue was resolved amicably. Although Bonnie did not know it at the time it was happening, nevertheless, this negotiation was to foreshadow the work in which she is now engaged, as we shall see. In her capacity as chair of BSU, she was also a member of the Student Council where she assisted in decision-making affecting the whole student community. She was also a member of different College steering committees, designed to review applications from time to time of candidates for certain administrative positions. Like Tara Fuller (class of '80 and now Mrs. Lamourt), Bonnie also wrote for the College newspaper, *The Amherst Student*, on, predictably, minority issues, but she also wrote on matters relating to sports. As one who was a sportswoman herself, she might have enjoyed this. She played basketball, varsity track and field while here at Amherst and she was also a "disc-jockey" on WAMH.

In her senior year, Bonnie was to become the first woman to win the Charles Hamilton Houston Prize. This was a highly competitive College-wide prize for which each competing student had to write an essay. This prize was established by a black alumnus, Steve Coleman, class of '78. Even while here at Amherst, Steve was already an entrepreneur; now he is chair and CEO of his own financial corporation, "Daedalus Capital LLC" in St. Louis. Steve's "company" while a student here at Amherst was called "The People's Choice Films," and it was from the profits of this endeavor that he established the Charles Houston Fellowship Fund as he had termed it.

Characteristically, Steve laid down strict guidelines on how the fund was to be utilized. It was, of course, to honor the achievements of Charles Houston, class of 1915. He wrote:

> First, the Charles H. Houston Fellowship Fund contains $3,000, of which $1,000 was given by People's Choice Films and an additional $2,000 was supplied by President Ward of the College. This means that by next spring, the interest from the endowment will have generated approximately $150. This $150 is the size of the award to be given out in the spring of 1979. In addition, the officers of People's Choice Films will make an annual contribution to the Fund each spring in order to increase the size of the award over time.
>
> Second, the criter[ion] for selecting a Houston Fellow is as follows:
>
> The Charles Hamilton Houston Fellowship Award is an annual gift awarded to a graduating senior from Amherst College who best personifies a commitment to realizing his or her humane ideals, much in the way that Charles Houston devoted his life to the fight for equal protection under the law for Afro-Americans in the United States. Candidates for the Houston Fellowship are required to submit a resume and to write an essay of no more than five pages on the question, "In what area of social involvement do you feel that you can best effect your humanitarian ideals?" There is no discrimination as to race, sex, origin, or religion.

Steve's most noble donation initiated the "Charles Houston Forum" which I chaired until 1982 when it was absorbed with the "Eastman and Lecture Committee."

We were very happy that President Ward, quite typically, had so generously backed up Steve's donation with funds twice as much as the original amount. The Houston Prize Committee came into being—with a committee also—which I chaired until 1989.

Bonnie's prize-winning essay of 1982, "Organizations to Help Black Youth," stressed the importance of education and self-help to motivate and revitalize youths in the inner cities. Her essay had the edge on intelligent pragmatism. She could use herself as an example of one who was helped by an organization called "A Better Chance" (ABC) that gave lower income youths the opportunity to attend qualified high schools, through scholarships. "I was fortunate enough," she wrote, "to receive a scholarship from this organization, and was able to attend a good high school in New York. Going there has laid the path for me to attend Amherst College, and the ambition to continue striving for the best." Bonnie believed passionately that a country's most important asset lies in its youth, hence the importance of organizations like ABC. "I have always believed that change lies in the hands of the youth, and I see it as necessary to educate black children so that they can study American life and find new ways to make life better for future generations."

Indeed, her extracurricular activities while at Amherst attested to this strong commitment to the education of the underprivileged: with the Police Athletic League, she tutored and counseled children who suffered from deprivations of all kinds; under the auspices of the Association of Christian Student Leaders, she sponsored conferences for black students at various colleges and universities; she assisted lower income families and she continued to assist the ABC organization in different ways throughout the time she was a student here at Amherst College.

Upon graduating, Bonnie went to Mercy College in New York City and there obtained a Paralegal Certificate in December of 1983, and with this Certificate she worked as a Paralegal/Medical Malpractice Investigator at the New York City Corporation Counsel. Then, during the summer of 1985, she worked at the New York City Legal Aid Society. Up to this period, it appears that Bonnie was still deciding on a career and to this end she had entered the Albany Law School in the fall of 1984, and a year later, she also enrolled at the Graduate School at the State University of New York at Albany where she obtained both the Master's degree in Public Administration (M.P.A.) and the J.D. degree in the summer of 1988. But during this period she was gaining experience in different part-time job situations. Between January of 1986 and June 1988, she volunteered as a Legal Intern at the New York State Attorney General's Office, and she even worked as a Judicial Clerk at the Supreme Court of Canada in Ottawa during the summer of 1987, and then, back to New York, where she worked as a Policy Analyst at the New York State Department of Transportation at Albany, and it was during this time she completed both the M.P.A., and the J.D. degrees.

At this point, Bonnie was to become involved in an employment which few Afro-Americans had ever been engaged in—certainly not even Harold Wade's impressive lot. It began with the "Presidential Management Internship," instituted to "attract to the federal government outstanding men and women from a variety of academic disciplines who have a clear interest in, and a commitment to, a career in the analysis and management of public politics and programs."

Bonnie applied and was accepted in the fall of 1988. She first worked on a rotational basis as Legal Advisor in the Office of the Secretary of Defense at the Pentagon, and as Policy Analyst in this same office, in this case stressing strategic initiatives; she also worked in the Executive Office of the President in the area of the Office of Management and Budget, as Budget Analyst. She was engaged in all this until June of 1990 when she began working on a more permanent basis as the Attorney/Advisor at the U.S. Arms Control and Disarmament Agency. In this high-powered capacity, Bonnie provides legal advice to U.S. Ambassadors and U.S. Delegations negotiating arms control treaties. As would be expected, this entails extensive travels abroad, since she would normally accompany the delegations to do the actual negotiations. (In the face of all this high-powered milieu we feel hesitant to remind ourselves, as promised earlier, of Bonnie's negotiating skills when she became chair of BSU!)

Despite all this work and travel, Bonnie enrolled at the Georgetown University Law Center in the spring of 1991, where she concentrated in International and Comparative Law and obtained the master's degree in law (L.L.M.) in 1994. She also spent a short time in 1995 at the Hague Academy of International Law at the Public International Law Division after having spent the summer of 1994 in Madrid, Spain, at the *Colegio Mayor Universitario San Pablo*, where she took courses in European Community Law, Comparative Law and International Environmental Law. She obviously felt the need to be constantly improving her expertise on these delicate negotiations with which she is involved.

In addition to participating in treaty negotiations, she also drafts treaty texts—or, more appropriately—she would be assisting in drafting the executive branch's official interpretations (since most signatories tended to have their own interpretations) of concluded arms control treaties. Such texts would then be submitted to the Senate for its advice and consent as the U.S. Constitution requires. She also provides legal advice to the interagency review process. In May of 1996 she was named Legal Advisor to the conventional forces in Europe for a wide-ranging conference that reviewed such treaties as: the Open Skies Treaties, the Chemical Weapons and the Biological Weapons Conventions, the Environmental Modification Convention, the Convention on Prohibitions or Restrictions on the Use of Certain Conventional Weapons (Protocol II on Mines, Booby Traps and Other Devices), the current comprehensive Test Ban Treaty negotiations, the present talks on a future Fissile Materials Control Treaty, the Bosnia Agreement relating to the work of the Organization for Security and Cooperation in Europe, as well as related International Court of Justice and United Nations issues. Bonnie is currently involved in most of these matters and so far she has traveled to countries in Africa, to Austria, the Bahamas, Belgium, Canada, Czech Republic, Finland, France, Germany, Hungary, Ireland, Italy, The Netherlands, Poland, Portugal, Russia, Slovak Republic, Spain, Switzerland, United Kingdom and Venezuela, and I have just received a card from her from Vienna where she is engaged in "a treaty negotiation" (Winter, 1996).

Not only is she involved at the diplomatic/negotiating levels of these matters, but she also finds time to write articles for scholarly journals on some of them. Her most recent (June, 1996) is on the Bosnia Herzegovina Agreement, titled "The Enhancement of Political and Military Stability in the Former Yugoslavia through the Use of International Law: Annex I-B of the General Framework Agreement" in the *Fordham International law Journal*. She has also published other articles such as, "The Role of the Attorney in the Treaty-Making Process," in *International Law Practicum*, Spring 1993; three articles in the *International Lawyer*, in 1994 and in the spring and summer editions of 1995; as well, she has published an article by the Geneva International Peace Research Institute, in 1994.

This extraordinary young person is indefatigable in her commitment to her intellectual and professional growth. We have already seen how many degrees and how many institutions she has attended in this country as well as abroad all with a view to the "tooling" of her skills. In a recent letter to me (July 16, 1996) Bonnie informs me that she will be attending the University of Virginia's Woodrow Wilson School next year "to embark on my Ph.D. in international relations." Already, for this, she has received two fellowships, the Dorothy Danforth Compton Fellowship and the Commonwealth of Virginia Fellowship, and she is seeking a third before attending the school. She is also intending to teach at the Georgetown University Law Center during the summer of next year (1997) and the anticipated course, for which she is already constructing a syllabus, is entitled, "Arms Control and International Negotiations." She is excited about teaching and is certainly looking forward to it: "As I write this letter to you I am immediately flattered that I can associate myself with you in that I will soon be a professor myself. Actually, I won't be a full-fledged professor as I will be an adjunct professor at the Georgetown University Law Center. . . . I look forward to it, and hope that I can be as inspirational for my students as you were to me when I was at Amherst College."

We can be quite certain that Bonnie is more than an inspiration to many youths "out there" already. We are happy to note that she has not abandoned the ideals she expressed in her Charles Houston prize-winning essay. She recently founded and organized a program called ACHIEVE, which provides minority youths with role models and mentors. In this regard, she organizes successful professional minorities to travel to elementary schools and other educational institutions, to talk to students about their future goals; and what is more, they help the students to plan on how to achieve them. She is also involved in volunteer work in Washington, D.C. (DC Cares) for the homeless. She helped with soup kitchen facilities for the homeless and with children in homeless shelters, and she finds these outreach programs "very rewarding."

She is also involved in many other activities of a more professional nature. Since 1994, she has been chairperson of the Arms Control and Disarmament Committee, of the International Law Section of the American Bar Association and co-chairman also of the American Bar Association Working Group on Nuclear Smuggling, since 1995. She is also Advisor and contributor to the American Bar Association Working Group on Improving the Effectiveness of the United Nations, among other American Bar Association programs. Her professional memberships include: Association of Attendees and Alumni of the Hague Academy of International

Law, Women in International Security, and Black Professionals in International Affairs.

Bonnie has received numerous awards and recognitions apart from those she received at Amherst College. Among them, she graduated "With Distinction" from Mercy College in 1983; she received the American Bar Association Law School Division Award in 1986; she was a "Distinguished Graduate" at the State University of New York at Albany in 1988; Arms Control and Disarmament Agency Meritorious Honor Award in 1992; Defense Service Medal—U.S. Navy Reserves in 1993; and Meritorious Unit Award—U.S. Naval Reserves in 1995, among others.

Bonnie is grateful to Amherst College for her achievements. She has expressed this to me repeatedly. "It enriched my life and instilled in me a sense of independence I have since carried with me. It showed me both the positives and negatives of standing up for one's convictions. . . . I still have fond memories of the friends I made, and I very much look forward to the publishing of this book so that I may read of what so many of them have done."

So far, therefore, apart from her extraordinary work experience, and her publications, Bonnie has chalked up many degrees and certificates since her graduation from Amherst: a paralegal certificate from Mercy College (1983); a Master's degree in Public Administration, MPA (1988); J.D., Albany Law School (1988); L.L.M., Georgetown University Law Center (1994) in addition to recognitions from foreign institutions such as the *Colegio Mayor Universitario San Pablo* in Madrid, Spain, and The Hague Academy of International Law, and, as mentioned earlier, she will be attending the University of Virginia's Woodrow Wilson School next year (1997) for the Ph.D. in international relations.

Bonnie gives credit to Amherst College for her successes. She basks in what she calls the "great reputation" of the College of which she was not aware until now she is "out in the 'real' world," and she is convinced that this assisted her in her employment opportunities. But even more important, in terms of her own personal development, she applauds "the liberal arts education the school fosters. I look back and appreciate the variety of courses I was able to take. I am glad I was able to do that at a time of real development in my life. I would highly recommend Amherst to anyone. It was a wonderful experience."

ᘓ

Kimberlyn Leary also belongs to that delightful, rare group that responded to my *first* letter in a timely fashion on June 25, 1995, in this case actually before the deadline. Kim majored in Psychology and, as she says, "Psychoanalysis has been a vital, energizing and creative companion in my intellectual, clinical and personal life." Yet, she tells us that her interest in psychoanalysis began, ironically, with a course at Amherst that really put her off. That is, during the first lecture "the professor began to describe what he thought of as psychology, saying that our concern in the class would be to study 'the prediction and control of human behavior.' Nothing in what the professor said sounded remotely like what I had foreseen, for I had expected psychology to be about *understanding* people rather [than] controlling them. I decided not to take that class but transferred into another taught by a psychodynamically oriented psychologist, Haskell Coplin, Ph.D. Interested in people's minds and not just their behaviors, this professor became an important teacher for me. Under his tutelage, I later read Freud, completed a thesis and formulated plans for graduate school. In crucial ways, his availability assisted me to take the first steps to become the psychoanalytic psychologist I have come to be."

Indeed no teacher could wish for greater acclaim.

It was this student that Professor Townsend wrote about so enthusiastically. He reflected—"I actually think—I *know*—I taught her something. Many have been the times when I have said to myself: Well, there was *one* student to whom I taught something." Kim first took a course, "Men and Women in Literature" with Townsend in her sophomore year. But she "couldn't bring into harmony the voices that spoke of Black Pride and of Feminism, but she heard both out, she questioned both, and then she wrote out her responses and reflections with remarkable poise and insight. That might have seemed enough, but she knew what (again) was not obvious to many at the time: that in order to understand and perhaps to improve the fate of African-American women, it would help to know more about the men. And so the next fall she took a reading course with me. She read (most importantly) DuBois and Wright and Baldwin and once a week over a long lunch in the old Fayerweather snack bar, we would talk. I say I taught Kim something. I should emend that: in this reading course I witnessed at first hand, in papers and in conversation, someone learning. There have to have been countless other occasions, but of this one I am sure. I have known few students who could explore and discover and—by the clear evidence of her articulations—achieve understanding the way Kim did, . . ." and it was here that Townsend quoted Whitman on teaching noted above, and indeed he saw Kim as a Whitman paradigm.

Despite her impressive work with Townsend in the English Department, Kim's mind was set on psychoanalysis. After graduating from Amherst, therefore, she moved to Ann Arbor, Michigan to begin graduate studies in clinical psychology at the University of Michigan, and was fortunate to have received two fellowships, a CIC Fellowship for Graduate Study and a Ford Foundation Dissertation Fellowship. She received her Ph.D. in clinical psychology in 1988, and this was to launch her career along the pathway of her choice. At this point, she accepted a post-doctoral fellowship at the University of Michigan's Psychological Clinic where she worked closely with Dr. Robert Hatcher and with whom she is presently working on a paper on psychotherapy. Her main post-doctoral work at the Michigan's Psychological Clinic involved her in psychotherapy research and, in addition, during this period she also worked as a clinical psychologist at the Michigan Psychoanalytic Institute's Treatment Clinic. Both of these positions, Kim tells us, enabled her to advance her clinical skills, while at the same time pursuing psychoanalytically-informed research and scholarship.

At the end of her post-doctoral fellowship in 1990, she accepted a sort of dual position: one was an Adjunct Assistant Professor of Psychology at the University of Michigan, and the other was to become a member of the Senior Staff at the University of Michigan's Psychological Clinic, and she has continued to hold both positions. Here, it seems to me, Kim is attempting to put in practice one of her fond theories: that is, to her, psychoanalytic life and academic life have much in common. "In both, there is the vitality of exchange, disciplined efforts to expand what is known and a deep commitment to be of service so that another person's life can be similarly opened up and enlivened." And who would want to disagree with this?

Apart from these two formal positions, Kim is also involved in many other things. She has a private practice in adult and adolescent psychotherapy in Ann Arbor; she does consultancy work with different institutions including the VA Hospital in Allen Park, Michigan, the Catherine McAuley Mental Health Center and at the University of Detroit.

Some of her works are represented in several psychological and psychoanalytical journals, among which are, *The Psychoanalytical Quarterly, The Psychoanalytic Psychologist, Contemporary Psychology* and *Women and Therapy.* And, at present, she is working on her first book which "will examine contemporary clinical theory in the light of postmodern discourses in the humanities." She has recently been selected as a Fellow of the American Psychoanalytical Association and this will certainly help to further enhance her career, especially since her future plan is to become a clinical psychoanalyst.

In this regard, she says, as "an African-American woman, I have also found in psychoanalysis new tools to broaden inquiry into other areas of my interest, namely, issues of race, ethnicity and social justice. Equally exciting to me, my interdisciplinary work in critical race theory and postmodern discourses in the humanities has led me back to psychoanalysis with new questions and a commitment to interdisciplinary dialogue with psychoanalysis as a critical participant." Her interests in these matters went outside the bounds of the academic world as seen in her outreach activities. In one of these, she works with a local community center, facilitating psychoanalytic psychotherapy to low-income residents of Ann Arbor and the surrounding community, many of whom "are members of minority groups. One of the innovative aspects of this program is that we send out interns and staff to the community center to provide services onsite, and in this way take a proactive stance about the utility of psychoanalytic therapy for a wide range of problems and its relevance for a wide range of people."

This highly professional woman has even found time for a private life. In 1994 she married Richard Hale Shaw, a computer journalist and consultant, and they presently live in a "brownstone" about ten minutes from the University of Michigan campus; and although we have not heard of any children yet they nevertheless have "two dogs."

৯১

Allison Moore-Lake   Like Angela Scott-Henderson, Allison belonged
to that special group who answered in a timely fashion with a letter dated
July 8, 1995. She is also enthusiastic about the project, as is typical of just
about everyone else who responded. The problem, therefore, is not one of
interest in the project. It has to do with the "p" word: procrastination. Remember our friend with the "magnetized fridge"?

Allison thought my letter "a welcome one," for, she said, "I have often
thought it appropriate to have a "Black Women at Amherst College"
book," since, obviously, there is one on black men. Graciously, she apologized for the delay, but hoped her letter would not be too late. Thankfully,
it is not for indeed her career so far is most intriguing, a small part of
which I have mentioned in the "Introduction."

Allison majored in Sociology and since then has done a number of
wonderful things including serving in the U.S. Peace Corps. To her, this
was a dream that came true because she had always wanted to do something of this kind. In just about a year after graduation, in the spring of
1983, she was assigned to Senegal in West Africa, for which she had to complete a training program of three months before leaving. Then she was
sworn in as a Community Development Analyst, assigned to work in a village in the region of Dourabel. This place must have been fairly isolated,
since it entailed a two-hour ride to the capital city of Dakar—but this is by
local transportation! She worked with a community group that was already established for the main purpose of designing income-generating
projects, and this is such fascinating work that she should tell it in her own
voice: Allison said:

> We built an irrigation system and vegetable garden/fruit
> tree orchard cooperative with several neighboring villages. I
> worked with the women's group on a chicken co-op, improv-
> ing their families diets' and building fuel conserving stoves.
> Upon completion of my tenure as a Peace Corps Volunteer I
> was contracted by Peace Corps to remain in Senegal for several

months as a Cross-Cultural Trainer for new volunteers. The three years I spent in Africa are to this day some of my most cherished experiences.

Not many alumnae of Amherst have had such a rich experience in giving useful service abroad—reminiscent certainly of the old missionary impulse which informed the College at its establishment back in the 1820s when Edward Jones was there.

In returning to the U.S. in 1985, the zeal for public service had not left Allison. She immediately took the position of Team Leader for a relatively new organization in New York City, called the "City Volunteer Corps." This organization is said to have based its program design on the Peace Corps model, but, in this case, its target was not the Third World but America's urban youth, and it should surprise no one that she found comparable situations. We will let her tell her story again:

> I supervised an ethnically diverse group of young people on service projects throughout the five boroughs and counseled them in personal and career development. This was an eye-opening experience for me coming back from a so-called "Underdeveloped Country" and finding so many similar situations in N.Y. City. It enabled me to get to know NYC and work with young people. Two young people have become like a brother and sister to me over the years.
>
> In 1986 I moved to the National Civic League in New York City as an Associate where I assisted in developing a national database of community development projects and administered the summer intern program. I was promoted to Director in 1987 for the All America City program honoring cities for civic excellence. I enjoyed my time at the League and was given the opportunity to perform many responsibilities working with community groups, board members and all those in between.

And even after the New York Civic League moved to Denver, Colorado, in 1988, Allison continued to work for non-profit organizations. She now took the position of Development Officer with Associated Black Charities (ABC) in New York City, which is a part of the United Way agency. Here she was "exposed to the world of fund raising" and probably did not like it very much, for after one year in this position she began applying to graduate schools. She soon won a full tuition scholarship and stipend from the Consortium for Graduate Study in Management to New York University at the Stern School of Business. In two years she graduated with a Master of Business Administration degree in Finance and International Business.

And now she is about to enter the private-sector world of commerce and finance. Will she like it? Her first position in this new field was with the U.S.A. branch of the Toronto Dominion Bank, where she was involved with the Utilities and Project Finance Group. "This was a challenging career change for me. The finance sector was new and exciting, but as in business school, my heart was not in my work. In hindsight I would have pursued a Masters in International Affairs or Public Administration. However, the MBA has given me flexibility in my career choices." Not too surprisingly, she left the Toronto Bank in September 1993, unhappy with the world of investment banking and the corporate sector.

In the meantime she had married Terence Lake of her class of '82 in July of 1988. The wedding was solemnized at the United Nations Chapel in New York City. He, too, had completed his MBA, but from the Georgetown University by 1986. And it was while working with the Toronto Bank that she had her first child, Sahara Theresa Lake, in October of 1992. When she left the Bank in 1993 she confessed that becoming a mother was a most rewarding "job" and if "finances allowed I would do it on a full-time basis." By this time she and her husband had also left Brooklyn, New York, although they liked it there, but decided that as a young couple starting a new family, moving to a suburb would be a better solution, and in May of 1993 they purchased a house in White Plains, New York. By this time not only did she want to spend more time with her one-year-old daughter but she also wanted to "get back into a nonprofit sector and community-based programming." And for a year she did some consultancy work with several nonprofit organizations in the New York area, assisting with fund raising and proposal writing, utilizing, no doubt, skills she had acquired from working with ABC and its affiliation with the United Way; she also consulted on matters pertaining to organizational development, board creation, and the like.

We should not be surprised to find Allison involved with nonprofit organizations again. Since 1994 she took a full-time position as Director of Outreach with the YWCA of White Plains and Central Westchester. In this capacity, she is administering an after-school program for African American and Hispanic school-age girls, with a view to helping them to develop self esteem, cultural awareness and educational and career options. She also acts as community liaison with different local agencies. Allison finds this work demanding and challenging, and made "even more so with recent budget cuts to youth programs."

Allison is undoubtedly one to whom service in the old sense of the term will always take precedence over monetary considerations. And I am sure she will pass this noble trait on to her daughter, Sahara, who will be four in October. She obviously enjoys interpersonal relations whether in her work or in her private life. She enjoyed her Amherst experience particularly stressing the friendships she made there. "I have to say that consistent throughout these twelve years since graduation have been African-American women, close friends, I made from my class at Amherst College including: Janice Cook, Adrienne White-Farnes, Jeanne Lisk-Friedman, and Susan McKeever (Class of 1986). These women have gone through my joys and hard-times with me. Although I am constantly reminded of the value of an Amherst education, it is because of these friendships, which I believe will last a lifetime, that I am forever indebted to Amherst College. Thank you for the opportunity to share these brief thoughts with you. Hopefully I can send the photos at a later date. If I can be of further assistance, please do not hesitate to contact me. I anxiously await *Black Women of Amherst College*."

It is letters of this kind that gave me the inspiration to continue with the project even during those moments of frustration over non-response as I mentioned earlier.

ॐ

Angela Scott-Henderson   Angela is among those precious few who responded to my *first* letter almost within the deadline, on July 6, 1995, hoping that her letter would not arrive too late "for inclusion in your book on the Black Women of Amherst. It sounds like a wonderful book and I hope to be able to provide any assistance that I can to the effort." Those who have edited any combined work for publication will know how a response of this kind is appreciated.

Angela majored in American History and after graduating moved to Akron, Ohio, away from the Northeast, where she was born (Worcester, Massachusetts) and educated. She really moved to begin work with B.F. Goodrich in the field of human resources, where she first received some training before assuming greater responsibilities, including recruitment, employee relations, labor relations generally and equal employment opportunities.

But Angela did not see this position, necessarily, as her final career goal. Thus, while working with B.F. Goodrich she enrolled at the University of Akron Law School. Conveniently for her, this was a program where one could obtain a law degree by attending night classes. After spending about four years with B.F. Goodrich, she left for a new position as a clerk in the civil section of the City of Akron law department. This was during the last semester of law school, and it was obviously a well-planned strategy. She passed the Ohio Bar examination in July of 1986, and having familiarized herself with the legal department at Akron, could now move on to bigger things.

In a very short time she was appointed Assistant Attorney General in the Ohio Attorney General's office in Columbus. In this position she found herself dealing with several government agencies. She had to represent the Department of Health, Education and Human Services in different areas of operation. For example, she became involved in litigating the difficult business of Medicaid overpayment to nursing homes, revoking foster care and day care licenses, and collecting interstate child support. She then shifted position by representing the Ohio Civil Rights Commission. In this role she was required to litigate Equal Employment Opportunity (EEO) complaints.

By February of 1989, Angela began to work for private companies. In moving to Cincinnati, Ohio, she obtained a position with Chiquita Brands International—a position which gave her the opportunity to combine her human resources skills, first learned in her first appointment with B.F. Goodrich, and her legal training. Here she was responsible for Equal Employment Opportunity issues and other labor relations connected with the firm. By 1994 she moved to New Jersey where she is currently Director of Diversity for Sony Electronics, Inc. in Park Ridge, New Jersey, and here again she is involved in labor and employment issues. Never forgetting the importance of self-improvement, she sat for and passed the New Jersey Bar examination in 1995.

In the meantime, Angela found some time for a private life. She married David Henderson in April of 1987, and now she has "a beautiful daughter, Carly Michelle Henderson who was born on May 28, 1990."

Angela's tribute to Amherst College is not unlike what we have heard constantly from Harold Wade as well as in this work. She said that her Amherst education "has opened many doors for me. Most importantly Amherst taught me how to think. . . . Amherst also taught me that I have the capability to do anything that I set my mind to. I valued the friends, professors and fond memories I have of my four years at the 'fairest college of them all.'" Harold Wade reiterated repeatedly how Amherst had "not destroyed the will to achieve in the Afro-American attending the College," and it is to be hoped that this will continue.

ॐ

Adrienne Elaine White-Faines actually responded to my first letter in August 1995, and yet she was conscientious enough to have regretted that it did not meet the first deadline of June 30, 1995, and hoped her letter was "not too late!" But she had just returned to work after having her second child, Karnau, born in June, and the first, Mari, was born in August of 1993. Adrienne has been married since 1992 to an Amherst alumnus, Dr. Larry Faines, of the same class of '82. Like so many others in their response, she, too, wished me "good luck with the project."

At Amherst, Adrienne majored in American Studies with a "minor" in pre-medical sciences. As if to demonstrate her interest in the sciences, during the fall of 1980 she took a study-abroad leave of absence to attend the City of London Polytechnic in London, England, where she pursued studies in Chemistry and Physics. Upon graduating from Amherst in 1982, Adrienne took a year off to work as an intern Dean of Students at Trinity College in Hartford, before going to graduate school. At the end of the year she entered the University of South Carolina in Los Angeles where she was awarded the Master's degree in Public Administration, stressing health services. But even as a full-time graduate student, this very conscientious young woman began her career in health administration in Los Angeles, California, working for 18 months as the Assistant Administrator for the Colima Internal Medicine Group (CIMG), and at the Los Angeles County with similar interests.

Adrienne then moved to New York City where she was employed in positions of great responsibility involving large sums of money. This was largely because of her special interest in hospital capital facilities. In 1985 she served as a Senior Planning Coordinator in the Corporate Office for Capital Planning where she developed long-range strategic plans, with a $1.5-billion ten-year capital plan. The main purpose here was to achieve a comprehensive renovation of five municipal hospitals with critical needs. Obviously her performance in this capacity was successful for in the following year, 1986, she was promoted to Associate Director of Planning and Development for Kings County Hospital in Brooklyn, New York. In this capacity, her added responsibilities even included supervision of designs and construction plans for a large municipal teaching hospital.

She left New York around 1988 to take up a new post in Chicago with the Northwestern Memorial Hospital and in 1989 became Director of the Redevelopment Project at this hospital. In this position she became responsible for the implementation of a $600-million project to replace facilities for the hospital's academic medical center. Her duties in this job situation are enormous. They include directing and supervising all facility planning activities to support replacement of inpatient facilities, diagnostic and treatment services, ambulatory care support and administrative space of vast dimensions. As the Director, she also coordinated the efforts of architects, engineers, construction managers, state and local regulatory agencies; she directed internal planning activities, managed project budgets, schedules, marketing initiatives and contract compliance on a daily basis—making it seem too much for any one person!

Currently, Adrienne is still Director, but in this case, it is of Community Services for the hospital, and whether or not the workload is lighter is not clear. She is now responsible for the establishment and maintenance of the academic medical center, which included among many other functions, involvement with community service, and other outreach programs of concern to the needs and health care trends of the wider community.

Adrienne also finds time to serve on several boards and committees: among these, she worked with National Association for Health Service Executives, where she co-chaired the National Educational Conference Program Planning Committee (1991-92) and is currently President of the Mid-West Chapter; she also served on the Committee to the Board of Trustees for Norfolk State College from 1987-1990; also, she is on the Board of Planned Parenthood in the Chicago area and the Near North Health Services Corporation. She is also a member of the Chicago Assembly and has served on committees sponsored by the Chicago Center for Urban Research and the Committee for Executive Leadership in Health Care sponsored by the University of Chicago.

Despite her enormous professional activities with the concomitant responsibilities, Adrienne also finds time to perform different voluntary community services: she has given much time as an Hospice Volunteer in the Northwestern Memorial Hospice Program, since 1989; she has served as a National Recruiter for the Judy Davis Bone Marrow Program. She is also an active member of her church, and she lectures regularly in the Chicago Public School system in their Youth Motivation Program.

Her professional affiliations include The American College of Health Care Executives, the American Hospital Association for Ambulatory Care Professionals, the National Association of Health Service Executives and the Chicago Health Executives Forum.

It should come as no surprise that she deservedly received the YMCA of Metropolitan Chicago Black and Hispanic Achievers of Industry Award in 1992 for her professional achievement and service to the community.

Class of '83

❧

Beverly Elaine Allen finally responded in August of 1996. In apologizing for the late response, she told me that she had been "reorganizing [her] professional life . . . trying to fine-tune and find my niche." She thanked me for doing the project and was looking forward "to the book."

Beverly majored in Black Studies and, apparently, was not very active on campus, quite possibly because she is proud to state that she worked her way through college: "Employed all four years of college," as she recounts it. I know Beverly very well as I was her advisor for her senior honors thesis, entitled, "Traditional Birth Attendants of Sierra Leone: Their Beliefs and Practices." She came to this topic while on a Study Abroad Program at the Fourah Bay College in Freetown, Sierra Leone, West Africa, and "was fortunate enough to take Rural Sociology taught by Dr. Moses Dumbuya," who introduced her to Traditional Birth Attendants (TBAs) in the remote areas far from the capital cities of this country. Beverly returned fascinated and excited with her new knowledge of these practitioners and was determined to do a senior thesis on them. Her major concerns were to identify what she considers the good points regarding the practice of traditional medicine as well as those that are downright harmful to good health. In the end she strongly recommended a merging of the best in traditional medicine with modern Western medical techniques and practices.

For this thesis, she returned with a thicket of disorganized interview notes from field research on these TBAs, as well as lecture notes and different reports, including some from the Peace Corps on traditional medicine in Sierra Leone. It was not easy to sort these out into a disciplined coherent thesis, and in her Acknowledgment she said that "without my faculty advisor, Professor Mavis Campbell, advising, chiding, correcting and especially caring about me, my thesis might have developed into a jumbled mess." The result was not perfect but her main theme was maintained. For her part, Beverly is certainly one of the most enduring of students that I have taught here at Amherst College. She was serious-minded, hard-working, responsible and determined to succeed. Yet she had a keen sense of humor and never allowed her ambition to consume her entirely or to detract from her humane beliefs. She had a strong sense of public service and was looking forward to the time when she could use her training and her skills to serve the wider community—as indeed, she is doing today. It is clear that she possessed these qualities from the influence of her mother to whom she dedicated her thesis:

> Most of all, I want to thank God for allowing me to be Mrs. Elaine Allen's daughter. My mother has loved me, nourished and advised me from before I was born. She is the first midwife I knew and the first person I have been extremely proud of. I wish that the two hundred babies that she has delivered had the opportunity to know her and to be inspired by her as I have.
>
> This work is dedicated to my mother and to all the mothers like her.

Beverly did not become a pediatrician as I had thought—because I was confident that she was going to be a doctor of medicine. Instead, she specialized in Psychiatric medicine but with a strong concentration in child

and adolescent psychiatry. After graduating from Amherst, she entered
the School of Medicine at the University of Maryland, Baltimore, in 1984
and received the M.D. in 1989. During 1985 and 1987 she was Treasurer of
the American Medical Women's Association. It is unclear whether or not
this was a position with a salary, helping to pay her way again through
medical school in this case. After receiving her M.D., she took an internship in Pediatrics at the Medical College of Virginia from June 1989 to July
1990, and then entered her General Psychiatric Residency at the University
Hospital, Baltimore, Maryland, from July 1990 to June 1992. With a Child
and Adolescent Psychiatric Fellowship (1992-1994) at the University and
Sheppard Pratt Hospitals, she completed an additional six months in the
Circuit Court of Baltimore City. Here she performed evaluations of adolescents and parents involved in CINA (Child in Need of Assistance), and
delinquency training.

But during this period of internship, residency and fellowship, she was
also involved in psychiatric evaluations at different institutions. At the
Florence Crittenton Group Home for Girls, Baltimore City, she treated
adolescent girls who were committed to the Departments of Social Services, Juvenile Services and that of Health and Mental Hygiene. At the
Maryland Army National Guard, she was the leader of the Mental Health
Platoon which was responsible for the mental health of the troops in the
entire division during annual training exercises; she also trained medics,
officers and senior NCO's about the nature of battle fatigue and its treatment, among various other activities involving medical support for the
troops.

Away from the troops, she entered another "battlefield," in this case,
sexual violence at the Sexual Assault Domestic Violence Center, where she
supervised others on cases dealing with incest, rape and domestic violence
generally. On another "battlefield," she performed court-ordered evaluations on detained and committed adolescents where she addressed psychiatric issues, treatment and appropriate placements at the Charles H.
Hickey Jr. School in Baltimore County.

Since 1995 to the present, she has continued to work on psychiatric patients, in inner-cities, suburban hospital emergency rooms, as well as providing consultations to other physicians about their hospitalized patients.
In addition to Maryland she has worked in Washington, D.C. performing

different services at the Child and Youth Services Administration, the Center for Mental Health and the Riverside Treatment Center, addressing issues ranging from forensic evaluations, delinquency, child and adolescent mental health programs, psychiatric treatment of substance abuse, and the like. Furthermore, she is always responsible for training and supervising clinical staff, and at the Residential Care Inc., in Washington, D.C. and Maryland she is also involved with the psychiatric treatment of children in foster care.

There is no doubt that Beverly's work is both onerous and psychologically demanding. But it is typical of her, with her strong sense of service, not to have chosen an easy or more lucrative position, but to be involved in what she thinks is right and necessary. She writes that Amherst has helped her to cope.

> Experiences at Amherst really helped me in that they were introductions of what was to come. I improved my ability to effectively deal with people who try to force me into a box, look at my options and make decisions. Of course there were problems at Amherst but they were a microcosm of the world. Working out and trying to address those problems made it somewhat easier when they showed up again. Looking back, my four years in college helped me to develop ways of dealing with society as a whole without losing me.

She also appreciated the liberal arts education she received from the College, involving courses in both the sciences and the humanities. She found that because she "was able to explore [her] interests, unencumbered by basic requirements, I was able to take information, synthesize it, and use it to do the best for the people who came under my care."

Beverly has medical licenses in both Maryland and Washington, D.C., and is a member of many professional organizations, including the American Association of Child and Adolescent Psychiatrists, the American Medical Women's Association, the Black Psychiatrist's Association and the Maryland Psychiatric Association.

Kathy Lorraine Frazier responded to my first letter with a short fax August 21, 1995, with something about herself. She has rather gone in for high finance which her major in Economics presaged. Following her graduation, she worked for two years at Morgan Stanley in the Corporate Finance Department—an experience she found gave her a good introduction to investment banking. She made the best use of this first encounter with corporate capital, observing as many aspects of the firm as was possible, even though she soon perceived that she would need more training for these endeavors. To this end, therefore, she left in 1985 in order to enter the Wharton School at the University of Pennsylvania, where she gained an MBA in 1987. At the Wharton, she majored in finance, and upon graduation, she took a position with Goldman Sachs in New York City, and, as she said, her activities "have been numerous." But it obviously brought forth good results, since she tells us that in "the spring of 1991 I became a vice president."

Her numerous activities found her in certain programs which should be socially satisfying to her: for example, she is a sponsor in the Student/Sponsor Partnership Program which provides scholarships for high school children in New York City. She is also involved in activities of the private school she attended, the Spence School, and last year was nominated to the board of trustees.

Unfortunately, we have no personal statement from her about her experience at Amherst College.

Class of '84

❧

Janet M. Buckner is among those who stoutly refused to reply to my numerous correspondence and telephone messages. But when, finally, I was able to speak to her on the telephone, in August of 1996, she said, as mentioned above, that she did not think that she had done much to write about! She majored in Black Studies but admitted also that she was not very active on campus because her clear goal was to pursue her pre-med courses and this consumed most of her time. In this she was successful, and within seven years of graduating from Amherst, she obtained the Doctor of Medicine degree from Morehouse.

Janet now practices medicine as a child psychiatrist, at the Jacobi Hospital in the Bronx, New York City, and I am sure that when this book is revised there will be a great deal about her to be included.

✑

Courtney Lynne Bullard Parks majored in Black Studies and Psychology, and although she has not been forthcoming with recent information, this was no problem because I know Courtney very well and am well acquainted with her views and activities since I was one of her advisors. She was an active participant in the life of the College community. She was actively involved in the leadership of the Black Student Union, and, in sports, she was a member of the softball team. During her junior year, she went to Howard University on educational leave, and there she became and continued to be a member of the National Psychological Honor Society and also of the Psychology Club of the Howard University. She was also always engaged in Children's Workshops as this was to be a part of her career goal; she worked with children as a counselor in summer camps and, for most of her years at Amherst, she was a volunteer with the Children's Workshop Program, a Saturday day-care center at Smith College, Northampton. "My work with children in these areas," she said, "and in day-to-day encounters has made me more sensitive to the personal qualities such as sensitivity, perceptiveness and patience that are necessary to interact successfully with and learn from children."

Courtney has always been interested in Psychology. "I have had a desire to study psychology since I was a child and my interest in the study of human behavior has strengthened with the course of time. Psychology appeals to me because it is a discipline that involves working with people and gaining a better understanding of the environmental and genetic factors that affect and influence human lives. The study of psychology requires a number of personal characteristics such as a skill in interpersonal relations, open-mindedness to new ideas and directions, sensitivity and perceptiveness. It also requires patience, determination and a commitment to serious research and investigation," she wrote in her senior year at Amherst College.

As usual, Courtney was clear-sighted about her choice of a double major in Black Studies and Psychology. She was certain that the combination would benefit her intended career goals, one of which was to conduct cross-cultural research on children. To this end, the psychology major gave her "a firm background in a range of psychological areas" and theoretical tooling while the Black Studies major gave her "a firm foundation of knowledge on the interactions of African, Caribbean, Latin America and European cultures and furthers my knowledge of the history, lifestyles and concerns of Third World peoples." She felt then that the study of culturally diverse people was a neglected area of psychology. And this concern was not merely academic. Serious investigations by committed psychologists in this area, she felt, could lead to the improvement of social conditions especially in the areas of education and public policy.

Parks, right, with Ms. Janice Denton

Although Courtney maintained an impressive grade average across the board and within both majors, she did not write a senior honors thesis because her aim was to pull from as many sources and disciplines as possible. Since developmental psychology was her area of specialization, she took one such course at Smith College, which, apart from everything else, gave her "the opportunity to be a part of the atmosphere of an all-women's college," while her junior year at Howard "exposed me to faculty doing research in a broad range of areas and enriched my knowledge in the new directions and foci of psychological study," and, of course, she is "proud" that it was while here that she was inducted into the National Psychological Honor Society.

She is also pleased with her experience at Amherst. "The relationships that I have had with Amherst professors have had a positive influence on my growth as an individual and have helped me to define my career goals. I am willing to learn and ask questions and have found that professors have responded receptively to my "quest for knowledge" and have helped me in any way that they could, inside and outside of the classroom. . . . My academic life at Amherst has helped me to further develop organizational qualities such as effective time management and the ability to express and organize ideas. These qualities will aid me in graduate study in psychology."

As would be expected, upon graduation, Courtney did pursue her goal of graduate study in psychology. She wanted to develop "a strong background and systematic foundation in developmental psychology: to gain breadth and specialization in the field as well as strong research and methodological skills," and for this she entered the graduate department in psychology at Howard University and gained the Ph.D. degree in 1991. During this time (between 1989 and 1991) she was a psychological consultant to the U.S. Department of the Interior, Medical and Health Services, and she also taught some courses in the Psychological Department at Lincoln University. At present she is a part-time faculty member of the Department of Psychology at Howard. Among her professional memberships are, the Association of Black Psychologists, the American Psychological Association, and the American Psychological Society, among others, and if she lives up to her undergraduate convictions, we know that she would also be involved in outreach programs: she had said that she wanted to use her education "to help make positive changes in human lives. I look forward to the challenges that lie ahead and am willing to commit the time and energy necessary to meet those challenges."

A year after receiving the Ph.D. Courtney was married to James E. Parks (July 1992) a graduate of Berkeley, '90, and the last time we heard of them they had a child. We hope that in the updated edition of this work, Courtney will be supplying a great deal of new information about herself.

෨

Yvette Cecilia Mendez did not reply to my two letters but when I telephoned her she responded with charm and promptness. She graciously apologized for not having replied but "was grateful for your reminder call since I do wish to be included in this momentous and worthwhile effort."

Yvette majored in Political Science and it is obvious that she has always been interested in the legal profession. Even while at Amherst her intern positions were with the District Attorney's Office in New York County and the Law Department for the City of New York, in January of 1983 and the summer of this same year, respectively. But Yvette was also engaged in other activities here at Amherst: She was a member of the Student Assembly, of the Black Student Union and she was elected a member of the Admissions Search Committee. She also played varsity volleyball.

Upon graduating, she attended the Fordham University School of Law and gained the J.D. in 1990. But during this time she was also actively involved with the New York Public Interest Research Group, Inc. (NYPIRG) where she was employed in different situations: she was a staff person organizer with varying responsibilities including supervising student-run lobbying organizations, and was soon promoted from entry-level to senior staff person; she then became Divestment Coordinator, where she conducted statewide grassroot campaign dealing with the extent and scope of New York State's divestment endeavors; she then went back to personnel affairs but in this case as Director and here she organized, developed and coordinated NYPIRG's recruiting program; later she became Legal Assistant to the group and in this capacity she organized and documented evidence and interviewed prospective witnesses in student-fee cases and finally, under this same group, she became Project Coordinator and was involved with the coordination of certain activities dealing with Hunter College in New York City.

All this she did between 1984 and June of 1987, when she took a new appointment with the New York City Charter Revision Commission as Research Assistant. Here she interpreted, analyzed and summarized various sections of the New York City Charter and, having done this, she would then write briefing papers, detailing and explaining charter provisions; she compared federal, state, and city ethics provisions and summarized the findings for the Commissioner's use; and she also researched and briefed case laws regarding land use, as well as the zoning and formation of greater New York City.

By May of 1988, Yvette found herself working with a private firm, Brown & Guilbert, as Legal Assistant. In this position she assisted the general practitioner, prepared complaints, affirmations, jury instructions, affidavits in matrimonial, real property and probate matters. She also compiled a successful opposition to a summary judgment in a multi-million-dollar personal injury lawsuit. During the fall of this year (1988) she also participated in Fordham's two-credit Judicial Clinical Program, where she researched and wrote opinions, observed trials and court procedures.

Upon leaving Brown & Guilbert in May 1989, she went on to another private firm, Gold, Farrell & Marks, as a part-time summer associate, where she prepared briefs and memoranda for entertainment litigation firms on issues of contract, construction, securities and attachment laws.

Having now received her Fordham law degree (J.D.) in May 1990, Yvette then went back to the public sector, in this case as a full-time Law Clerk for a federal district court judge in Boston in September of 1990. In this capacity she attended court sessions, acted as courtroom deputy on bench trials, in addition to which, she briefed issues for motion sessions and prepared memoranda and opinions. She also acted on different occasions as a judge for trial advocacy classes and summary jury trials. She was also involved in the training and coordination of student intern programs, which must have reminded her of her own intern service in New York in 1983. She remained in this position until September 1991, when she went back into private practice, in this case with Goodwin, Procter & Hoar, still in Boston, but on a part-time basis. Again she is involved in trial practices, mostly civil, including discovery, trial, preparation of motion practice, in environmental, insurance and personal injury matters; she also is court-appointed counsel in contempt and First Amendment cases.

In the meantime, Yvette has been involved in some teaching. From September 1992, she signed up with the New England School of Law and became a writing instructor to law students, teaching them, on an individual basis, how to gain skills in legal writing and reasoning. She also became a writing specialist, through the Legal Practice Skills Program (LPS) at Suffolk University School of Law, and is still involved in this teaching program.

At present she is working with the firm of Sugarman, Rogers, Barshak & Cohen, as an Associate. This firm concentrates on insurance coverage, insurance defense and discrimination cases. Although Yvette leads a very busy life, she nevertheless finds the time for some *pro bono* activities, including the presidency of the Massachusetts Black Women Attorneys, and membership of the Metropolitan Black Bar Association of New York. She is also a member of the American Bar Association, the Boston Bar Association, and the Massachusetts Bar Association, among others.

She is very concerned about hiring practices in the legal profession and has always been an advocate of more diversity. This is well reflected in an article she wrote, "Affirmative Action and Diversity: A Hand in Glove Situation," published in the *Boston Bar Journal*, vol. 39, no. 4, September/October, 1995. It is a level-headed, well-reasoned article that made positive suggestions on how the situation could be alleviated.

Like so many of these alumnae of the College, Yvette has paid tribute to her Amherst education: "At the time that I graduated from Amherst College in 1984, I was merely pleased that I had endured four years of college and had received the payoff—my Bachelor of Arts in Political Science. Now, as a practicing trial attorney at a 24-lawyer firm in Boston, Massachusetts, I am grateful for my Amherst experiences—both inside and outside of the classroom—and for the benefits that the Amherst reputation has sent my way." She felt that the sense of community service that has become a part of her lifestyle was "spawned during my Amherst years, during which I served on the Student Assembly and played an integral part in the planning and execution of many of the rallies and community events that occurred in the Five College area during my [time there]. Today, I can say that my Amherst education and experience played a supreme role in my development as an attorney and has made me a concerned and active citizen. It has also given my family, who emigrated from Panama, a sense of great pride in my accomplishments. I owe many of these accomplishments to my Amherst experience.... I encourage all Amherst students and graduates, indeed, all young people—college-educated or not—to pursue their dreams and make their voices heard."

ॐ

Barbara Jean Smoot (nee Liggon) is easily one of the most outstanding students to have crossed Amherst's path. She was exceptional not only because she majored in Physics with a cumulative average grade of A-; not only because she received the highest grade across the board in her junior year and was a Phi Beta Kappa (1983–1984); not only because of the numerous awards she received in Mathematics and Physics—and one could continue—but also because she was a marvelous person who gave much joy both to her peers and professors who taught her. In speaking to some of her colleagues in the process of writing this book, invariably, when Barbara's name was mentioned, there was some exclamation of praise for her. It usually took the form of "she was so bright, yet so nice!" Alice Middleton-Merrick '87, for instance, was one such who found Barbara a refreshing and nice person who helped her with her mathematics.

The composed and dignified professor of Mathematics, Jim Denton—never one for excesses—"had the pleasure of having Barbara . . . in class as a third-semester calculus student and as a first-semester statistics student. She did a consistently outstanding job in both classes, receiving a well-deserved 'A' in one and an 'A-' in the other." Denton considered her "an outstanding person [who] never became so serious that she lost her sense of humor or so impressed with her own achievements that she abandoned her friendly, easy-going manner."

I, too, know Barbara very well because I had the pleasure of being her advisor for the four years she spent here at Amherst College. This was (and is) unusual but it came about because even after she declared her major in Physics and was accordingly assigned an advisor in this discipline, she insisted that I continue to be her advisor also, and fortunately the then Deans of Faculty and Students agreed. I thus became her general advisor and confidante, and she knew she could contact me at any time. From the first few meetings with Barbara in her freshman year, I soon discovered that she had exceptional qualities. Apart from the fact that she was totally unafraid of challenges but rather welcomed them, she had a zest for life which was remarkable. Each day seemed to her a new adventure in the business of her intellectual development; her desire to know, to explore, to challenge, to learn was her very *raison d'etre* and yet all this Aristotelian approach to life did not affect her keen sense of humor.

Barbara was not among the first to have responded to my letters and numerous telephone calls. Indeed, it was only after a very firm call from me that she finally responded. In extenuation, she is being kept excessively busy with her job, a loving husband and two children, the second having been born (July 18, 1995), just about the time I sent out my first letter, asking for a reply by June 30, 1995. But when she did reply, typically, it was thorough and fascinating—some 20 handwritten pages! In it she gave some interesting anecdotes, one of which was the very manner in which she had perforce to be writing to me. Her children, husband and job kept her so busy that she had to be "squeezing in a few minutes here and there. . . . As a matter of fact, I'm currently sitting on the floor of a Discovery Zone Center while my children and nephew play on all the toys and climb through all the tubes. Thank goodness for Discovery Zones. The noise level in here from the kids can be deafening at times, especially when kids find out it's time to leave and their parents try to drag them out. (My kids *never* do that! [funny face here]) This explains why this writing is so choppy and that I seldom complete a thought once starting it." Although she calls this writing very "choppy," nevertheless, it is a sensible and sensitive account which I have hardly edited when direct quotations are made. The most I did was to rearrange, reorganize and give contexture to the material. Then, although many of the students involved in this work have commented on their professors here and there, she, on the other hand, did a short separate biographical sketch of those professors here that she felt have influenced her most. These will be entered later.

Barbara was a member of the Black Student Union and if she were not very active on campus, she nevertheless influenced and helped many of her peers on a one-to-one basis; but it is also understandable for a student who was getting straight "As" in subjects like Mathematics, Physics, Calculus and the Japanese language in any given semester. On the other hand, because this young woman was so brilliant, she was soon subject to certain attitudes and actions that were the result of the usual combination of jealousy, envy and downright resentment, all of which consumed a great deal of her time. In all this, she was fortunate to have had some sterling support from Professors Gordon and Jagannathan of the Physics Department. In an understatement of the year, Barbara said wryly, "I ran into a couple of situations at Amherst (which Professors Gordon and Jagu can attest to)." Some of the incidents she encountered came from white male students in the Physics Department, "who," as Barbara said, "could not accept me as an equal—that I was quite competent, that as a black woman I could 'satisfactorily' meet the requirements of a Physics major at Amherst, and that I certainly didn't receive any favors from anyone." Both Professors Jagannathan ("Jagu," as we call him) and Gordon have related some of the unpleasant situations she encountered. Professor Jagannathan wrote:

Barbara (Liggon) Smoot '84 graduated as a physics major. I came to know her in Fall 1981, my first year at Amherst, and her second year here. She took the second semester of Introductory Physics with me at that time. It was obvious to me from her work in the course that she was a very bright student, with a solid command of the necessary mathematics and physics for the course. She was also articulate and well spoken. Needless to say that we took a liking to each other very quickly, and she became my physics advisee. I also remember that my colleagues in the physics department too had a high opinion of her. As I got to know her better, she sensitized me to a number of large and small ways in which she, as an African-American and female student, faced particular burdens and prejudices on this campus. For example, there were a few white students in her class belonging, if memory serves me well, to a particular sports team, who recognized that she was very capable in physics, and wished to "work with her" on their problem assignments. But it soon became clear to Barbara that their idea of working with her was that she would do the problems, and they would copy the solutions. When she balked at the idea, she faced some verbal hostility, the exact nature of which I never learned. She told me about these students, and how similar things had gone on the previous semester in a different course as well. It was clear to me from talking with one of those students that they could not bring themselves to treat Barbara with respect or equality, but would rather look upon her as a resource to be exploited for their benefit. It almost seemed to me that they could not comprehend that there might be something deeply wrong with their outlook. After all, since their "buddies" would be available to them, without fussing over the niceties of intellectual responsibility, why should Barbara not do the same thing. Yet, of course, Barbara could not be one of their "buddies," nor would she even remotely wish to be. From our perspective, Barbara and I sensed that the manner of inclusion and exclusion—their in-group of "buddies" and others—on which these guys were acting out had everything to do with race and gender although nothing explicitly racist or sexist was said as far as I know. As a result of some actions I took against one of the students involved, they resented Barbara for the rest of her career here, and during Senior Assembly, when Barbara received some award, this group of students actually hissed and booed, a rather unusual occurrence.

In spite of a number of such overt and not so overt insults and injuries, Barbara could take great pride in her many accomplishments, the respect of the faculty who knew her, and the high regard in which most students held her. She volunteered to give a talk on her work during the previous summer at the beginning of her senior year. We invited her to give the talk as part of the physics seminar series. Though a bit nervous, she gave a well-prepared and articulate account of her research work.

After consultations with Jagu I read the above to Barbara, and, at a flash she said, "every word is true," and approved of its entry.

Professor Gordon also dealt with another incident which was even more overt. In this case Barbara received a letter (a copy I now possess) from one of these students who "basically said I owed it to him to give him the answers to Gordon's final exam since it was quite clear I was going to get an A. I am glad I had the sense enough to do the right thing in seeking out Professor Gordon." In telling me this story, Barbara remarked that she "had never seen Professor Gordon so angry!"—as well he might be. A part of the letter ran:

Dear Barb,
Well in any event, at least Physics 13 is completely over for you! Listen, normally I really wouldn't be asking you this favor but now I am quite desperate. I'm going in to Wednesdays (sic) final with a C average & simply cannot afford to get lower than a B on that test. You really don't have to if you don't feel right about it, but seeing that it will hardly effect (sic) your "A" in the course, do you think you could give me a good idea of exactly what to study. This way I can concentrate on the relavent (sic)

topics & not waste precious time studying things that are not on the test. I would be most grateful for any help & advice you can offer & will surely be in debt to you. Remember that you'll always have a favor coming to you!

P.S. If you don't want to talk about the test but wouldn't mind helping maybe you could write some of the material included in the questions on the back of this sheet & slip it through my door. PLEASE HELP ME!! Thanks again.

In writing to me about this letter, Professor Gordon said he could not quite "recall why the author of the letter was to take the exam after Barbara. Possibly I had given him an extension for (purported) illness or something. I know that Barbara was very upset by the letter, as was I. She left it with me to deal with, but I think the letter's effect stayed with her for a long time." Gordon did not tell me how he dealt with the matter but it is well for him to know that Barbara was greatly impressed by his action/s. She said, "I learned to handle a situation like this with class and integrity. After a conversation with him [Professor Gordon] I felt that I could hold my head high regardless of the critics. And this is how I carry myself today. I know I confounded some people when I did get my degree in Physics and I know I confounded some people when I received my F.S.A. (Fellowship in the Society of Actuaries) after I completed all of the actuarial exams and the ethics class (March 1992)."

Although she is now satisfactorily employed as Senior Actuary, I was very disappointed as I told Barbara repeatedly that she did not pursue physics to graduate school, and I am gratified to find that Gordon also felt the same way:

> Barbara did well in Physics 13. Her midterm exams placed her in the top 10 percent of the class. Her work in the lab and on the homework was consistently very good. The final exam I gave that year proved to be quite difficult. Barbara's performance was affected rather more than that of most of the other good students in the course—hence she received an A- rather than an A for the course. Nonetheless, her overall performance was one of which she had every right to be proud. I had high hopes

for her prospects as a future physicist, and I think I let her know this (at least I hope I did). Still, whatever pleasure she might have had at having done well in Physics 13 was marred, I am certain, by that letter.

You know Barbara far better than I, so you will know whether or not I'm correct in thinking that she felt increasingly isolated from Amherst in her subsequent years here. A sense of apartness was (and is) felt by every woman who majors in physics at Amherst, and elsewhere. The problem is compounded for black women. Yet, Barbara had the ability to become the first woman to go on to physics graduate school from Amherst. It would have given me great pleasure and pride had she chosen to do so. I've wondered whether, despite our genuine good intentions, my colleagues and I made physics seem to be a truly viable and inviting career option to Barbara, as well as to a number of other able women who passed through our courses, but who chose to pursue other careers. Still, I gather from you that Barbara is happy, successful, and stimulated in her life and in her career. I am not so parochial as to believe that physics offers more. So please give Barbara, and Kevin, my hearty good wishes.

[Now, it should have been my turn to relate what is easily the most unpleasant and unnecessary situation that could have happened to any student—anywhere. In this case it involved a most outlandish and bizarre decision made by a few, not students, in this case, but administrators. I discussed that matter closely with Barbara regarding whether or not we should mention it in this work, and although she left the decision entirely to me, I decided not to enter it, in part, because it was I who helped in the final resolution of the ugly case. But it is certainly a wonder to me that this remarkable young woman does not evince any bitterness in looking back at the episode.]

Apart from the support of her professors, Barbara also had the support of Kevin Smoot, class of '83, who became her husband in her junior year. I well remember Barbara raising the question of getting married while still in college with me. As usual, I discussed the pros and cons with her and

then let her make the decision. This has always been my manner of dealing with most issues with Barbara, because I trusted her judgment. No
wonder she said of me: "While she did not answer all questions for me, she
did give me a map that I could use as I found my own way." On those occasions when she would burst into my office (or call me late at night) to
say she could not take any more and was leaving Amherst, I would employ
irony by reminding her that she should never even think of leaving the
place without first saying goodbye to me, and this would invariably bring
on a tension-relieving smile.

Barbara and Kevin were married in her junior year. It is a happy marriage and they now have two children, a daughter, Tanya Kevonne Smoot,
born December 12, 1991, and a son, Kevin Frederick Smoot, Jr., born July
18, 1995. She loves her husband, her children, her family: "I am fortunate
enough to be married to the most wonderful man to have graced this
planet. (Well, maybe, 2nd most; my father is #1!)" Kevin has also done well.
At present he is Associate vice President of the Fifth Third Bank of Columbus, and he, too, is obviously good at figures (although an English major
at Amherst), for he has already obtained a Certificate in Public Accounting (CPA), and is teaching accounting classes in the evenings at a local
state college. Kevin is also very active in the community, serving on a large
number of boards. But, to Barbara, his most prestigious position is to be
"the father of our two wonderful children. . . . There are no words that can
describe the height of our excitement, the depth of our love, or the
breadth of our joy the day our daughter was born. From that day forward,
I have been here to do right by her. She keeps my husband and me young.
As a child, I was 'too mature' to enjoy dancing to *Schoolhouse Rock*. Today,
everything in the house stops when *Conjunction Junction* or *Interjection*
comes on so I can dance like a crazy fool with the kids."

After her graduation from Amherst College, Barbara took a position at
the Kingswood-Oxford Private School in West Hartford, Connecticut,
where she taught Mathematics, Algebra and Physics. She recounted that
she was the only African-American instructor at "the upper campus that
held the 9th-12th grades," and she sensed some resentment. But, according
to her, she was well prepared for this. One of the things "I learned in my relationships with my professors and advisors at Amherst that most helped
me was the importance of being a role model. My professors and advisors

seemed to always know when it was time to give me a swift kick in the butt and when it was time to let up. I learned that regardless of how tough the road was, there is no excuse not to set a high standard for your goals and expectations of your performance. This is what I tried most to impart to *all* my students and especially the African-American students at the campus. The funny thing is, the places and the players may be different, but the battles you fight are all still the same."

Barbara wrote that she enjoyed teaching very much and would like to pursue it "some day." She had "some excellent students who really had a thirst for knowledge and wanted to do well. The most difficult situations arose with students who had very wealthy parents who would protect and defend them even when the students obviously were in the wrong. Money talks and always will continue to do so. Luckily though, these situations were the exception rather than the rule."

She stayed at the Kingswood-Oxford School for two years (1984–1986), leaving to pursue the actuarial career. She did this for several reasons as stipulated by her. Not surprisingly, she "needed intellectual challenge. Teaching high school algebra was fun, but I knew I could get burned out doing it year after year. When I am not in the process of learning new things myself, I feel that I may as well be dead. The actuarial examination process provided me a rigorous approach to learning a new discipline. The actuarial exam process is such that you are just a candidate number to those grading the exams. They don't even know your name let along your gender or race. When my peers witnessed my success with the exams, they could not ever dispute what I did and so try to pass it off on 'racial or gender favoritism.'"

Then, with her usual good humor, she related the circumstances surrounding one of these very difficult examinations: "Not to digress from the main point here," she declared, "but I do need to share a story with you," describing how:

> The exams are graded with a score of 0–10 (integers) in which
> 6–10 are passing (10 = the highest possible passing score). I,
> and several of my peers, sat for an exam on advanced pricing
> techniques. The examination room had several problems with
> noise. A fire alarm went off several times (I was sitting directly

beneath it—the closest one in the room). Many other distractions occurred, and I was sitting in the worst position in the room. Well, when exam results came out, there were a few of my peers who were very "used to passing and doing well," either failed or received just a six. What a blow to their egos. They were so distraught that they wanted to petition the Society of Actuaries to "give them some slack" because of the exam room disturbances. Assuming that I also did not do well or that I failed, they sent a friend of mine to ask me if I would join them in this effort. My response was, "Gee, I'd love to, but since I got a 10, I don't think my testimony would be of much help—especially since I was sitting in the worst position and should have been most negatively affected." There is a large part of me that doesn't believe in excuses.

Another reason was that I was always fascinated with the corporate world. (I've since grown up and gotten over that, though.) The actuarial career would let me pursue a career in business as well as keep up my math skills I had worked so hard to get.

I was not born into a wealthy family so I did not have a trust fund I could dip into when my annual salary of $14,000 couldn't meet the bills.

So I became an actuary.

Professor Denton has informed us that the field of Actuarial Science is no joke. Yet, Barbara passed "the first three actuarial examinations (there are ten of them) within two years (normally these examinations are taken one to two years apart)." Denton also invited Barbara, about four years ago, to return to Amherst to "discuss the Actuarial career possibilities with interested students," which she "graciously accepted," and he is expecting to invite her again soon.

In receiving the highest grade (a score of 10) for her first actuarial examination, Barbara credited this as mentioned earlier, to Denton of the Mathematics Department and to her majoring in physics at Amherst. "Professors Gordon and Jagu's exams made the actuarial exams seem like 'cake' by comparison. Many of my peers didn't have the pleasure of being in a Gordon/Jagu physics class so they didn't have a good benchmark for fear!"

Since 1986 (to the present) Barbara has been employed at the Nationwide Insurance Company in Columbus, Ohio, first as an Associate Actuary but now promoted to the position of Senior Actuary, in the Group Annuity line of business. She has done Guaranteed Investment Contract (G.I.C.) pricing, financial reporting of different kinds, underwriting, development of contracts, among many other activities. She considers this position as having "some challenging opportunities.... My supervisor can tell you that its best not to let me get bored and unchallenged. I like to be learning new things all the time and use what I've learned to contribute to the operation and performance of the line of business. My boss ... can always count on me to dare to be different and produce a positive outcome as a result of it." In recognition of this praiseworthy quality, in March of 1995, she was presented with the Robert N. Powell Award, for "Recognition of a high order of innovative, non-traditional thinking and excellence in performance."

But this is only one of a number of awards Barbara had been receiving even before entering Amherst College. While still in high school, she was the recipient of the Rensselaer Mathematics and Science Award (1978), and the year before coming to Amherst she was a Semi-Finalist in the National Merit Scholarship. At Amherst, she won the American Physical Society Scholarship for Minority Undergraduates (1981–1982); the Amherst College Bassett Physics Prize she won in 1982. This is awarded to a student who has demonstrated outstanding ability in the first Physics course taken; she was Phi Beta Kappa, 1983–1984, and in her senior year, she received the Amherst College Addison Brown Scholarship awarded to a senior student "who has attained the highest academic standing of the freshman, sophomore and junior years," and when in 1992 she received her Fellowship in the Society of Actuaries, she was awarded A Certificate of Recognition from the Columbus Chapter of the Association of Black Insurance Professionals for completing the Actuarial Examinations, and we can expect her to chalk up many more awards in the future.

She is also a member of different professional organizations, including the Society of Actuaries, the American Academy of Actuaries, the Columbus Actuarial Club, and the International Association of Black Actuaries.

What has Amherst done for Barbara? She has high praise for her Amherst experience as we have already seen. Even those outrageously negative experiences that she encountered have conduced to her benefit. She saw them as contributing to her growth in strength and self confidence—making her "one tough cookie"—in her own words. She is happy that she worked hard and never shirked her assignments, and this has brought her rewards in the workplace. "I thank God I had the sense enough to keep at it at Amherst and the wits to follow the advice of my professors. . . . Amherst saw to it that I was challenged to my limits, broadened my background and forced me to participate in things in which I wasn't necessarily a star. Dealing with the socio-economic/class differences as well as the racial/gender differences also meant that I had to develop an inner strength to make it through Amherst. Today, I can tell you I'm one tough cookie! I feel at ease in a wide diversity of situations. I can walk the walk and talk the talk in an executive conference room filled entirely with extremely highly compensated white males. I am confident enough to participate in fundraising discussions in a board/staff meeting at the MCK (?) Arts Complex of which I am a board member. Don't get me wrong, I might be a little nervous [when] starting out, but once I get going I'm in my element and I *perform*."

As said earlier, she thinks some of her Amherst professors "deserve their own special sections," and here they are:

My Amherst Professors:
Professor Gordon: I loved Prof. Gordon's classes. I think he took great joy proving all sorts of theories on the board, making up his own rules of mathematics. Many of the things he did were not intuitive and many times I left his classes feeling as if someone played a theoretical prank on me that I still hadn't figured out. Prof. Gordon approached his classes with such enthusiasm. I could tell that he really enjoyed what he was doing.

Professor Denton: I believe I had Prof. Denton for three math classes. I regret not having taken more math classes. I honestly feel like you can never take too many math classes.

I have two stories in particular to share with you regarding Prof. Denton. I remember my freshman year in Math 11 at a time when he sauntered into class carrying our first set of exams to take. He had them piled on the desk, and the class was fairly quiet waiting in anticipation of the destruction of egos yet to come. It seemed like forever to me until he passed out the exams. While I sat frozen in my chair, still looking at that stack of exams, I said to him, "The exam looks hard." And Prof. Denton said, "But you haven't even seen it yet?!" My reply was something to the effect that it didn't matter whether or not I had seen it. The mere fact that he created the exam probably meant it was difficult.

The second story has to do with a statistics class I took from him. How humbling! As I read the questions on the first exam, I realized I was in trouble. You know it's bad when you read question after question and don't even understand what is being asked! Needless to say, that exam was a real tear jerker. I went back to my dorm room afterwards and I was inconsolable. My husband, Kevin, my boyfriend at the time, knew it was hopeless. He ended up calling my dad to come up and cheer me up. My parents only lived about 20–30 minutes away so it was a fairly easy drive to make. Since I was always a daddy's girl, it was always my father who I turned to when I was down.

In any case, I received an 81 on that exam. I think this was one of the highest scores. I thought I had flunked it. To me, however, anything less than a 90 was failing. I've since grown up!

Prof. and Mrs. Denton were so kind to have Kevin and me over for dinner one time. That was a real treat given the college student's yearning for home-cooked meals. Mrs. Denton made these excellent corn bread muffins and a soup—all from scratch.

Prof. Denton was the first African-American instructor I had ever had in my life. I was awestruck when I first saw him, and I felt extremely proud. Because of him, I could see myself succeeding at Amherst. I can't ever overstate the importance of having African-American professors at these small liberal arts colleges. At Amherst, they were a lifeline to me.

To this day, I can still remember the sound of Prof. Denton's voice, his gait, his laughter, and even his writing. When you meet someone like him whom you admire so much, you try to focus on every detail of the person in hopes of picking up even a fraction of his/her being.

Professor Hirota: I loved the Japanese language and Prof. Hirota helped me learn quickly by setting extremely high standards. To me it was important to dare to be different. Why be like everyone else in taking European languages? To me, taking Japanese put me at the outer extremes of diversity.

Prof. Hirota was extremely disciplined and made special attempts to get to know all of her students. High participation was required. Because I had her at 9:00 a.m. four days a week, I became disciplined from the very beginning to rise early to get ahead of the game and to attend *all* classes. I was never one to cut class.

Prof. Hirota taught me a lot about the Japanese culture. She went all out to expose us to as much as possible—from the attire to tea ceremonies to the food. She worked hard at this.

I was sorry that she was forced to leave. Last I heard, she pursued her Ph.D. at a university somewhere in California. I'd be interested in knowing how things went for her.

Professor Jagu: What can I say except for the fact he was excellent. I don't think that there will ever be a way for me to repay him for all the time and guidance he has given me. He knew when it was time for him just to listen to me so that I could vent some of the extreme frustration that African-American students go through while at Amherst. He knew when I was making excuses for poor performance rather than owning up to an occasional lack of discipline. He knew when it was time for him to tell me to shut my mouth and listen to him give me what I had coming. He knew when I just needed a shoulder to cry on. He knew if I were slacking off and not being all that I could be. He knew when I grew tired of fighting for myself and justifying my right to be at Amherst and instead, needed him to do it for me. And I believe he did this at risk to himself at times. For that I will always be grateful.

Like Prof. Gordon, Jagu (as we called him) always gave freely of his time as I needed it for guidance or for help with classroom material. Jagu took a keen interest in the students and was always there to help us sort out all kinds of problems. If any of us failed, it would not and could not have been because of anything done or not done by Jagu. I remember when Jagu had a group of students over his house for dinner. He is an excellent cook. His meal was the first Indian meal I had ever had. It was so healthy and it was also spicy—just the way I like it. My only regret is that I didn't have more time or make the time to learn as much as I could from him about his culture and his roots. I feel that these two components are such a huge part of a person that to ignore any of it is to not fully know or understand the person.

Prof. Gordon did an excellent job whipping me into shape as to how to learn, understand, and appreciate Physics. By the time I entered Jagu's class, I was more relaxed and enjoyed Physics a lot more. When I saw Jagu work out problems using some of the same "mathematical tricks" Prof. Gordon used, I started to wonder that perhaps Gordon wasn't making up his own theories to prove his assumptions.

To Jagu, I say, "I'm okay now. I made it all right. All of your work with me did not get wasted. You made a real difference in me."

Professor Campbell: She was my mother while I was at Amherst and still is today. Amherst did the right thing in having her be my advisor. I could not hide my feelings from her because as an African-American woman, she knew them all too well. She was aware of the "nay sayers" and how cruel they could be. I felt a sense of protection with Prof. Campbell. A mother defends her child at all costs and puts everything she has into the development of that child. There were many times at which point I entered her office all broken inside. Bit by bit she would help put me together again in such a fashion that the final product was stronger and wiser than before.

Professor Campbell definitely met my vision of a true scholar in every sense of the word. She was disciplined and insisted that I take the toughest of classes that provided the most rigorous learning experience. I thank her dearly for setting high expectations for me and for refusing to accept any failure on my part.

Prof. Campbell was very good at detecting when I was feeling sorry for myself. She would have none of it. During those times, she always reminded me of all the wonderful gifts that I had and all the people I had pulling for me. I would say my greatest challenge was the time that I took one of her classes. As both a mentor and mother figure to me, Prof. Campbell and her view of me and my work meant a lot to me. More than anything I wanted to do well in her class so that I did not disappoint her. This is why I saved taking her class to later on in my schooling at Amherst. I wanted to be ready. Her class was the true test of all that I learned in the way of synthesizing volumes of information and producing a document reflecting serious analysis and thought processes.

Closing:

My parents, Walter and Mary Liggon, worked hard to raise me. I can only imagine what it must have felt like to them to send me off to college. I just took my daughter to kindergarten for her first day of school. When your children go away or off on their own, they take a big piece of your heart with them. On my daughter's first day of school, I took the first step of a long journey in the process of letting go.

My parents sacrificed a lot in their lives as they raised me and it was not easy sending me to Amherst. Although I was 18 at the time and only 20 minutes down the road, I was still their baby girl. I am sure that you heard the African proverb that it takes a whole village to raise a child. Well, Profs. Campbell, Jagu, Gordon, Denton, and Hirota formed a large part of my village at Amherst. All of them contributed pieces of the puzzle which when finished will be my life.

Yours Always,
Barb Liggon Smoot '84

ॐ

Margaret Rose Vendryes replied within less than a month of my first letter, and like all the others who responded, she too is excited about the book and is very happy to make her contribution.

Margaret is quite probably the first *married* Afro-American student—at least woman—to have attended Amherst College. As she will state it, "I came to Amherst under very different circumstances. . . . In 1979, I was the wife of an alum (. . . Leslie Cohen '76 . . .) and the mother of a four-year-old son when I began there as a sophomore transfer from UMass. By the time I finished the degree in 1984, I had a second son who was three and had been through lots of changes."

As an older, more experienced student, and one with much leadership capability, Margaret contributed a great deal to the College community. She was, for example, president of the Women's Center in 1983-84, and she founded a "union" for Older and Married Students. Her main purpose in founding this organization was to supply a "need for 'non-traditional' students to have events (usually of a social nature) to offset the academic workload." This "union" was appreciated by all the older and married students—most of whom then were white males and these students were fortunate to have had a President like Julian Gibbs, who was very responsive to and supportive of their special needs. Margaret did not know if this organization was still existing. "I have no idea if it still exists," which forced me to make inquiries and was directed to Mrs. Charri Boykin-East, Associate Dean of Students here at Amherst College, and it could not have been a more fortunate contact. She was very gracious and cooperative and in no time she supplied me with current information on this very important organization. But first I should note that Dean Boykin-East is very enthusiastic about this book on black women at the College: "The news about your impending book is very exciting. I'm sure it will be a tremendous contribution to the community. Thank you on behalf of all of us for doing this important work." Her interest in the book also extends to her own professional research which she is conducting for a dissertation toward a Ph.D. degree on black women in administration in this country.

The organization which Margaret Vendryes founded now carries a slightly different title from the one she had given it. "The Married/Older/Transfer Student Support Service," Mrs. Boykin-East was "pleased to say . . . is doing very well. Over the years, this service has attempted to enhance cohesiveness among our transfer and non-traditional students. Funds have been set aside to assist and support transfer and non-traditional students. Staffing has also been provided. Kathy Mayberry, Associate Dean in Admissions, and Charri Boykin-East, Associate Dean of Students, co-advise this group and plan appropriate events.

> In the past, the College has accepted as many as 20 transfers in any given year, of which the average age is 21. Each year we have 8–10 older (age 24+) and married students attending Amherst. These students have entered either as transfers or first-year students. Some of them live on campus, and others live off campus. Some have families with small children. Issues our non-traditional students have faced include housing/rental problems, balancing work and family . . . returning to school after being away for an extended period of time; the need to identify a quiet place to study or rest as commuting students, and several commuter issues. Over the past few years, older and non-traditional students have NOT had many problems as a group in acclimating to campus. However, when individuals and group members have identified personal and/or group concerns, this support service continues to be available to provide assistance.

I am sure that Margaret will be pleased to find that one of her contributions to the College has now become institutionalized. Equally I am certain that she will be grateful to Charri for supplying this information that will also be very useful to students of the married/older/transfer categories who may be contemplating coming to Amherst. This information is thus of good service to the College

Margaret Vendryes has that intriguing ability to be able to stand back and watch herself pass through different stages. Before coming to Amherst College she saw herself as a wife and mother almost within the traditional context—at least so she thought then. She saw herself as capable of doing "a lot of things but I did not see myself on the intellectual level of the men around me. My ex-husband was in one of the last classes to graduate without women.... I also remember not really caring much about the co-education issue. When I was asked about transferring to Amherst, I only thought of being offered an opportunity to catch up with the men who had become our close friends ... those arrogant black men in the class of '76." But it was Amherst that was destined to raise her level of consciousness and, in the process, help to inform her sense of self. In examining the whole experience, therefore, she could surefootedly assert: "Needless to say, I finished Amherst having attained an intellectual level leaps and bounds beyond most of them. I had grown as a visual artist, an opinionated thinker/writer and a woman. I changed. I outgrew married politics and the imbalance of sacrifice it required from me. I also became seduced by the academic life." One could almost hear her cocoon shell bursting open and see her soaring forth.

She is attracted to the academic world for precisely the same reason as so many others. "I enjoy the freedom to read and voice my opinion in the open forum of the classroom." And even more important for her, she wanted "to find a place in the academy where the voice of a black woman will be heard. We are few in academia. The humanities are suffering with lopsided/one-sided views of the world because more people of color do not choose to be here. I may never make a million dollars but I'll be damned if the next few generations of leaders will not know that there is another way of seeing America besides the dominant one."

Margaret then expressed a view of the Amherst experience which has become a constant in many of the statements of these black alumnae, as it was with Harold Wade's black alumni. In her own expressive way, she said: "Yes, Amherst changed me. It made me believe that I was Ivy League material and that there were more than a few things that I could do to contribute to society. The classes were always about give and take. I forced myself on the teachers as I was, already cynical and skeptical. They let me say it my way and for that Amherst holds a fond place in my heart."

As would be expected Margaret is now in the Academy. She began to prepare herself for this by first attending Tulane University in New Orleans, where she was awarded the M.A. in Art History in 1992. The thesis she wrote involved her with the Amistad Research Center in New Orleans, where she became Assistant to the Visual Art Curator, while researching her topic. But she also did some teaching. As a Teaching Assistant at Tulane University, she taught courses in Western and American Art Surveys, from Cezanne to the present. The title of her M.A. thesis clearly foreshadows her current Ph.D. dissertation: "Art in the Archives: The Origins of the Art Representing the Core of the Aaron Douglas Collection from the Amistad Research Center," where she documented "over two hundred and fifty works of art by notable African-American artists housed in the archives of the Amistad Research Center, New Orleans, La."

Margaret has given many lectures and presentations on African-American art: among them are, "Hanging on Their Walls: An Art Commentary on Lynching; The Forgotten 1935 Exhibition," "Reading Images of Women Constructed by American Sculptor, Richmond Barthé," "Under Cover of Darkness: Black Male Nudes Under the Gay Gaze," "Landscape Painting; Nature and Culture at their Intersections" and "The Primitive in Art Deco: The African and Native American Influences." She has also published some of these presentations in magazines such as *The Art Deco Weekend Magazine* (of Miami) and "Hanging on their Walls . . . " is a chapter in a book with modifications to be published by the New York University Press. She has also contributed a piece in *Thomas Eakins and the Heart of American Life,* edited by John Wilmerding for the National Portrait Gallery in London.

At present she is completing a dissertation in the Department of Art and Archaeology at Princeton University, toward a Ph.D. degree. Her topic is an interesting and important one on the art of the Afro-American sculptor Richmond Barthé (1901–1989). The title, "Expression and Repression of Identity: Race, Religion and Sexuality in the Art of American Sculptor Richmond Barthé," promises to be a significant contribution that will certainly broaden our knowledge of American art history in general, as it will hopefully, also help to establish new techniques (or should one say, new aesthetic principles?) that could be brought to the service of analyzing and interpreting African-American art. A part of the abstract of the Ph.D. dissertation she sent me will give some insight into the nature and scope of the work:

> The dissertation will investigate how expressions of race, religion and sexual orientation were confined to and subsequently

exposed in the art of America's most celebrated black sculptor Richmond Barthé (1901–1989). Conflicts brought about by racial and cultural difference erupted in America during the years bridging the two World Wars. These were Barthé's years of public popularity and self discovery. Social conflicts have inspired fine art expression for centuries. A clear-headed examination of these years through an African-American visual art filter has not been done.

Barthé used his art to advocate racial integration and assimilation. In the 1960s, separatist Black Power movement writers embraced Barthé as a race artist but suppressed his promotion of integration. The treatment of African-American visual art by historians has been overwhelmingly race centered in an attempt to correct past exclusionary practices. As a consequence, much of what has been published was consciously uncritical. An application of alternate methods of approaching African-American art, using Barthé as a catalyst, will serve to broaden the discussion of difference as it applies to race, religion and sexuality.

Barthé was distinguished, in his early career, as both a Roman Catholic and a black role model. Members of the Roman Catholic hierarchy commissioned Barthé's work and devoted articles to his progress in their publications. However, Barthé's biographers have avoided addressing the significance of religion in his art. Writers who have addressed religion as an expression of race found it difficult to reconcile Barthé's black art expressions with Roman Catholicism, a religion unchanged and unchallenged by black folkways.

Altogether therefore, since her graduation from Amherst with a B.A. in Fine Arts, she also has now acquired an M.A. in Art History at Tulane University (1992) and has now received her Ph.D. degree from Princeton in June of 1997. This information I have just received from her in a letter dated June 25, 1997, and, naturally, she felt it a great "relief." Congratulations, Margaret! We know that you are going to make your mark on society!

Class of '85

☞

Karen E. Cole responded to my first letter in August of 1995 with a short note expressing appreciation about the project and promising to send me further information. But, unfortunately, despite all this good intention, it was only after the third letter and a telephone conversation that I finally received a reply in October of 1996 for which she apologized. Karen majored in Anthropology and Black Studies and was quite active on campus: she held different positions in student government, including being a representative for the Library Committee, and the Black Women's group. She was also a very active member of the Black Student Union where she held leadership positions. Her non-political activities saw her participating in sports, mainly the varsity basketball team and she also sang with the Amherst Gospel Choir and participated in some of the activities of the Women's Center.

Karen spent a part of her junior year studying abroad at the University of Nairobi, Kenya (under the St. Lawrence University program), where she took courses in government and Anthropology. At Amherst she wrote a thesis that looked at "Black Women in Baptist Ministry" from an anthropological perspective. It mainly consisted of interviewing black women in the Baptist ministry, analyzing their experiences as well as an historical look at the Black Church and its leaders.

She graduated from Amherst in May of 1985 and in July of this same year she became a Field Coordinator (CVC) apparently in New York City. Here she supervised work-site projects designed to aid the city's homeless, senior citizens, developmentally disabled and the physically challenged; she also counseled volunteers in personal, academic and social skills, as well as assisting in the development of in-service training. Leaving this position in October of 1986, she became a Divisional Manager with the National Service Corporation in New York City. Her responsibilities included the supervision of field coordinators and the monitoring of the performance of field staff and volunteers. In addition, she also served as liaison to agencies throughout the New York City area, where she communicated operational standards to staff and provided training and technical assistance where needed. She also developed and coordinated new projects and provided leadership and motivation, which, in some cases, resulted in teams winning service citations from the city. She has also been invited to present programs on youth corps initiatives at the Children's Defense Fund Conferences. She remained in this position until September 1988.

At this point Karen obviously felt the need to develop her skills further, and, to this end, she entered the University of Rochester and took a Master's degree in Business Administration in 1990, concentrating on organizations and markets. With her new M.B.A., she worked for a year (June 1990 to June 1991) as a Research Assistant, apparently in New York City for ICL (?) where she provided market analysis and technical assistance to private as well as public organizations and businesses. She also drafted business plans for small businesses. Upon leaving this position, she became a Training Associate with The Women's Centers and AIDS Project, where she identified and screened potential national sites for such centers. She also planned and developed project programs and prepared progress and final reports. She continued to be involved in women's concerns when in July of 1991 she took on the new position as Associate Director of the Women's Alcohol and Drug Education Project of the Women's Action Al-

liance, Inc. (WAA), in New York City. Here she monitored program and revenue expenditures, and supervised project assistants and site staffs. Equally, she prepared proposals, programmatic and fiscal reports, and developed new budgets.

Upon leaving this position with the WAA, Karen became a consultant with Public/Private Ventures (P/PV) in Philadelphia in April of 1994, and was engaged in different activities: these included the coordination of staff and corps member leadership training for AmeriCorps; providing technical assistance and training to different staffs; developing and compiling materials for individual training modules and hiring additional trainers when and where needed. She remained in this position until June of 1995 when she moved to Arlington, Virginia, and became a consultant again, in this case, to TvT Associates. As she has done in many of her other job situations, she researched and developed program blueprints that set performance guidelines and standards again for AmeriCorps.

Since April of 1996 Karen has returned to New York City, as administrator to Women in Need, Inc.

Karen is appreciative of the professors of Black Studies and Anthropology (her majors) with whom she interacted. She named Professors Childs, Rushing, Dizard, Gewertz, Pitkin from these two departments and Professors Basu and Kateb from the Department of Political Science, as those who were particularly accessible to her with their advice and guidance. She also has much praise for those black alumnae/i who "extended themselves to us as black students." Educationally, she is appreciative of the size of Amherst College: "The small intimate nature of the college provided many opportunities to interact with professors on a one-to-one-basis. In retrospect I feel I did not take enough advantage of these interactions for both my scholarly and personal development."

From the social point of view the Amherst experience, though complex, was also valuable:

My time at Amherst College can best be characterized as a constant quest to reconcile ambiguities. As a young person raised in a predominantly lower middle class, immigrant neighborhood in Brooklyn, New York, I saw Amherst as a respite from city life. Its almost surreal New England picture-postcard surroundings gave the appearance of the quintessential environment for nurturing young minds; and in many ways for those who could appropriate all that Amherst had to offer, this was the case. If one was willing to defer multiculturalism, true individuality, and acknowledgment of a world outside Amherst, one could truly have "the Amherst experience" in all its grandeur.

However, for those of us who could not defer, it meant a time of struggle, daily struggles—struggles in the classrooms to educate classmates and professors that there were valid views outside that of white mainstream America—struggles in the dining hall for understanding that groups of black students sitting together did not mean rejection of others, but an affirmation of each other—struggles among ourselves as black students that mirrored every societal conflict concerning "race" identity, class and gender.

One had several options in dealing with these struggles, options that ran the gamut from denial to out-and-out warfare on the College and its values. There were far more casualties of this warfare than I think the College will ever recognize. For the most part my responses to challenges at Amherst vacillated along a continuum of wanting to be just like everyone else to challenging the Dean's office to find and retain qualified nonwhite personnel for positions throughout the College. My Amherst experience was a lesson in choosing battles; they are lessons that continue to serve me well.

ॐ

Phyllis Marie Cureton majored in Economics and was fairly active on campus; she held offices in the BSU, SAC and the Student Government as well as serving as a Resident Counselor. She regrets, though, that she did not study abroad and would wish to have gone to Africa: "I did not play sports. I sang in the Choir and Chorus and took three wonderful years of voice lessons (made possible through the generosity of the College). I met individuals, both students and faculty, for whom I developed a tremendous respect, like Norton Starr my calculus professor, Dean Case, Dean Moss, and fellow student Uhuru Kenyatta; I also met those whom I have chosen to forget." She found Drew House a "comfortable haven," and enjoyed eating at the "black" table at Valentine, among her friends. She felt that it was here that "the majority of 'schooling' took place between the upperclassmen and the lower-classmen," but was aware that they were criticized for "separatism."

But her attitude to the College is rather mixed largely because of some unfortunate situations she was exposed to in some classrooms: "I reflect distastefully," she wrote, "even today, on my Amherst Economics Department experience, in particular being told during an international economics class that someone had studied the size of brains, related intelligence to largeness, and that blacks had the smallest brain mass and Asians the largest. To this day, I still cannot see how that theory relates to economics, although it is very easy to see its relation to ignorance. Or being lectured by a prominent sociology professor on women in the work force, read 'white women' in the workforce, he having ignored the prior and continuing contributions of black female labor." But she is mature enough to say that "I am neither bitter nor effusive about my Amherst experience. The small class size and bright minds around me created a stimulating and probably unparalleled learning environment. The individual attention, for me from persons such as Susan Snively (the writing counselor) and Prof. Yolanda Henderson, made contributions to a student's growth that most will never know. For these things I am grateful."

Upon graduating, Phyllis became involved in "high finance." But even before she graduated her interest in this direction could be identified when she spent the summer of 1984 as an intern with the Goldman Sachs & Company, Corp., in New York City. Between 1985 and 1987 she worked with the Morgan Bank in New York City first, as an analyst, and then as an Assistant Treasurer. Here she was involved with large sums of money. She identified, analyzed and negotiated billion-dollar financing for Fortune 500 clients; she organized loans in all their different manifestations; she also dealt with letters of credit, leases, and asset "securilizations." In the process, she received an intensive nine-month Commercial Bank Management Training Program. Here she received training in advanced

course work, in accounting, corporate finance and credit analysis. She was again a Financial Analyst during the summer of 1988 but apparently, during this period, she had already entered the Harvard Graduate School of Business Administration, concentrating in Finance and General Management, and receiving the M.B.A. in 1989.

Between 1989 and 1991, she was Senior Treasury Analyst, Corporate Headquarters. This seems to overlap with her employment with Scott Paper Company and Scott Health Company. All these appointments embraced many facets of finance, which she listed as: strategic planning, capital budgeting cash flow analysis, domestic and international tax structures, off-balance-sheet financing, commercial credit analysis and commercial risk analysis.

She is also associated with different professional organizations. In 1995 she was the Finance Chair of the Board of Directors, Charter Oak Terrace/Rice Heights Health Center; she was President of the National Black MBA Association, the Philadelphia, Pa., Chapter, 1993-94, and the Greater Hartford Chapter, 1995; she was a member of the Harvard Club in 1995 and since 1989 to the present, has been a member of the Harvard Business School Club.

Her experience at Amherst, as said earlier, was mixed, but what is it in retrospect? "More than ten years later," she said, "... I feel that Amherst was a wonderful experience but question whether I would recommend it to my children if I had any. Yes, one could attain one of the best undergraduate educations in the world, but one had better be armed with a strong sense of self; a loving and supportive . . . family; an ability to call on a higher spirit, preferably God, when times got rough; and an ability to stand for something and separate the truth from the silliness."

ॐ

Lisa Evans is decidedly on the side of the angels in that she replied to my first letter on June 15, 1995, even before the deadline! Lisa majored in Black Studies and Political Science and was always interested in matters concerning Africa and its diaspora. She was proud to tell us that she was born in East Harlem and was raised along with her two siblings by her mother alone after the parents were divorced when she was only ten years old. Her mother was obviously an exceptional person: "My mother instilled in all of her children a sense of respect for learning and pride in the achievements of black people—a value that is often lost in the process of assimilation and higher education." These children were taught that they could "rise above the cycle of poverty through disciplined scholarship." To this end, she saw to it that her children were sent to the best schools available to her through scholarships and any other programs that were being offered. Lisa responded beautifully and soon found herself accepted at the Hunter College Campus School, reputed for its high standard. And it was this good foundation that gave her access to Amherst College in 1981.

At Amherst Lisa was to become a very active student, making her contribution to the College community. But from the freshman year, she was very preoccupied with pursuing the possibility of going to Africa on a study-abroad program. Typical of her focused concentration on goals, she soon found that she could go to East Africa under the Saint Lawrence University program, and in the sophomore year she was admitted to the University of Nairobi in Kenya. Lisa took many courses here including the

Kiswahili language. She also had "the unique opportunity to live with a pastoral tribe, the Samburu of northern Kenya as with the agricultural Louya people of the western province." This was a very maturing experience for her and she was able to make the best use of other opportunities. For instance, at the end of the first semester at the Nairobi University, she succeeded in creating an internship with the American Embassy in Nairobi as a research analyst. Equally at the University she approached different professors especially those from the Institute for Development Studies because she was also very interested in Kenya's then "Five Year Plan." This was a rewarding trip for Lisa and a part of its result was that she wrote her senior thesis on the development of nationalism in Kenya, in her final year back at Amherst.

Lisa herself tells us that her exciting trip to Kenya gave her new perspectives about Amherst College, raising questions of its place as well as her place in the wider world, and even if she did not arrive at definite answers, nevertheless they appear to have informed her participation with campus activities. She was soon elected to the position of the Black Student Union representative to the Student Assembly—the political liaison between students on the one hand and the administration on the other. She must have been a successful representative since she was re-elected in her senior year. She also became involved in activities other than political ones: she was a soloist in the Gospel Choir of the College; she hosted the "Jazz Plus" show on the WAMH radio station, and she even joined up with the Third World Theater Ensemble at the University of Massachusetts and was engaged in some acting for a time.

After graduation, Lisa became engaged in different "public interest activities in Brooklyn, and thereafter, in my community, East Harlem." In 1986 she took up employment at the Brooklyn office of the Legal Aid Society as a paralegal in the Administrative Law Unit. This was not the first time she was involved with the law profession. Even before Amherst, while at the Hunter High School, she was employed on a part-time basis as an intern at the law firm, Christy and Viener in New York City, and this, as she says, gave her the "first practical glimpse of the legal profession. I did quite a bit of case reading on my own, and was impressed by the way that justices reach their concurring or dissenting opinions." She was therefore no novice to the law when she took the appointment with the

Legal Aid Society. In this position she worked with women who were receiving Aid to Families with Dependent Children (AFDC); she counseled them of their rights under state regulations and federal laws, including how to challenge improper case actions. She also was an advocate for clients at local Income Maintenance Centers and even represented clients at State Fair Hearings.

Still with the Legal Aid Society, between 1987 and 1989, her functions were shifted to other areas. Now she became involved with housing. She coordinated the Emergency Assistance Rehousing Program (EARP), which helped to place families living in shelters into permanent housing, particularly in East and Central Harlem; she located vacant apartments, hired city-approved minority contractors to make renovations and facilitated public assistance disbursements to cover moving and other expenses.

After four years with paralegal affairs it is clear that Lisa, with her strong determination to succeed and a healthy work ethic which aimed always at self improvement, would want to proceed further. It is also clear that the legal profession would be her "calling" and to this end, she entered the Columbia University School of Law in 1989 and obtained the J.D. in 1992. But during this time she became involved in civil rights activities: She was one of three students selected to participate in the Columbia Law School Human Rights Internship Program and was placed in the New York office of the NAACP Legal Defense and Education Fund (LDEF). Here she researched issues dealing with the Voting Rights Act and the provision of equal municipal services to minority communities. She also dealt with even more delicate matters pertaining to teenage pregnancies and parenting as they applied under the Family Support Act. But in her second year at law school, she was back with the Legal Aid Society, working many hours a week in the Criminal Appeals Bureau (CAB). This could not have been an easy appointment, for her main task here was to prepare appeals for indigent prisoners incarcerated in state correctional facilities. In the main, she would draft motions with a view to reducing their sentences.

Throughout the summer of her second year and during the third year at law school, Lisa, perhaps quite understandably, had a stint with a private law firm. This firm, Vladeck, Waldman, Elias and Engelhard, specializes in plaintiff-side employment dealing with discrimination in the workplace and also in labor laws dealing with unions.

Upon graduating from the Columbia University Law School in May of 1992, she took the appointment as a *Pro Se* Law Clerk with the United States Court of Appeals for the Second Circuit in New York City. Here she assisted litigants without attorneys, advising them, for example, on procedural matters. Most of her work however, consisted of evaluating *pro se* legal claims, and formulating opinions on those cases to circuit judges. She stayed in this position until 1994, when a great opportunity opened to her.

This opportunity began when in November of 1993 she was one of ten attorneys selected through the Attorney General's Honors Program of the United States Department of Justice to become a Trial Attorney in the Civil Rights Division. In this new position, where she has remained to the present (July 1997), her work seems complex and certainly very topical. Her appointment, she tells us, is with the Educational Opportunities Litigation Section "where I monitor school districts under desegregation orders. . . . In addition to race-based discrimination, our office litigates on behalf of students alleging discrimination based on gender and disability." This kind of work is obviously most meaningful to Lisa and it is interesting that she saw a connection with it and Amherst College. "I am proud of this achievement," she wrote, "because in a way, it has brought my life to a full circle, and back to Amherst. It was because of Amherst's graduates like Charles Hamilton Houston and William Hastie that I was able to attend Amherst and go on to enforce the laws that they directly helped to create. I plan to continue my work in the area of civil rights by teaching or working in a public interest law firm, dedicated to advocacy on behalf of African Americans and Latino clients in the areas of education and employment." Indeed Charles Houston would have been proud of Lisa.

Lisa is now married, since 1991, while still at law school, to Joseph Scantlebury, a graduate of Cornell University who majored in the Africana Studies Program, comparable to Lisa's Black Studies major. He is also in the legal profession, having graduated from the New York University School of Law/Wagner School of Public Policy.

As would be expected, Lisa has been awarded many honors. While at

Evans receiving Special Achievement award from Attorney General Janet Reno and Assistant Attorney General for Civil Rights Deval Patrick

the Columbia University School of Law, she was named the Charles Evans Hughes Fellow, was the Earl Warren Legal Scholar (1989-1992) and was also the recipient of the C. Bainbridge Smith Fund about the same time.

Perhaps Lisa's most prized award is that which she received from the present Attorney General, Janet Reno. On October 8, 1996, the Attorney General presented her with a "Special Achievement award in appreciation and recognition of meritorious acts or service performed in behalf of the Department."

Class of '86

ॐ

Phyllis R. Barber-Smith finally wrote me a delightful letter in October of 1996 with a very sincere personal statement. She apologized for the delay in responding largely because of a certain personal experience: "I have been avoiding writing or even thinking about writing in response to your request and I am very sorry to have inconvenienced you. I write this letter as an explanation of my quandary and hope you can extrapolate something that will be of use in your publication. I really just don't know what to say about Amherst anymore. You see, so much of my Amherst experience is intertwined with a failed marriage to a classmate (after a four-year relationship there). I have, to a great extent, come to terms with much of this: I have remarried and have a beautiful family and a potentially fruitful career, however, I remain confused about a chunk of my life that seems wasted. When last I saw you at Amherst during the reunion, that was one of my steps toward reclaiming what was mine."

Phyllis majored in Sociology and was quite active on campus. She was a co-founder of the Amherst College Gospel Choir, and from 1982 up until her graduation in 1986, she was the manager of this Choir. She was also a member of the Black Student Union and during her junior year was its admission's liaison. Her interest in sports saw her actively engaged in the Intramural Basketball.

Her participation in the Gospel Choir meant a great deal to her both socially and spiritually. She tells us that it was "One of the most important things" she did at Amherst. "The opportunity presented itself to us in our first year. A group of us learned there was to be a Gospel Music Festival at the school and Amherst was not to be represented. With a handful of voices, a lot of determination, and very little time, we pulled it off. For me, this was not only the beginning of something that continues today, but it was an outlet which actually helped me survive Amherst. We met regularly, even when schedules became difficult. It became a support group and a means of expressing ourselves and praising the Lord through song." This combination of initiative and successful follow-through was very much a part of the pioneer spirit of the '80s which was a continuation of the positive activities reminiscent of Harold Wade and his group.

Upon graduating, Phyllis took a position with the State of Connecticut as Program Coordinator at the Department of Mental Retardation. In this situation she coordinated and implemented weekend activities including trips for developmentally disabled adults, and charted their daily progress and behavior. While here, she was also involved with the Arthritis Rehabilitation Center and New Haven Hand Therapy Center as Office Manager. Here she simultaneously managed two offices for their new and growing companies, maintaining in the process, financial and client records. Between July 1988 and December 1990, she was a Lead Children's Services Worker at the Department of Children and Youth Services, counseling child-clients in personal and interpersonal problem solving. She also wrote progress reports on behavior for inclusion in permanent records, along with the supervision of the staff of four or five workers.

But it is clear that Phyllis was now thinking of a career in law, and for this purpose she enrolled at the University of Connecticut School of Law and graduated with the J.D. degree in 1994. During this period she worked at different legal clinics in Connecticut, and as a Law Clerk with a private law firm, Sullivan, Lettick & Schoen. At this firm she researched and wrote office memos in areas of law relating to labor and education. She also assisted attorneys with the Board of Education in their preparations for various contracts dealing with teachers and administrators, all of which could have the potential for arbitration. At present, Phyllis is remarried and is taking care of her two children but is also looking forward to returning to the practice of law soon. Her concentration is in family and juvenile law.

In looking back on her experience at Amherst College after ten years, altogether, she has some very positive things to say:

> Amherst was the place where I developed most of my longest-lasting friendships, most of which survived even the divorce. It was the first place I ever felt the need to seek out and foster relationships with people of similar experiences and culture and beliefs. Having grown up in a very small town with parents who refused to let us believe we were different, I had not felt the effects of prejudice or at least was able to brush it off with the support of a tight-knit family. Alone at Amherst was a different story....
>
> It was at Amherst that I first believed that I had something to offer the world. Sitting alongside some of the best and brightest (so we were told) and actually holding my own. I cannot say that Amherst equipped me for real life, but I know it ultimately helped to open the door to law school.

And it was at this point she mentioned that she was looking forward to returning to the practice of law.

৵

Renee M. Baron majored in English and French and wrote a senior thesis, "Jessie Redman Fauset: The Misreading of a Woman and Her Novels" in both departments. Renee was one of those students who made the most of the opportunities the College provided. She was keenly interested in research and at one time thought she would major in History and this was how I came to know her very well. Her first internship was at the New York

Public Library's Schomburg Center for Research in Black Culture during January of 1983. This she enjoyed so thoroughly that she applied again to be back for the summer of this year.

In writing a reference for her on this occasion, I could remind the Director that it would have been impossible for me to have exaggerated her enjoyment of the experience at the Schomburg Center. "Never reticent in verbal communication, she would buttonhole an audience at any convenient time (and sometimes not too convenient) to tell of the delight she had, and the inspiration she gained from working at your institution. Renee has already developed a strong sense of history which will be strongly enhanced by working at the Schomburg.... She will be an asset and you certainly will enjoy this very charming yet so well-organized young person," was a part of what I wrote about her. She was awarded the internship and was back again during the summer months of 1984 and 1985. As an Archival Assistant, Renee assisted the Archivist in the processing of papers and private collections of various writers, leaders and organizations; she helped with the organization of exhibitions, as well as assisted in conducting tours to visitors and school children of the Research Center.

Renee also had another bee in her bonnet which she discussed with me from her sophomore year at the College. This was to study in France to improve her skills in the French language. And soon she was an exchange student during her junior year at L'Institut D'etudes Europeenes in Paris. She also took courses at the Sorbonne and L'Institut d'Etudes Politiques, and she returned proficient in the French language and with a great deal of self-confidence. We also have a photograph of her before the Arch d'Triumph in Paris. Renee also has a good knowledge of the Portuguese language.

After graduating from Amherst, Renee enrolled with the Yale University Graduate School, and was a recipient of two fellowships for this: the Amherst Memorial Fellowship, 1986–88, and the Yale University Graduate Fellowship, 1986–88. At Yale, she entered the Master of Arts program in Afro-American Studies and wrote a thesis, "Understanding the Stepchild: Wallace Thurman's Correspondence and Novels," for which she was awarded the M.A. in May of 1989.

But during this time she was also engaged in some research and part-time teaching. During the summer months of 1986 she was a Market Research Analyst with the Data Development, Inc., at New Rochelle in New York. Here she conducted research and edited surveys dealing with the compilation of data on various consumer products and services. The research skills she gained at the Schomburg must have stood her in good stead for this position. But she also gained new research techniques here when she was involved in learning the fundamentals of statistical methodology all with a view to improving the products and services of the markets.

Her teaching experience is very varied. Between 1986 and 1988 she was a French Instructor at the St. Martin De Porres Elementary School in New Haven, Connecticut. Her classes emphasized French language, written and oral, as well as French culture and institutions. During the same period she was also a tutor at Yale University. Her main focus here was to provide individualized instruction for first and second year students who were experiencing difficulties with written and oral expressions in French.

In 1987 she was a Teaching Assistant at the Yale Graduate School, doing more or less what teaching assistants normally do—assisting in organizing classes, grading papers and the like.

Between January 1989 and June 1990, she was in Washington, D.C., teaching at the LADO International College. Here she taught upper-level classes of English as a second language; the classes emphasized the achievement of full linguistic performance in speaking, listening, reading and writing. She also conducted elementary literature survey classes and preparation classes for the Test of English as a Foreign Language (TOEFL). During this time she was also teaching at the Benjamin Banneker Model Academic High School, also in Washington, D.C., for the District of Columbia Board of Education. In this position she taught English at the ninth and tenth grades, stressing grammar and composition. But she also introduced students to the basic elements of literature and literary canons, as well as creative and critical writings.

Since 1990 she has been a part-time Instructor in the Department of English at Howard University and is a member of this University's English Department Executive and Curriculum Committees.

Renee is a doctoral candidate at The George Washington University. She is completing her dissertation, "Redefining the American Self: Autobiography in the Postmodern Moment," which might well be completed before this work goes to the press. In the process, between 1991-1994, she was awarded the prestigious George Washington University Presidential Merit Fellowship and, in 1994–1995, the Thurgood Marshall Dissertation Fellowship.

She has also reviewed a number of books for the *American Studies International* since 1992, and has made presentations at different conferences. She is affiliated to many organizations including the College Language Association, the American Studies Association, and the Modern Language Association. She was also a member of the Executive Committee of the Amherst College Alumni Association in Washington, D.C., as well as Coordinator for the Amherst College Area Recruitment for Washington, D.C.

We are sorry that we did not receive a statement from Renee telling of her experience at Amherst College.

༕༠

Susan Lynn McKeever replied in October of 1996 after numerous communications. As a consolation, she thanked me "for the continued effort." Susan majored in Political Science and French and went on a Study Abroad Program in June of 1984. Her destination was the Universite de Dakar, Senegal, West Africa, from where she received the Certificate de Specialisation, Literature d'Africaine et civilations Africaines. She did not write a thesis at Amherst but worked on a special topic dealing with West African Francophone Literature. Her language skills include French, Wolof and American Sign Language.

Susan was also very active on campus, participating in a variety of organizations, including the Black Student Union; she was also elected to the judicial board of the College Council, and was on the very active President's Committee then installed to examine whether or not the College should divest its holdings in South Africa. In addition to these heavy responsibilities, she was also very much involved in the theater, acting in plays such as "A Raisin in the Sun" and others. But she was even more interested in Dance, and actually became a Professional Dancer, upon graduating in 1986 up to 1992. At Amherst she choreographed a piece for a spring dance concert, and as a professional dancer, she was involved in a variety of performance activities, including dance operas such as "Mother of Three Sons," to the Houston Grand Opera at the New York City Opera at the Lincoln Center, and even abroad, in Germany, at the Munich Biennale Deutches Theatre and Staad Achen.

It appears that from the fall of 1992 Susan began to consider a career change and took a position with a private firm, The Oglesby Towers Management Co., as a Building Manager. Here she managed some 191 rental apartments and was also responsible for account management and supervision of office and maintenance staffs. Within the year (summer of 1994), she took another position with Sidley and Austin in Chicago. Apparently a law firm, she researched and drafted legal memoranda dealing with trusts, estates and litigation matters. She also researched tax issues and corresponded with the IRS on behalf of a client, and drafted briefs relating to issues concerning labor. At this point, having worked at a law firm, she enrolled at the Northwestern University School of Law, Chicago, Illinois, and was awarded the J.D. degree in May of 1996. Here she had the academic distinction of having been on the Dean's List twice, during the fall and spring of 1994 and 1996 respectively. As is usual with many graduate students at law schools she also became an intern before her law degree. She did this from August 1995 to May 1996 with WTTW Channel 11 Chicago, and she researched and drafted memoranda at this radio station relating to a range of broadcast issues. She also prepared reports on copyright infringements and screened potential advertisements for compliance with federal regulations.

In not responding to my letters earlier, Susan cited her recent law degree as having contributed to this. As would be expected from her many and varied activities while at Amherst, she had an enjoyable life here. She said:

> I enjoyed my years at Amherst: the friends I made at Amherst are still my closest friends. It was not until after graduation that I realized how competitive the atmosphere at Amherst was. I remember realizing that it is not normal to break down in tears at the *thought* of a low grade. I also realize that the "isolation" of black students at Amherst can take a toll on one's psyche but the positive effect is the strength of the relationships which develop (friends who are black and non-black). I also found a great deal of support from professors and administrators. I do not have negative thoughts about Amherst generally because I have very strong memories of positive interactions with my black peers. My non-black friends from Amherst are those who felt isolated and different from the majority of Amherst Students."

ॐ

Anne Marie Pocock was among those who responded to my letter in good time. Her note of June 19, 1995, was a few handwritten words, that expressed a time-honored philosophy of the really busy person: that is, let me do it now or "I wouldn't have done it otherwise. So I thought, better this than nothing." The "this" here is a not-too-up-to-date curriculum vitae with numerous handwritten emendations, additions and explanations, thus giving a certain "life" to the usual bland character of C.V.s. She hates to write "things like that about myself," nevertheless, she is sending the material along and was gracious enough to have wished me, "Good luck . . . it sounds like a neat project."

Anne Marie majored in Economics and since graduating, has spent her time teaching and counseling high school children. She is definitely committed to this, and has expressed much job satisfaction in such a pursuit. Between 1987 and 1992 she taught at the Stony Brook School in New York. Here she taught pre-algebra to the 7th grade and algebra I to the 8th and

9th grades. But apart from teaching algebra she was also Academic Advisor as
well as Resident Hall Director at one of
the dormitories. In this capacity she
resided with and was responsible for 32
female students ranging from the 7th to
the 12th grades; she also served as an administrator when she directed student
activities and student services, on- and
off-campus. In her marginal notation
on the C.V. she tells us that she enjoyed
a high job situation at this school because she had a strong sense that she
contributed to society by having a positive impact on the lives of the young
students. As Resident Hall Director, for
instance, she tried to maintain an environment conducive to the students'
personal and intellectual growth.

After leaving the Stony Brook School, she registered at the University of
Washington to work toward the Master of Education and the ESA in
School Counseling. As usual, Anne Marie has given us her views on these
programs, in this case, in interlinear notes on her C.V. She saw the M.A. in
Education as "definitely a means to an end. The program was fine but I'm
definitely not a scholar/researcher at heart." While preparing for the Master's degree, she became a Teaching Assistant at the same College of Education at the University of Washington, and from August 1994 to January
1995 she was a counselor at the Kamiakin Junior High School in the Lake
Washington School District. In February of 1995 she began counseling at
the Saghalie Junior High, at the Federal Way School District, which she is
doing up to the present.

She received the M.A. and the ESA in School Counseling in June of
1995, from the College of Education, University of Washington, and is also
teaching at this institution. In addition, she has been a counselor at the
Totem Junior High since September 1996, involving her in academic, social and emotional counseling for a widely diverse group of students.

Her volunteer work also involves her with high school and junior high school students. From 1994 to the present she sponsored a Senior High School Group at the University Presbyterian Church, and is a volunteer tutor at the Northgate Elementary and the King's Junior High Schools, both in Seattle. She also went on a Mission trip to Tijuana in Mexico, April 1996, helping to build homes for poor families.

Anne Marie is among the fortunate ones who enjoy real job satisfaction. She tells us that she has a "genuine enjoyment of and affinity towards kids"—a sentence she has placed at the top of her C.V. under the heading "Summary of Qualifications," and indeed it should be seen as a part of one's qualification when dealing with "kids." In her handwritten notation, in this case, a marginal one, she says: "I believe that working with youth allows me the opportunity to make a tremendous contribution to society. I think that a large measure of the solution to many of the problems facing our society lies in educating young people and instilling within them a sense of value and purpose. My desire to become a school counselor has been motivated by my desire to be involved in this process in kids' lives," and indeed the country could do with more of her type.

And how does she view Amherst? She replied:

I loved Amherst.

It represents to me good friends, discovery in areas that I had known nothing about, incredible opportunity to learn and grow and experience.

Amherst taught me how to think. Through hard work and diligence, I had managed to graduate first in my class from my high school without ever really learning this. I received a rude, but important awakening when I arrived at Amherst.

It was at Amherst that I decided to "come out of the closet" and pursue my Christian faith in a more overt way. My involvement with the Christian Fellowship at Amherst was a huge milestone in the serious development of my faith, a faith which greatly impacts the life I choose to lead today.

As much as I did love my experience there, Amherst was very challenging for me. I never felt as gifted as others. I always had to work so much harder than everyone else. Graduate school was like that too in a lot of ways. But this was harder to deal with at Amherst, I guess because I wasn't used to it.

Interestingly enough, although my skin is dark and my parents are from Jamaica, while at Amherst I never identified myself with the Black Student Union. I tried to, but it was not a natural fit for me. I guess I should not have been surprised. I never really had identified myself that way before. But I felt wrong somehow for not connecting in that way, and that was hard too.

She hoped I will find this useful and that it will "enable the class of '86 to be better represented."

࿊

Gwendolyn D. Reeves replied to my first letter on June 27, 1995, expressing her willingness to participate in the book on black women at Amherst College. Although "extremely busy and cannot write as thorough a biography as I would like," she nevertheless, sent me a curriculum vitae, along with some answers to some of the questions I had posed in my first letter.

Gwendolyn majored in Psychology and after graduating from Amherst, she took a position with a private investment firm, the First Investor's Corporation in Chicago, Illinois, as an Investment Analyst. Here she investigated and analyzed different investment vehicles, and advised clients on how to reach their financial goals. In this position she also had herself licensed with the National Association of Securities Dealers, giving her the right to sell mutual fund investments and annuities. Having spent about a year with this firm, Gwendolyn was ready to take on a bank, and in 1988 she found employment with the Northern Trust Bank, also in Chicago. She came into this job as Investment Manager Liaison Representative, and as the title suggests, one of her duties was to act as a liaison investment manager of corporate and trust accounts and the bank. The responsibilities seem enormous: they involved relaying account information to all the different sectors, processing securities, and assisting in problem resolutions; and she was also expected to see that deadlines were strictly met. After about three years in this position Gwendolyn felt that she was obviously up against the proverbial glass ceiling. "I left my position at Northern Trust Bank," she wrote, "because I found myself frustrated in my inability to advance professionally. The bank presented a very conservative, very political environment. I do believe race played a role in my lack of mobility."

She was thus at the point where she wanted "a challenge and a career, not just a job. So I went to law school." She enrolled at the San Diego School of Law from where she obtained the J.D. in 1994. Even before receiving her law degree she began working in law firms. During 1993, between May and August, she worked as an intern at the Superior Court at San Diego, where she conducted research, drafted memoranda on juvenile delinquency, interviewed personnel from county and social service agencies on potential court reformation, and observed court proceedings; this internship overlapped with other part-time positions she held in the legal profession during 1993. For instance while still with the Superior Court she took another position, in this case with a private law firm, Gunner and Richardson, as a law clerk. Here also she was involved in research, motion and memoranda drafting for attorneys in the field of criminal defense. Between September and December of this same year, she became an intern with the Federal Defenders of San Diego, performing more or less the same duties as with the others but in this case she was also trained in court procedures and trial techniques. Her next part-time position was at the University of San Diego School of Law where she was a Research Assistant to Professor Donald Weckstein from November 1993 to May 1994. Here again she conducted research and gathered data for compilation into a casebook on labor law, and her last appointment before receiving the J.D. degree was between January to May of 1994 as a legal intern with the American Civil Liberties Union Foundation, also in San Diego. Again she was involved in research; in this case, her search had to do with issues that affected civil liberties and constitutional rights. She also drafted memoranda for the proposed reformation of the administrative procedures of county school districts.

Gwendolyn's first full-fledged legal appointment came in November of 1994 (to the present, July 1996) at the Office of the State Appellate Defender in Chicago, Illinois, as an Assistant Defender. At this First Judicial District, she represents indigent clients who are on appeal from convictions for criminal offenses, where she must try to maintain contact with these clients; she must also read trial records, perform legal research, analyze meritorious legal arguments, and write appellate briefs.

Let us now try to find out her views regarding her appointments in the legal profession. She frankly admitted that up to the time she was responding to my questions, she had not yet "found the 'perfect job.' I'm not sure such a thing exists." In her usual honest manner, she writes: "I'm not satisfied in my first job out of law school either. As an appellate attorney, I spend my time conducting research and writing. I thought I would enjoy this work, for in law school I enjoyed conducting research and I was interested in working with indigent clients. Further, I'm more interested in defending someone's constitutional rights as opposed to finding a loophole which would make a rich client richer. . . . However, I've found that the pace is too slow for me. Right now, I'm pursuing other options. As a matter of fact, I'm networking with Amherst alums in the area."

To my question of what contribution she thought she has made to society she said that she was "still working on that. God has a prominent role in my life and I'm constantly striving to be a better person. . . . My professional goal is to be the best attorney I can be and always render quality service to my clients. My personal goal is to be a better person and continue to be happy." And with this, she wishes me, "Good luck on the piece!"

We can be certain that Gwendolyn's striving to be a better person is already demonstrating itself in the type of community work in which she is involved. She serves the Chicago Youth Success Foundation in different ways: she provides assistance with a view to fostering academic advancement and reducing the dropout rate in the Chicago Public High Schools; she helps with fund raising to facilitate some of these community services; she counsels students in their preparation for college; she judges their essays among a number of other ongoing school activities. This is in no small way, making contributions to society, and we hope that Gwendolyn will soon, if she has not yet done so, find greater job satisfaction.

Class of '87

ᗛ

Dahna L. Batts-Osborne was among those influenced by Dr. Kimberlee Wyche to respond to my letters, and this she finally did in August 1996. Dahna majored in Anthropology, and it is clear that she had no doubts about her career goals, for upon graduation, she went straight to the Thomas Jefferson Medical College in Philadelphia. In her senior year at Amherst, with her career in view, she was awarded the John Woodruff Simpson Fellowship for the study of medicine. By 1991, only four years after Amherst, she was the recipient of the Doctor of Medicine degree, and what was more, she was honored with the "Outstanding Third Year Student" award from the Medical Society of Pennsylvania.

Between 1991 and 1994, she entered the Howard University Hospital in Washington, D.C., for her Residency, and soon became the Chief Resident for Emergency Medicine. During this time she was also a Provider for Advanced Cardiac Life Support, under the auspices of the American Heart Association (1991) and a Provider also for Advanced Trauma Life Support with the American College of Surgeons (1992) and likewise for Pediatric Advanced Life Support, again for the American Heart Association in 1993.

In 1992 and again in 1995 she obtained other certificates called "Diplomats" at the National Board of Medical Examiners and the American Board of Emergency Medicine.

Upon leaving the Howard University Hospital in 1994, she became an Attending Physician in the Emergency Department at the St. Agnes Hospital in Baltimore, Maryland, and she held a similar position at the Greater Southeast Community Hospital, Washington, D.C., and at the Fort Washington Medical Center, Maryland, between 1994 and 1996. Since mid-1996 to the present (September 1996) she has been employed with the Agency for Toxic Substances and Disease Registry, at the Center for Disease Control Exposure Investigations Section at Atlanta, Georgia.

Dahna has also been engaged in other activities: in 1993 she was an Instructor at the George Washington University at the Emergency Medical Technician and Paramedic Department; in this same year she sat on the Practice Management Committee of the American College of Emergency Physicians and in 1994 to the present she has been on the Commission of Public Health as a Volunteer Special Events Physician.

She is at present a member of the American College of Emergency Physicians, the National Medical Association, the American Association of Women Emergency Physicians, the American Professional Practice Association and the Alpha Kappa Alpha Sorority, Inc.

Unfortunately, Dahna did not send me a statement on her experience at Amherst, but, hopefully, when this work is revised, she will have something to tell about it.

༄

Carol A. Gray finally responded, thankfully, through Kimberlee Wyche's intervention. Her letter of August 22, 1996, did apologize for the delay in sending information to me, and it also acknowledged that Kim did remind her. But Carol redeemed herself when she generously offered "to contact some of the other women in New York and get them to send you some info[rmation]." She also hoped that the book was coming along well. And, true to her word, she did contact some women of the class of '87 who have since sent me information.

Carol majored in Psychology at Amherst and during her junior year she went on a Study Abroad Program to the San Luis Universidad in Madrid, Spain, where she studied the Spanish language and literature. Her positive opinion about her study abroad experience is shared by just about all the women who took this route. She writes, "It might seem strange, but I think that I grew up most while away from Amherst. My junior year, my semester abroad in Spain, was the most enlightening part of my college experience. The traveling, experiencing different cultures, and the people helped to mold me into the individual that I am today. I recommend that everyone try to take at least a semester abroad as I found it both enriching and rewarding."

She is also among those who found that the Black Student Union helped her to adjust to the College. Through this organization, she and her colleagues participated in many activities, but she must be particularly pleased with her participation in making Amherst "divest out of South Africa"—a central issue of the decade of the 1980s. "Going through these things together," she said, "made many of us a close-knit bunch, and the forging of these friendships is what made Amherst interesting and bearable."

After graduation, she worked as a Caseworker with the Child Welfare Administration in Queens, New York. In this position, she appeared as witness in Family Court cases, evaluated and determined extensions of placements, managed caseloads of some 35 clients, interviewed parents and children with respect to allegations of neglected or abused children, counseled families and conducted bimonthly home visits. She remained in this obviously difficult situation from August 1987 to September of 1989. Her next position, during the summer of 1990, was at the Queens District Attorney's Office where she served as an Intern. Her responsibilities included all aspects of trial preparations for a number of attorneys in the Major Offense Prosecution Program. Her duties involved responding to motions, drafting legal memoranda, preparing subpoenas and witnesses; she also conducted legal research and was in attendance during trials.

It is clear that Carol's career so far was leaning toward the legal profession and she became enrolled at the New York University School of Law and obtained the J.D. degree in May of 1992. In the process, she was awarded the Earl Warren Legal Training Scholarship, the Public Interest Committee Fellowship and the Ann Petluck Poses Clinical Award.

Before obtaining the law degree, she continued to gain legal experience through practice by working in other attorneys' offices. Thus, in the summer of 1991, she was a Law Clerk in the U.S. Attorney's office, SDNY, New York City. Here she assisted attorneys in the difficult Special Narcotics Division with preparations for trial; she also conducted legal research, developed theories of cases, assisted in depositions and interviews and attended trials. From August 1991 to the time of her graduation in 1992, she worked with the New York Criminal Defense Clinic at the New York University School of Law. In this capacity she represented clients with misdemeanor cases and participated in programs aimed at developing litigation skills.

With her new law degree, Carol entered the Neighborhood Defender Service of Harlem as a Staff Attorney. Her activities involved: assisting in the development of innovations for the public defender's office; representing indigent defendants in a wide range of criminal matters from pre-arrest through to all aspects of trials in Supreme, Criminal and Family Courts. Her responsibilities also include researching, analyzing legal issues, writing memoranda of law, grand jury presentations and suspension hearings. She held this position up until August of 1996 when in her letter to me (dated August 22, 1996) she said that she would be starting "a new job next week [September, 1996]" at the Brooklyn Defender Service.

Carol is also engaged in legal outreach programs, assisting in mentoring services for deprived groups; she also taught a course on "Conflicts with Cops" from 1992 to 1995.

At present, she is a member of the American Bar Association, the New York Bar Association, and the BLAPA Notary Public, and, she tells me, "Life after Amherst has been exciting and fulfilling."

And how does she view Amherst in retrospect? She writes:

> Life at Amherst was exciting–NOT, exhilarating–NOT, interesting–sometimes, okay–a learning experience–DEFINITELY. I learned a lot during my years at Amherst, and if I had to go to college all over again, I can honestly say that I would choose to attend Amherst. In retrospect, first semester, Freshman year

was a culture shock for me, especially coming from New York, being a black woman in "the valley." I distinctly remember trying to adjust to roommates in James Dorm and having problems dealing with extremely drunk people in my room when I wanted to go to sleep. Talk about being homesick—that was my middle name. Yes, it was indeed a period of adjustment. However, I, like many others, did indeed manage to adjust. . . .

I recently returned to Amherst to attend an Alumni weekend. One of the things that was striking to me was that some of the issues for black students generally remain the same as when I was a student at Amherst. Back in '87, there were also problems about who would live in Drew House. I remember that this house was a safe haven for us, it was a place where we felt free to discuss with each other the problems of the day. It was a place to re-energize, recuperate, and find strength to address the trials and tribulations that we had to face at Amherst. On my recent visit it was also interesting to see that the social life for a black woman in the valley was basically the same. With women still outnumbering the men by about 3:1, let's just say that Amherst seems to be a place that a black woman still can "really" concentrate on her studies.

❧

Alice Middleton Merrick majored in Economics and was quite active on campus. She was a member of the Black Student Union, a part of the Gospel Choir, a member of the Christian Fellowship Association, and she participated fully on the Committee on Social Life. During the summer months of her junior year, she went on a Study Abroad Program to the Institute of Political and Economic Studies in London, England, which was very important for her with a major in Economics. At the Institute, she concentrated in Economics and International Organizations with special emphasis on the European Economic Community.

After graduating from Amherst, she took a position as President/Financial Consultant with the Middleton and Associates company in Fairmont Heights, Maryland. In this position she helped already established businesses to provide financial advice to small fledgling business entities as well as to non-profit organizations. She also established a referral relationship with the consulting attorney for the Small Business Administration of Maryland; she recommended creative financing alternatives and developed formal business plans with clients that included a building contractor, a ballet company and a large church. It is no wonder that Alice received the Maryland State and Optimist Club Award for community service.

Her next position was with the American Security Bank in Washington, D.C. Here she worked as Assistant Treasurer in the Department of Communications Lending Group (Corporate Division). With this group, she co-managed some $200-million loan portfolios involving cable television and radio station operators; she analyzed operating performances and financial strengths of potential borrowers to determine, among other things, credit risks; she earned primary account responsibility on acquisitions to the extent of $5 million, and she also led division seminars on how to construct and sensitize cable television projection models.

At this point in her career, Alice obviously felt the need for further training to pursue a career in business, and, accordingly, enrolled at the Harvard Business School in 1989 and was awarded the M.B.A. in 1991. She had a successful career at Harvard and is very positive about her experience there. As with Amherst, she was involved in different extra-curricular activities at Harvard. She was, for example, active with the African American Student Union, and in no time was elected chairperson of its admissions committee.

With new successes, new experiences, and added confidence, her first position after her Harvard M.B.A. degree has been with the Exxon Company, U.S.A., from 1991 to the present. At this firm she has held many positions. Working at the New Orleans branch in Los Angeles, she was Senior Financial Analyst, where she evaluated major expense projects, negotiated joint operating agreements with Shell Oil, designed and implemented financial and accounting management systems at new oil fields, and even saved Exxon some thousands of dollars by successfully challenging the cost allocation method at the jointly owned property in the Gulf of Mexico.

Her next position with Exxon was at the Greenbelt, Maryland, branch,

where she worked as a Retail Practices Specialist in the Northeast Marketing Division. Her responsibilities here included the coordination of some
100 "Customer Appreciation Promotions" from certain states such as
Maryland and Virginia. She also negotiated with advertising, publishing
and temporary agencies, and arranged suitable advertising with print and
radio. In addition, she was engaged with managing both employees and
contract workers. Her efforts in this situation were obviously successful
and within a year (1993–1994) her promotion initiatives resulted in a revenue increase of 10 percent for the firm.

She then moved on to becoming Territory Manager since 1995 to the
present. She has managed some 10 retail outlets in Northern Virginia with
annual revenues totaling $40 million; she supervises managers, 11 in all,
non-exempt employees totaling 130, and is responsible for all aspects of
operations, involving profitability, promotions, customer service and
safety. Altogether, she has some very good results: she has generated
$3 million in profit in 1995, representing a 10-percent increase over the
prior year; she has successfully opened two new stores in 1995, and "grew
sales from zero to $300,000 per month within four months," and she has
also developed and implemented certain innovations within the territory
which increased sales by 10 percent.

Alice is a smart, highly motivated person and we are bound to hear
much more of her in the future. She has kept in touch with the "philosophy" of the College—even if she has not been visiting—and is heartened
by this book on black women at Amherst, as she is in tune with the views
of the new president, Tom Gerety. In replying to my letters, she said, "I am
compelled to write for two reasons. First I applaud and appreciate your
work on this undertaking. Second, the current president of the college
made me proud to be an alumna when he articulated Amherst's support
of Affirmative Action during the commencement of 1996." This resonated
with her because of her own personal experience.

"I grew up in a black neighborhood. Attended black schools—including Head Start. . . . Had a father who owned and operated his own black
business. My family was not well off, but I am not underprivileged. I graduated valedictorian from my high school . . . didn't everyone at Amherst! I
am not bragging, I am simply trying to say when I arrived at Amherst I was
a strong, confident, proud woman. My foundation was strong."

As for her experience at Amherst, although mixed, especially in social terms, nevertheless, she is "proud of [her] academic and professional achievement. I am grateful to my professors at Amherst for adding to my toolbox. . . . Amherst honed my academic skills. I was fully prepared for the rigor of the Harvard Business School."

᠀

Lisa A. Smith (nee Williams) responded promptly after my telephone conversation with her in August of 1996. Lisa majored in Economics and was very active on campus. During 1985–1987 she was a disc jockey on the campus radio station; as well, she was Treasurer for the Straight Ahead Executive Committee for most of this time period. Equally, during this period she was elected a member of the Economics Advisory Council, and throughout 1986 and up until graduation, she was a Resident Counselor.

Following her graduation, she took a position as an Analyst with the First Interstate Bank of California. In this employment she assisted in structuring and financing bonds and short-term notes for municipalities in the Bank's Public Finance Division. Here she prepared both actual and projected cash flows for issues; performed "all due diligence" for official statements and oversaw the remarketing of floating rate notes with bond traders. After a year in this situation (June 1987–June 1988) she became a Corporate Banking Officer and held this position until January 1990. As a Corporate Banking Officer she analyzed general financial conditions and helped to structure loan needs for companies with sales from $5 to $300 million. She also negotiated loan terms and conditions with prospective and existing customers; managed a $20-million portfolio of commercial loan relationships; marketed the bank's financial service products to existing customers, and was responsible for generating new customers through referrals and prospect lists. In the process she also successfully completed the bank's nine-month's commercial credit training program.

From January to September 1990, she moved to *Societe Generale*, still in Los Angeles, as an Analyst/Corporate Banking Officer. Here she prepared projections and analyses for the bank's participation in the Fortune 1000 commercial credits, with an average loan size of $10-$25 million. She monitored and reviewed existing corporate relationships and marketed new customer relationships with account officers.

In the meantime, Lisa enrolled at the Anderson Graduate School of Management at UCLA, and in June of 1992, she graduated with the Master of Business Administration degree. She was a two-year recipient of the First Interstate Bank Fellowship.

With her newly acquired M.B.A., she took a position with the firm of Donaldson, Lufkin & Jenrette Securities Corporation as Associate, Public Finance Division. In this employment she prepared analyses of bond debt service schedules; she reviewed all legal documents, assisted in the structuring and financing of issues and coordinated and managed all pertinent parties. In addition, she initiated, managed and developed proposals for presentations. The specialized areas included housing, redevelopment and lease financing. After nearly two years in this position, she took a new job at Stone and Youngberg in February of 1994 to the present (August 1996). As an Associate at this firm, Lisa is responsible for the technical and daily maintenance of bond financing for the company's Southern California municipal clients. Again she is involved in the structuring and financing of issues; in the coordination and management of all parties, including bond and underwriter's counsels, bond insurers, rating agencies, trustees, institutional and retail investors. She also prepares analyses of bond debt service schedules and reinvestment alternatives for financing and reviews all legal documents. Lisa is skilled in both Apple and IBM computers, and is a Certified Municipal Securities Representative (Series 52 and 63).

Lisa, whose maiden name was Williams, is married to Derek Smith, "a native of California," and they now have a one-year-old daughter (Sydney). They live in Pasadena, California, where Derek has his own business. He also has an M.B.A. degree from the Anderson Graduate School of Management.

Lisa looks back at her experience at Amherst with "mixed emotions" and some nostalgia:

> I now only remember the fun times, lasting friendships and challenging, but stimulating classes. Unfortunately, when I

was still a student, I didn't feel the same way. I believe the reason is twofold: First, the ignorance and naiveté of youth. What an opportunity I had and this was truly the best time of my life, unfortunately I was too young and not experienced enough to realize it. Second, I do believe that being an African-American woman affected my feelings as well. There was an overriding sense of not truly fitting in with the wider school population and these feelings tarnished my thoughts at the time. Almost ten years later, I realize that this feeling would permeate throughout the rest of my life, but now I know how to handle as well as overcome it. Amherst proved to be the best training ground for life, preparing me to be successful professionally as well as personally.

Life was not that bad in the Pioneer Valley when I think about it now and how I do wish to have the freedom, the vast resources and many opportunities again. I am proud to be an Amherst alumna and would love for my daughter to have the same opportunity.

This is a tribute to Amherst that has been repeated over and over again by these graduates and the College should be proud of this.

ॐ

Sheree D. White, as would be expected, responded to my first letter in good time (July 1, 1995) apologizing for replying after my deadline date, but hoping her letter was "not too late to make a contribution." She is excited about the book: "I am delighted that you are undertaking this project, and quite honored by your invitation to me to participate. . . ."

Sheree White majored in Black Studies and Political Science and is now a librarian although many of us who knew her well while here at Amherst College, thought she would have been involved in some international organizations or activities. Even she would seem to be surprised by her new career. She said that she would never have guessed it when she left the College "that I would ever relish the thought of being a librarian."

Sheree participated fully in the extracurricular life of the College while she was here: she was involved in the Amherst Student Assembly, the Black Student Union and she was a Five-College student representative for some time; she also assisted in recruiting minority students and athletes to the College for it should be noted that she also had a keen interest in sports, particularly varsity basketball of which she was a team member. It is clear she has continued this interest, for in her present job situation she writes that her "extracurricular activity will be coaching one of the basketball teams here, which I am quite tickled about."

During the summer of her junior year in college, Sheree had an internship in Brazil, where she took a great interest in learning the Portuguese language. As a result of her experience in Brazil she became a sort of consultant or spokesperson for the YMCA Intern Abroad Program from 1986 to 1991. In her senior year she was awarded the Edward Jones Prize which required the writing of a college-wide competitive essay.

After graduating, Sheree enrolled with the Johns Hopkins School for Advanced International Studies, Washington, D.C., and in 1991 she obtained the M.A. in International Studies with a major in African Studies and a minor in Economics. For this she was awarded two very important fellowships: the Amherst Memorial Scholarship for Graduate Study and the Alpha Kappa Alpha Sorority, Inc. Scholarship, also for Graduate Study. During this time, before she received the M.A., she worked as a Research Assistant, 1988–1980, with Independent Sector, where she collected and abstracted material on philanthropy in religion. She also conducted research, interviews and editing for special projects on minority churches, in addition to planning and organizing national conferences and academic retreats. But when Sheree took a position of Library Assistant at the Johns Hopkins School for Advanced International Studies, and not the usual Teaching Assistant position that most graduate students would normally undertake, perhaps she had already decided on her career goal as a librarian. While at Amherst, she also worked as a student assistant in our Robert Frost Library. So, despite her keen interest in international affairs at the articulation level and her graduate pursuit, there was obviously the librarian within rearing to emerge. At the Johns Hopkins Library, she was part of a team that converted the card catalogue of the Library to the OCLC network. She processed, searched and retrieved bibliographic information on OCLC; as well, she catalogued and processed newly received acquisitions.

But she has not totally neglected her international perspective, especially on matters bearing on Africa, because we find her, while still at Johns Hopkins, becoming a Special Events Consultant with *Africane Inc.* Here she was busily engaged in numerous activities: planning of annual dinners, assisting in fund-raising, involvement with public relations campaigns with African Ambassadors as well as with area clergy; she drafted programs for different events including press releases and the like, in addition to which she maintained project database and managed office bookkeeping and supplies.

Still in Washington, D.C., for the greater part of 1991, she took on another appointment after leaving *Africane Inc.*, with the Center for Development and Population Activities as Assistant Coordinator at its International Development Forum. Again, she was involved with some of the same kinds of activities as with *Africane*, such as, for example, the preparing of drafts for programs, press releases, brochures and so on. She also supported different program chairs and planning committees with logistical and administrative assistance; she hosted international participants and aided with forum proceedings at conferences.

After receiving the M.A. in International Studies, Sheree took an appointment with the University of Pittsburgh's School of Medicine as an Administrative Assistant. Here her duties were varied. They involved general office management, making her responsible for internal financial records, inventories and supplies, composing and editing memoranda, correspondence, reports and grants; she also managed two student-run programs and supervised student workers but she was also responsible for organizing and maintaining a departmental library.

While working for the University of Pittsburgh, she enrolled with its School of Library and Information Science and received her Master's degree in Library Science in 1994. For a part of this year (1994) she took a position with the Carnegie Mellon University as Information Assistant, where she provided reference service to students, faculty and staff. She also performed assigned projects, such as the preparation and listing of journals, conducted library collection surveys, and participated in different searches.

From the latter part of 1994 to the present, she has held a position at The Ellis School in Pittsburgh, in the dual role of both librarian and teacher. She is a Mary McCune Edwards Fellow in Teaching. "Though my primary duties will be in the school's library, I will also be overseeing a minority internship program at the school, and working towards getting other schools in the Western Pennsylvania and Ohio areas to be more open to the notion of accepting minority teacher interns." And we may remind ourselves that it is here that she will be a coach for the basketball team.

Sheree has now chalked up two M.A.s since leaving Amherst in 1987, one in International Studies and the other in Library Science, and it is clear that she has found her bliss. She says, "I am very satisfied with my current position. . . . Being both a solitary person and at times an extrovert, I love the opportunities I have of withdrawing into my books (which is part of my job) or dealing with students and other patrons by sharing the joy of knowledge, fairytales, or adventures through books with others. Finding information that people want and need is an empowering position to be in."

Sheree has become proficient in numerous arcane library skills, including WordPerfect Dos and Windows; Macintosh; DBASS11+ and IV; Lotus 123; Internet; Unix. VMS. Procite; Proquest; Guide 3.0; CD ROM; PHD+ (scanner program); and OCLC. She is affiliated to associations such as the American Library Association, Special Libraries Association, Black Caucus of the American Library Association and the Alpha Kappa Alpha Sorority, Inc. She has attended numerous conferences, made presentations at some, and was a Keynote speaker at the Adams Elementary School graduation in Washington, D.C.

♫

Kimberlee Denise Wyche was among the selected few who responded to my first letter on time. She too was appreciative of the book on black women at Amherst College: "The project is a great idea whose time has come," and, perhaps understanding the difficulty of getting people to respond, she offered to help in the outreach process should I have problems in contacting members from her class.

Kimberlee majored in English and Spanish while fulfilling premedical requirements, making her exemplary within the context of a liberal arts education. She further demonstrated this balanced approach to education, when, in the winter of 1985, during her sophomore year, she went on a study-abroad program to La Universidad de San Luis in Madrid. Here she entered an intensive exchange program studying and gaining fluency in the Spanish language; she also studied Spanish literature and composition.

In her senior year she won two important competitive awards: The Charles Hamilton Houston Award and the G. Armour Craig Award for Excellence in Prose Writing. Upon graduating, she went to the Tufts Medical School, Neuroscience Department, in Boston, and there she studied neonatal substantia nigral degeneration in the Weaver mouse as a model for Parkinson's disease in the human world. In the summer of 1989 she enrolled at the University of Massachusetts Medical School in the Department of Preventive Medicine at Worcester, then in the following summer we find her in Quito, Ecuador. With her fluent Spanish, she could attend the University of Massachusetts Medical School there, and from the Department of Cardiology studied the dietary and environmental cardiac risk factors of urban vs. rural Indian children.

In 1993 Kimberlee received the Doctor of Medicine from the University of Massachusetts Medical School, and entered the Children's National Medical Center (CNMC) in Washington, D.C., the same year as a Primary Care Resident, which was to be for the next three years. During this time (the summer of 1994), she also worked with the Department of General Pediatrics at the CNMC where she collected data regarding the accuracy of evaluating Mantu TB skin test by parents.

In her letter to me Kimberlee had advised that after 1996 she would be returning to Boston to do a M.P.H. (Master's in Public Health) with a concentration in maternal child health care, with a view to "working in an inner city clinic environment doing Pediatrics, Adolescent Medicine and Child Health Advocacy."

But in pursuing her medical career as a Pediatric Doctor of Medicine Kimberlee was also actively engaged in community service. Since 1988 she has been working with the Region I Minority Action Committee, where she helped to identify specialists who can address issues of minority access to health care and in many cases she represents Region I at national conventions; during 1988–1991, she assisted the "under-served" in health screening, flu shots for the elderly, AIDS information sessions, child development seminars, clothing drives, canned food drives, soup kitchen volunteers for inner city homeless population, and the like; between 1989 and 1990 she was Chapter President of the Student National Medical Association, where she organized fundraising, as well as educational and student events dealing specifically with people of color. And it is no wonder that she received the Student National Medical Association (SNMA) Chapter Award in 1990. From 1991 to 1993 she became the Regional Director of the SNMA, where the activities were much more varied and more geographically spread. For instance, now she had to oversee the work of eight New England chapters; to serve on the national Board of Directors, and she even initiated a Regional Director newsletter.

For all this service she was deservedly awarded the SNMA Regional Award for Outstanding Leadership in 1992. Since 1993 she has volunteered to serve with the Zacchaeus Free Clinic, providing primary care to indigent infants and children in N.W. Washington, D.C.; also, since 1994, she has provided a low-to-moderate literacy educational guide outlining child development, nutrition, parenting, common infant and childhood health issues, adolescent health maintenance, and so on. She has also helped to initiate and launch a new Children's National Medical Center dealing with a comprehensive program geared toward the complete wellness of adolescent parents and their children.

Kimberlee has also been active in non-medical community service by volunteering to serve with organizations like the United Way; she also assisted with Teen Mother Mentorship Programs or the Jessie's House for the Homeless, where she provided advice, companionship and life style alternatives for adolescent women with young children. She even contributed to the *RX Art Literacy Magazine,* by composing and editing literary pieces for publication.

Her professional affiliations included membership with the American Academy of Pediatrics, American Academy of Family Practitioners, National Medical Association and Student National Association.

Class of '88

The class of 1988, I am sorry to say, has the dubious distinction of not having even one alumna responding to (1) my letters, or (2) telephone messages and the urgings of other alumnae who promised to contact some of them. Their names are listed in the appendix and we hope they—at least some of them—will participate in the updated edition of this book.

Class of '89

ⲋ

Crystal R. Brown (nee Jean) could not respond to my first letters because she was in the throes of her marriage preparations which took place September 2, 1995, and, in the process, was relocated. Yet, typical of this conscientious young woman, her reply to me was dated October 17, 1995; therefore, under the circumstances, she should be given top ratings for response. She even apologized for her late reply and wished me good luck with the book and, in another letter to me (September 21, 1996), said that she felt "honored to be a part of it."

Crystal majored in English, and in her note to me said that she had a "full" experience while at Amherst, and so it would seem. To begin with, we have already heard her expressing appreciation for the support she received from Professor Cody of the English Department, who "devoted so much time to helping me understand Shakespeare. . . . You've gone beyond the call of duty."

Crystal was quite active on campus. She was a member of the Gospel Choir and the Black Student Union and, in her junior year, was nominated to the Executive Board and was its Admission's Liaison, where she helped to coordinate "effective recruiting devices." She also helped with the planning of Early Orientation, Minority Open House and Pre-Freshman Weekend. Her junior year also saw her a licensed disk jockey with her own radio show under the Minority Media Project. In the field of sport, her great love was tennis, which she used, as she said, as her "outlet." But she was good enough to have played on the Women's Varsity Tennis Team.

Crystal graduated from Amherst with the distinction of being nominated the Eugene Wilson Scholar.

It seems she has always been interested in health care management and services. Even while at Amherst she worked between September 1987 and May 1989 as a Student Health Educator where she helped with organizing contraception education classes and awareness programs. During the summer months of 1986 through 1988 she was an Inroads Intern with the American International Group in New York City, where she gained good managerial and planning skills. In this capacity she was involved with planning, coordinating and executing public relations projects; she produced and wrote for an in-house publication, interviewed senior management for articles and worked with the legal department for opinions on some sensitive issues. She also supervised a high school intern on special projects.

After graduation, she became an Underwriting Trainee, obviously with a view to becoming a part of the health care insurance system, and from February 1990 to August 1991 she was Associate Health Care Specialist with the Continental Insurance Company of New York City. Here she completed the Initial Development Process, established a client base and broker relationships and evaluated new as well as renewal accounts.

During this time she enrolled at the New York University, New York City, and in 1992 obtained the Certificate in Health Care Administration. By September 1991 she was promoted to Health Care Specialist and was in this position until February 1993. In this capacity she was involved in managing large sums of money, and within a month (March of 1993), she was again promoted, in this case to the position of Senior Health Care Specialist. Her duties were many: she specialized in underwriting medical malpractice insurance, she evaluated hospitals, physician groups, and managed-care organizations. Equally she was responsible for accounts

that generated millions of dollars, for evaluating and marketing health care products and services and she also provided technical support for the underwriting department.

Once again, Crystal felt the need for more preparation for the job so she took a graduate course in Health Services Management and in May of 1995 obtained the M.P.A. degree (Health Services Management) from New York University. With the M.P.A. in hand she obtained a new position with the CNA Insurance Companies in Chicago, where she has worked since September of 1995 to the present. Here she is Senior Underwriter and is managing hospital accounts generating millions of dollars.

Crystal has a very highly developed social sense and is always involved in outreach programs. "Community leadership," she tells us, "has been an essential part of my upbringing. I am particularly interested in the welfare of our youth. Personally, I understand how difficult it could have been for me growing up in Harlem in New York City. Luckily my family ties were very strong and positive. My mother and sisters opened up many pathways for me and made sure that I continued to be challenged and well educated. . . . It has been rewarding for me to give back to my community and try to help someone else along. Over the years I have always made a choice to align myself with organizations that hold community service in high regard." With this in mind, she was actively engaged with INROADS even before graduating from Amherst as noted above. As a national organization whose goal is to develop and place talented minority youth in business and industry, and prepare them for corporate and community leadership, INROADS has made positive contributions throughout the country. While a member of the New York City branch, Crystal participated in a variety of INROADS projects. These include: facilitating workshops for inner city students and recruitment of students from high schools and participating in the interviewing processes for replacements, among many other voluntary activities. Now that she has moved to Chicago (since September 1995) she planned "to make contact with them in the future," and one can easily surmise that she has already done so.

Her dedication to community service also led her to membership of the Delta Sigma Theta Sorority, Inc., a national organization that seeks to better black communities across the country. As a part of this organization, Crystal expresses her interest in "the welfare of our children with regard to their academic and professional achievement, and the availability of positive role models and mentors in their lives, the welfare of black women with regard to health issues, family stability, educational achievement and success within professional fields. . . ." Again, she became involved with the Sorority during her senior year at Amherst by becoming a member of its Springfield (Massachusetts) chapter. Her enthusiasm for the organization, and the work in which it is engaged, comes through with sincerity as she tells us in a lengthy description:

> During my senior year (1989), I became the *first* member of the Pi Iota Chapter (Springfield City Wide Chapter) of Delta Sigma Theta Sorority, Inc. from Amherst College. I admired the community service and goals that these women established in the Pioneer Valley as well as their work I'd discovered on a national level through articles and books about the women of Delta Sigma Theta Sorority, Inc.
>
> While in New York, I was a very active member of the North Manhattan Alumnae Chapter of Delta Sigma Theta Sorority, Inc. (10/89–8/95). The following are activities that I participated in: Delta Teen Mentoring Program; Health Fairs, Career Development Workshops; College Search and Application Process with our teens; Black History Month Programs; United Negro College Fund Telethon; Scholarship Drives; Creative Writing Workshops; Visits to a nursing home in Harlem; School America (reading to children at the library); Spending Martin Luther King, Jr. Day at a Homeless Shelter for Men; Semi-Annual Clothing and Food Drives; Zawadi for Children—Hale House; Celebrating Kwanza with our teens; Voter

Registration Drives; Contributions to Africare and Habitat for Humanities; Holiday Raffles; "May Week" (Teen Talent Show free for the community) and many social gatherings.

I was co-chair of the Delta Teen Mentoring Program from 1990–1995 and Corresponding Secretary from 1993–1995. Near to my heart while a member of the North Manhattan Alumnae Chapter was the Delta Teen Mentoring Program. This program was designed for young women between the ages of 13 to 17. The Delta Teen Mentoring Program was established January 28, 1989 at the Polo Grounds Community Center with 11 young women from the Ralph Rangel Colonial Houses and the Polo Grounds Projects located in Harlem. We met on a monthly basis and focused our programs building educational, cultural, and political awareness. The majority of our young women came from single-family households and somewhat unstable surroundings. This program was personally rewarding because it gave me an opportunity to touch so many lives. Although emotional and challenging, I enjoyed the interaction, feedback, and sense of sisterhood. With our constant reinforcement, many of the girls are now in college and are the first in their families to do so. Three of the teens that I was paired up with are doing well in school. One of our first teens just graduated from Hofstra University. I am very proud of them and look forward to hearing about their future successes.

A few years ago, our chapter also participated in a service project in conjunction with New York Cares. We helped to clean up a drug-infested park for children located in Harlem. This park was called Dream Street Park. This was another emotional project. There was a section of the park with headstones in memory of children who had lost their lives to drugs or drug-related crimes. We removed debris including IV needles, empty crack vials, and overgrown shrubs. The kids painted and planted flowers. It was beautiful to see at the end of the day.

As we saw above, Crystal attributes her zeal for the public welfare of others to her family "growing up in Harlem," as she did: her mother, sisters and others, and Professor Cody would seem to agree. When I read Crystal's sincere and enthusiastic appreciation of Cody, I called him to tell him about it and to inform him that it would be entered in the book and wondered if he remembered Crystal enough to give me some impressions of her, and he very graciously and willingly agreed. Cody observes that:

Crystal came to Amherst already well-educated in values as well as in the elements of the curriculum. Her mother, Mrs. Ethlyn Jean, of Brooklyn, a teacher, and the Sacred Heart High School of Yonkers had prepared her well to take part in the life of this college. Her brother-in-law, Dr. Richard V. Sims, is an Amherst graduate of the class of '70. Crystal was not, as a first-year student, notably very good at anything (except perhaps tennis, in which her athletic gift made her notable among Amherst women), but she was wonderfully open to suggestions for improvement; she was well-rounded as a student; and she had the poise that comes with having learned what it is to be sensible.

She took the first course for English majors with me in the fall of 1985, and during that semester of reading and writing about poetry, short fiction, *King Lear*, Emerson's essays, and Cather's *The Professor's House* her performance as a reader and as a writer improved very markedly from a C- to A-. She showed that she knew well how to learn, and could put this knowledge to good use. When she declared an English major in her junior year I replaced Professor Rose Olver as her advisor; and so I began to see how she was faring across the curriculum. Her grades now rarely reached the level of A; she was to the end of her career at Amherst a B or B+ student, even as a senior in courses in her major; she had difficulty with the notorious Chem. 11, with Calculus, and with Econ. 11, but she did much better in humanities and social sciences. As an English major, she defined herself somewhat marginally by the courses she chose when a junior and a senior in Black Studies, Anthropology, and Sociology. These, probably, and not the more conventional English courses she took in American Men's Lives, Literary Criticism, Shakespeare, were what, in the English department, we would now call her "concentration." But in her Amherst transcript Crystal is not concentrated; however, in her all-round performance as a student in numerous departments, at U. Mass. in Five College registrations, and as a member of the college community, she was, as they say, a very "together" student indeed. She was a good citizen in everything she did, across the curriculum and beyond.

Crystal's husband, Damon Brown, is a graduate from Cornell University, where he earned the B.S. in Chemical Engineering in 1988, and is now working for the DuPont Company. He, too, like Crystal, believes in giving back to the community. "Helping others" he said, "has always been fulfilling; from recruiting and mentoring new minority employees to teaching high school students physics at DuPont's Minority Regional Incentive Training Program (M.E.R.I.T.) In Seaford, Delaware, I've always taken pride in knowing that I've helped another. I have a print in my office by an artist named Gilbert Young. It is called *He Ain't Heavy*. The original painting depicts one brother reaching over a wall to pull another up. . . ." He, too, seems to have a strong sense of self combined with a high degree of social responsibility, as Cody has characterized Crystal. To him, "Crystal values and possesses individuality: she recommends and practices the virtue of knowing who one is and pleasing oneself; but she does so modestly and responsibly with an active awareness of how much the individual in practice depends upon and owes to other people, or a group, or society. She knows the importance of working together, as well as of playing fair."

ॐ

Sonya Y. S. Clark responded to my first communication on July 3, 1995, yet she graciously apologized for not meeting the first deadline (June 30, 1995) but explained that she had changed her address and therefore my letter took some time to catch up with her at the new address.

Sonya majored in Psychology with a concentration in African Studies, and there is no doubt that she was very clear about the way she wanted to integrate Psychology with African art and her own personal background and experience as a first-generation American of African-Caribbean heritage. "In my artwork," she wrote, "I have brought together several aspects of my background. As an undergraduate student I became interested in social psychology, specifically identity formation and chose Psychology as a major. At the same time I took African Studies courses with Professor Abiodun and Professor Pemberton at Amherst College, Professor Femi Richards at the University of Massachusetts and the late Professor Pearl Primus, Five College Professor. I would be remiss if I did not also mention the influence of Professor Cobham-Sander and Professor Rushing. Under these two women I gained an entrance into African, African-American and African Caribbean literature. Often it is from literature that I get inspiration for my work."

Even her extracurricular activities in college reflected her deep involvement in African art generally but particularly African textiles, which to her should be seen as "physical manifestations of social identity in African culture. This interest expanded into a fascination with the retention of African aesthetics in African American arts and crafts." Her African Fashion Show in the Fall of 1988 in the Charles Drew House, which she called "Adornment of African People," was meant to demonstrate this point. She tells us that "[a]lmost all the members of the Black Student Union participated or attended this celebration and discussion of traditional African garb." Later, she designed a "pieced quilt," called "Kuumba: the Burden of the Mother is Life." This was a truly communal endeavor where the women of the Black Student Union participated in this quilt-making effort. In this operation they "spent hours together talking, sewing and working toward a common goal." It is no wonder she referred to the whole process as "a celebration of the creativity of black women." It is also fitting that the end product, the quilt, was hung in the Charles Drew House for a number of years.

Sonya had no ambiguity about her future career: it was to be in African Art, with a concentration in African fabrics. But she was also doing well in the other prong of her major in college, for during her junior year she was awarded the "Incentives for Excellence Scholarship Prize in Psychology."

She also made the smart decision to have spent the summer of her

sophomore year in Portugal, although studying abroad was nothing new to her. While at the Sidwell Friends secondary school, before coming to Amherst, she went on the school's study abroad summer program to Spain in 1983, and studied the Spanish language in an intensive course. In addition, she studied art history and music, thus laying a good foundation for her African art and culture studies. From Amherst, she went to Portugal under the "Religious Youth Service Development Aid Program," and there she studied Portuguese culture and history, although she was also involved in more practical matters such as the building of sanitary facilities as a part of the Development Aid Program. Now, with some background in Iberian history and culture, it seems the logical step would be that her next travel would be to Africa. And so it was.

Sonya graduated in the Spring of 1989 and the summer of this year found her in West Africa, at Cote d'Ivoire (the Ivory Coast). Here she entered the summer program of The Parsons School of Design, and studied art, music, religion and traditional textile designs. This must have been a most perfect environment for her—the experience of seeing African textile designs being undertaken in time-honored traditional ways, and understanding more closely the African cosmology that intimately combines art, music, literature, and religion without making the sharp distinctions as with Western culture—all this must have helped to inform her own artistic development.

When she returned from Africa, she took an interim position during the autumn of 1989 through to the summer of 1991, as Assistant Director of Admission at the Williston Northampton School. During the winters of 1989 and 1990 she was involved with the Amherst College Interterm Program, where she taught African surface design techniques for textiles. Between the winters of 1991 and 1992 she held two part-time teaching positions: one at the Williston Northampton School Intersession Program, Massachusetts, where she taught not only traditional African art but also had a more comparative dimension when she also taught Japanese tie dye and shibori techniques. The other part-time position was at Nick Cave, Deer Isle, Maine, as a Teaching Assistant, teaching surface designs as well as organizing workshops.

Her commitment to the study of textile designs and fine arts in general was such that she was prepared to go for another first degree (in addition to her Amherst B.A.) in fine arts. To this end, she enrolled with the School of the Art Institute of Chicago and in May of 1993 obtained the B.A. degree in Fine Arts (Fibers). During the summer of this year, she became an Apprentice with the Fabric Workshop in Philadelphia. As an apprentice, she performed dye lot tests with pigments and fiber reactive dyes and assisted with High School apprenticeship programs, among other things.

Perhaps understanding the need for a more comparative approach, especially in light of the pervasive and apparent similarity between African art and certain Oriental art (particularly with batik and tie dyeing techniques), in the winter of 1993, Sonya visited Indonesia. Under the auspices of the School of the Art Institute of the Chicago Intersession Program, she studied music, religion, textile design and history, thus tooling herself further for more comparative teaching and practice. She also extended her expertise while working for the B.A. in Chicago when she was Studio Assistant at the "Joan Livingstone," where she assisted in the sewing, patterning and production of industrial felt sculptures.

After her B.A. in Fine Arts, Sonya soon enrolled at the Cranbrook Academy of Art in Bloomfield Hills, Michigan, and obtained the Master's degree in May of 1995 in Fine Arts, again specializing in Fibers. While preparing for this degree she was also a Teaching Assistant at this same Academy. In this position she supervised and organized technical workshops and maintained studio equipment.

Also, during the summer of 1994, she obtained a Graduate Internship at the Smithsonian Institution in Washington, D.C. where she was obviously kept very busy: she organized and helped with children's workshops, teaching African art; she established networks among museums with African Art collections and she conducted research on African headdresses. In addition, in the winter of 1994, she was Exhibition Coordinator at the National Graduate Fibers Symposium at Bloomfield Hills, Michigan, where, among other things, she helped with the hanging of exhibits.

After the M.A. degree she took a teaching position at the Pontiac Creative Arts Center in Michigan. Here she taught children's workshops on kente cloth and weaving, presented gallery talks on different exhibitions, for example, that on "African Objects of Use and Spirituality."

Sonya's experience is rich and varied. She has traveled widely, and her exhibitions are many. Indeed she began giving exhibitions while still at Amherst when she organized a Textile Design Show at the Augusta Savage Gallery at the University of Massachusetts in 1989. Thereafter, she has had exhibitions in Michigan, Chicago, New York, Detroit, Washington, D.C., among other places too numerous for all to be mentioned. She has had some of her art work collected in different private and public places, including the residences of Ms. Mary Denison, Mr. Sam Gilliam, Mr. and Mrs. Sidney Hanson, and for public places, we have the Hampton University Museum in Hampton, Virginia, and even the White House.

Sonya has also been the recipient of many awards and fellowships. In 1992 she was awarded the Undergraduate Recognition Scholarship by the School the Art Institute of Chicago and the Jack Lenor Larsen Scholarship by the Haystack Mountain School of Crafts; in 1993 she was awarded The Philip Morris Fellowship by the Cranbrook Academy of Art; in 1994 she was awarded the Minority Fellowship by the Smithsonian Institution and also the Nita "Billie" Barak Memorial Merit Scholarship again by the Cranbrook Academy of Art, while in 1995 she received the New Initiatives for the Arts Award.

Sonya's devotion to fibers goes very deep into her own personal philosophy. "My interest in fibers as a medium," she writes, "and the concepts of syncretism, double consciousness and retention of cultural aesthetics is firmly rooted in my exposure to African Studies and textiles, readings in Pan-African literature, studies in Psychology and my personal experience as a first generation American of African-Caribbean heritage. . . . Throughout all of my experiences my Amherst College education has been an invaluable resource and foundation to my growth as a visual artist." The personal philosophy of her work is intriguing.

In what she calls the "Artist's Statement" she informed us that:

> Culture is dynamic. It flows from the external to the internal and from the internal to the external. That which is carried on the head is often indicative of that which is carried within the head. The head is a sacred place, the center where cultural influences are absorbed, siphoned and retained, the site where we process the world through the senses and the house of the spirit. The sculptural headdresses and hats I create are metaphorical funnels for the fluidity of cultural heritage and cultural melding as well as vessels for the entrance of spiritual energy (ashe) into the head.
>
> Visually, I draw my source material from African culture and its retention in the African Diaspora: images of women carrying loads on their heads, African hats and headdresses, Caribbean carnivals, African symbolism in form and materials are as important to me as process. I use copper because of its symbolic spiritual power as the "red gold" of Africa, its red color denoting blood, life energy and lineage to the ancestors. Likewise, I am interested in copper pennies which make reference to African American history and economics because of Lincoln's profile and their status as the least valuable form of currency. I employ textile techniques from African crafts into my work as a means to address the history of the African craft and African American craft legacy.

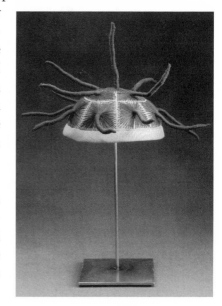

She is a member of the American Craft Council, the College Art Association, the Surface Design Association and the National Conference of Artists. She has lectured widely on different aspects of African Art.

Sonya is now married to Darryl Harper, class of '90, *summa cum laude* and Phi Beta Kappa, whose major was music. She tells me she has been too busy to start a family "yet."

&

Monica M. Colvin responded September of 1995 in a very short note to say that she was "very interested in the project," but was about to change her residency and "was unable to send any information at this time." However, after two or three more letters to her I have not been able to receive a response.

Monica majored in French, and wrote a Senior Thesis and her advisor, Professor Leah Hewitt of the French Department, was kind enough to supply the topic for me: "Les Effets sociaux sur le roman antillais: Une Analyse de l'aliénation dans le roman antillais." The "thesis discusses," Professor Hewitt says, "the ways in which socio-political issues inflect discussions of Antillean identity in the novels of Haitian writer Marie Chauvet and Guadeloupian writers Michèle Lacrosil and Maryse Condé. Monica concentrates on themes of alienation and of flight from the islands in these writers' works."

We hope Monica will be able to respond fully when this work is updated.

Class of '90

～

Nicole M. Moore apologized, citing "personal obligations and career changes," for her late reply. But, like all the others who responded, she wished me "the best of luck and much success" with the book.

Nicole majored in Psychology and Black Studies and was very active on campus. In sports, she participated in Women's Varsity Track and Volleyball, while she held executive positions in the Black Student Union. On the campus Entertainment Committee, she represented the Black Student Union and she was also consistently involved in coordinating cultural events for this Union. Since her graduation, she has volunteered to participate in the Amherst alumni fund-raising activities.

After graduating, Nicole went to work with a private law firm in New York City, Cahill Gordon and Reindel, as a Corporate and Litigation Legal Assistant. She participated in all phases of corporate transaction; organized closings and prepared documents for government filings, assisted attorneys in different areas of the litigation process, and, among other duties, summarized depositions and edited briefs. She remained in this employment until September 1992, when she left to join another law firm.

At Simpson Thacher & Bartlett, still in New York City, she was employed as a Case Manager. In this capacity, she conducted "factual" research for the New York Bar Association, federal archives, engineering and insurance libraries. But she also attended trials, supervised legal assistants and temporary employees for trial preparation, proofread motions and organized "tables of authorities," among other activities.

Nicole obviously had her mind set on the legal profession. After leaving the above firm, in August of 1995, she took another appointment at another law firm, also in New York City, as Senior Litigation Legal Assistant at the Tenzer Greenblatt, LLP outfit. But she remained there for just over a year before moving to the Winston and Strawn firms, still in New York City and with the same title. In this appointment she worked extensively with partners and clients in preparation for arbitration and trial. She now considers herself "skilled in cite checking and shepardizing briefs," in drafting affidavits and in responding to requests for documents—skills she learned in her second appointment.

Still with the above firm, Winston & Strawn, she has now enrolled at the Washington and Lee University School of Law and is anticipating her J.D. degree in 1999.

Nicole is proficient in Spanish and has acquired computer skills including—IBM systems such as WordPerfect, Immagic, Quicken and Lotus 1-2-3; also trained in Lexis/Nexis and Westlaw.

How does Nicole remember Amherst College? She writes:

> As an undergraduate at Amherst, I was determined to take advantage of all that was offered. I concentrated on the humanities and social sciences, took challenging courses and actively engaged in class discussion....
>
> At Amherst, I realized many of my strengths and limitations and it is here that I experienced tremendous personal growth. I am indebted to Amherst for what it has offered me educationally. I had an opportunity to conduct an independent research topic on gender biases in psychological testing, to attend lectures by Chinua Achebe and learn about Afro-centric

literature and authors absent from my public high school curriculum. Amherst has also offered me more than I expected culturally. I was exposed to gifted students from a variety of cultural and socio-economic backgrounds. I fondly recall Kwanza celebrations in Drew House and African dances choreographed by Professor Primus. I also recall "souls release," an event in which we would gather in the Octagon, hold hands, bow our heads and take turns expressing what was on our minds. I remember Dean Moss reminding us to persevere and to not merely survive, but to thrive at Amherst and in whatever we chose to do.

Although historically, Amherst was an institution dedicated to the education of white males, black women can claim Amherst as their own because of what we have 'brought to the table' academically, athletically, culturally and socially. We should be proud of our tenacity, our ability to excel in an environment that has not always been welcoming or comfortable. I am reminded of the words of Maria W. Steward in the *Liberator*, 1831, "Shall it any longer be said of the daughters of Africa, they have no ambition . . . ?"

ॐ

Keila C. Tennent finally responded to my letter of September 1996. But she did have the good grace to say that she was sorry it all "took so long." Keila majored in English, and was very active in sports, especially in the Women's J. V. Lacrosse and Rugby. In her junior year she availed herself of the Study Abroad Program and went to the University of Edinburgh, Scotland, where she studied Scottish and English literature.

Following her graduation, she accepted employment with a private insurance firm, "The Travelers Companies," in Hartford, Connecticut, as an Associate Account Manager. Her duties involved research as well as analyzing insurance politics where she investigated the facts and circumstances relating to policy holders' claims. She also made coverage determinations, taking into consideration the terms and conditions of the

contract as well as relevant hazardous waste and environmental pollution laws. She remained in this position until August of 1991 and then she entered the Vanderbilt University School of Law in Nashville, Tennessee, and graduated in 1994 with the J.D. degree.

During the summer of 1993, before receiving the J.D., she was an Associate at the law firm, Strang, Fletcher, Carriger, Walker, Hodge & Smith, in Chattanooga, Tennessee, and after receiving the law degree, she became a full Associate with this firm. In this position which she holds to the present, she is engaged in assisting clients with environmental regulatory compliance for underground storage tanks as well as obtaining environmental permits. She also represents clients in environmentally related administrative proceedings. But she is also involved in the drafting of pleadings and motions, in addition to providing general litigation support for commercial, environmental and employment law-related litigations. In the General Sessions Court, she regularly represents clients in dispossessory-related matters. Personnel policies and contracts are equally reviewed by her with a view to ascertaining compliance with federal and state laws.

Keila is a member of the Tennessee Bar and the American and Chattanooga Bar Associations. As an outreach activity, she is a Board Member of the Kidney Foundation of Tennessee, while her hobbies include tennis and running.

In looking back on her experience at Amherst, she said: "The older I get, the more I appreciate my experience at Amherst. I certainly didn't appreciate Amherst while I was there—I was too overwhelmed, immature and unexposed to make the most of what the college had to offer. The miracle is that despite these obstacles, I managed to develop a love for learning, life-long friendships and a constant desire for self-improvement. Yes, I know there were plenty of days when I felt that Amherst was too small, isolating, stressful and certainly too damn cold! Funny though, I have no specific bad memories. Now when I think of Amherst, I fondly remember what it felt like to run the [first?] mile on a beautiful, sunny day; spending hours chatting with my friends in Valentine on those dark winter evenings; sitting on the lawn watching a lacrosse or Rugby game; and last but not least dancing my butt off at a new dorm party."

Altogether, one suspects that Keila had a rather enjoyable time at Amherst. In a second note to me she again expressed appreciation for the book and is looking "forward to reading about the experiences of other black women at Amherst."

Class of '91

꒰

Valerie Jean Daugherty responded to my final "call," and just in time
to be entered in the book.

Valerie majored in Philosophy and her extracurricular activities saw
her participating in sports such as lacrosse and squash. In addition, she
was a vocalist for the Amherst College Jazz Ensemble.

Since her graduation from Amherst, Valerie has traveled on different
occasions to Greece. She spent the first year away (1991–1992) on a Teaching Fellowship at Athens College where she "discovered that teaching is as
much about learning as about imparting knowledge." She obviously had a
marvelous experience in this country, recalling nostalgically "getting up
very early to meet a bus taking me to the grammar school on a hill and
greeting first-graders carrying 30-pound backpacks as they boarded at appointed stops after mine." She also took the opportunity of the proximity
to the Middle East to visit Turkey for a Thanksgiving weekend (1991) and
then to Egypt for "Orthodox Easter" (1992).

Upon returning home, she first moved to Boston and took up an appointment as an intern/researcher for a documentary called *American War on Poverty*, produced by Blackside Film and Television. As an archival researcher she pulled together "newspaper and other clippings that helped to detail the tale of the U.S. government's tryst with equal opportunity," as she states it. Then, reflecting her love of Greece, she soon began to work as the U.S. Director for the Ithaka Cultural Studies Program in Crete, where she encouraged high school and college students to repair to this beautiful place. "Rugged Crete," to her, "was easy to sell not least because it held such bright blue memories for me," and she even managed to return there before enrolling for graduate studies.

At present she is a graduate student in Philosophy at Columbia University in New York City, and is just about finishing her course work (May 1997). Her dissertation proposal is along the line of "defining moral facts."

How does she view Amherst College in retrospect? "My years at Amherst," she writes,

> have remained vivid through my network of close friends. My best friends today were my best friends then. We've kept in contact despite distances actual and theoretical. If I thank Amherst for anything, I thank her for my friends foremost. Just last weekend, we gathered for a wedding shower for my future husband and me, and Amherst came up toward the end of the evening. Talk brought back our nights in Valentine, our after-dinner strolls to the playing fields and back, and long, long conversations about whether being at Amherst was the right thing for us, whether she cared at all to be supportive enough for us. Amherst gave me those friends to keep who sustain me even now. We all agreed: Amherst taught us to believe in our own abilities, perhaps at times despite herself.
>
> I don't know what to make of what I learned there or really how I learned it. Perhaps later on, distance will be prismatic, and I will be able to distinguish what of the person I will have become is due to Amherst. I can't say now: I'm still becoming.

But it is clear that Valerie Jean Daugherty is a woman who knew what she wanted, and is perfectly capable of assisting in the process of unfolding even from her Amherst days—otherwise how could she have taken on the redoubtable Professor of Philosophy, Bill Kennick? Well, I will recount asking Kennick if he had taught any black women here who impressed him for one reason or another, and without a moment's reflection he remembered Valerie and agreed to write a piece on her, which he gave to me in record time, and it is herewith reproduced:

> In the spring semester of 1988 I was surprised to see a young black woman appear in my course on early modern philosophy (from Descartes and Hobbes through Kant). Very few black students take my courses, and this was the first time for a black woman at Amherst to do so. (One of the very brightest philosophy students I taught at Oberlin in the early fifties was a black woman, but that was another place and another time.) The reading load in my course is very heavy, and students are required to write a paper every other week—and my grading standards are high. I thought this young woman must have made a mistake, and I expected her to drop the course during the two-week grace period. But Valerie Daugherty stayed with it. And not only did she appear at every class, she came up after class to ask questions about points she did not understand. I was at first slightly put off by her manner of asking questions—it was unusually aggressive (not for a woman, but for any student) and seemed to carry an undertone of flippant challenge. I replied to her questions accordingly in a rather chilly and dismissive way. To my surprise, she was not put off. There was a kind of spunkiness there that I grew to admire, and as my manner softened so did hers. We had found a way of talking productively to one another, and the semester went off without a hitch. Valerie did not do above average work that semester, and, although I ended up having a good relationship with her, I was sure I would not see her again.
>
> She showed up, however, in the fall semester for the companion course to the one she took, ancient and medieval philosophy (from Plato through Aquinas). Since we already had a smooth working relationship, we got off to a good start, and

Valerie did above average work in this course. To make what could be a longer story short, she went on not only to take two other courses with me (Aesthetics and a seminar on Wittgenstein) but to major in philosophy. She even started to write an honors thesis in her senior year but, I think only because she did not get the right counsel from her thesis advisor, she ended up dropping the thesis. Otherwise she was a good philosophy student—bright, willing to work, well motivated, and intellectually interested. When she graduated from Amherst in 1991 she took a job that she did not find satisfying; thought of doing graduate work in music (she was a singer) but gave that up; and finally decided to go to graduate work in philosophy at Columbia. I was happy to recommend her for admission, and, as far as I know she is doing well there. She turned out to be as gratifying a student as just about any I have taught and more gratifying than most.

Valerie is indeed doing well at Columbia, just finishing her final examination, and is involved in extracurricular activities, including working with the Harlem Tutorial Project, and is now a member of the Riverside Choral Society.

ॐ

Marvalyn E. DeCambre responded to my final call just in time to be included in this book before it goes to press but, in extenuation, she told me that she had been traveling for some time.

Marvalyn majored in Psychology and contributed a great deal to the college community. She sang with the College Gospel Choir, was "Most Valuable Player" of the Amherst Women's Rugby, and played in the Amherst College Track and Field events. She was also a part of the Third World Theater Group/Spectrum III, and was responsible for founding the magazine, *Points of View*, a provocative and lively journal that she co-edited. In addition to all these activities, Marvalyn also chaired the Black Student Union in her junior year, and she also served with the Amherst

College Admission Office as tour guide, interviewer, and director of minority "pre-fresh" weekends.

Yet, this well-rounded student also wrote a Senior Honors Thesis. In it she said that she conducted a survey comparing white and black first-year students at Amherst from predominantly white and black communities respectively, identifying the "comfort level and success" of each group at the College.

Marvalyn rightly said that she "put a lot into Amherst and got significant dividends." To begin with, she graduated with the awards, "Outstanding College Student of America," and Sigma Xi (Scientific Honor Society).

No beating around the bush here, Marvalyn was a "pre-med" student and she knew it. Upon graduating from Amherst, therefore, she promptly enrolled with the School of Medicine and Dentistry at the University of Rochester in New York, where she is expecting the M.D. in May of 1997. Her internships while still at Amherst, during the summers of 1989 and 1990, at the Mount Sinai Medical Center, New York City, and the Harvard Health Professions Program, respectively, were certainly preparatory to medical school.

At Rochester she is already involved in various activities. Those of an extracurricular nature include her participation in the Rochester Women's Rugby Club; in the Club Caribbean of Rochester, where she has served on the Scholarship Fund Committee; on the Curriculum Committee of the Aids Education Task Force, among others. She has also served, between 1992 and 1993, on the International Health Programs, in Rochester: she developed fund-raising and marketing ideas for international health scholarships for medical students and helped to organize the first International Health committee run by students. Between 1992 and 1994 she was a member of Crossroads, Rochester, where she founded and organized programs for students and faculty in curriculum development, and she is now elected to the ten-year accreditation committee by the Dean of Student's Office at the University of Rochester. Since 1992 to the present she has been a member of The Student National Medical Association (SNMA), Chapter IX, Rochester, where she helped with organizing forums on medical topics; in addition, she attends national meetings as a delegate from her chapter.

As would be expected, Marvalyn has received many awards and fellowships. In the summer of 1993 she was awarded two fellowships: one, as an International Health Fellow, which took her to the Dominican Republic (Santo Domingo). As a Graduate Researcher here, she was engaged in demographic surveys of the female population, "using OB/GYN Services." The second fellowship of this period was the Alpha Omega Alpha (AOA) Fellow, where she was again a Graduate Researcher, apparently at Rochester University, looking into "Isolation of Interleukin-1B receptor mRNA in rat spleens."

Summer of 1994 found her again a Graduate Researcher as the "Strong Children's Research Fellow," doing assessments of Race and Glucose metabolism by MtDNA analysis." During 1995 and 1996 she was the beneficiary of the NIH Medical Research Fellowship, and as a Graduate Researcher she has inquired into "Glucose Homeostasis and the Partial Hepatectomized Animal."

Although originally from the Anglophone Caribbean (Jamaica), she is also interested in the Spanish-speaking zone. Her knowledge of the Spanish language facilitated her fellowship to the Dominican Republic in 1993. But she had also spent some time in another Spanish-speaking country, Venezuela (Caracas), between the time of her graduation from Amherst and her entry into the University of Rochester (1991–1992). In Caracas, at the Escuela Campo Alegre, she was an instructor but not of subjects relating to medicine! In fact, she taught Algebra to seventh-grade students, and coached them in intramural sports.

She tells us that her hobbies are reading and the writing of poetry. How does she view her experience at Amherst College? She 'liked" it. "Amherst was good for me," to a great extent because, as she said, she had invested a lot of her time and energies on the campus. She went to Israel from Rochester, a trip, she said, "that had a lot to do with my time at Amherst. I was called an anti-Semite by folks from Hillel because I agreed to have Kwame Toure/Stokely Carmichael speak at Amherst as the main speaker for Black History month. I was so hurt by the activities by Hillel surrounding that event, I became fearful of going to a predominantly Jewish medical school in NYC. Who wants to be labeled an anti-Semite throughout their medical education. I did not understand Zionism. My trip to Israel helped me to appreciate the desire for a Jewish state. It also helped me appreciate the desire for a Palestine state. I probably would not have changed Kwame Toure's engagement at Amherst knowing what I know now, but looking back, I was certainly influenced by my Jewish classmates at Amherst to increase my understanding."

Class of '92

༄

Akinyi Adija majored in Psychology, and was obviously interested in the sciences. For this she was fortunate to have taken Professor Pat O'Hara's introductory chemistry course in her sophomore year. Professor O'Hara found her "anxious about her ability to master some of the more abstract and mathematical aspects of her science courses. She was a most reliable visitor to my office during office hours and we would go over her prepared questions again and again until she had gotten it right. Through conscientious hard work and perseverance, she was successful in completing her first college chemistry course, receiving a respectable grade of B-."

O'Hara knew that Akinyi went on to the next course in the Chemistry Department, "Thermodynamics and Kinetics, which is undoubtedly one of the most abstract and difficult courses offered in our introductory sequences at Amherst College. I know the same traits of hard work and perseverance got Akinyi through this course as well; I would often see her working hard with the professor of the course during his office hours and beyond."

When it is remembered that Akinyi is from an inner-city neighborhood, one "that can be hostile to those not materially blessed," in O'Hara's words, then, to find her grappling with the sciences is even more remarkable.

Akinyi's story must serve as an example to women in general who tend to fear the sciences. She did not clearly accept the negative expectations generally from the sciences here, but went in with her own determination to succeed through hard work and was intelligent enough to seek help when needed.

Professor O'Hara also finds Akinyi "a delight to have in the classroom. She is always bright and cheerful no matter what the hour, day or situation. She doesn't seem to get frantic and panicked like so many of her peers at the end of the semester. There is a calm, patient, determination about her that keeps her focused. In lab, I saw many of these same characteristics lead her successfully through the experiments and the lab write-ups. When she needed to do something over because of confusing or contradictory results, she did so without complaint."

We do not know what Akinyi is doing at present; we know that she applied for a position at the Northfield Mt. Hermon School in Massachusetts, to teach biology at the 9th grade level, and we wish her well. As O'Hara says, "She will master any challenge she accepts and make the world a brighter place while doing so."

Tracey D. Briscoe was among those special ones who responded to my first letter in a timely fashion. She was "extremely pleased to hear about your exciting new project. I look forward to reading about the accomplishments of Amherst women; in particular the achievements of black women graduates over the past twenty years. Thanks very much for thinking of me although my experiences to date are modest given my recent entry into the financial services industry."

Tracey majored in History and I was her advisor for her Senior Honors thesis. In her junior year she went on a Study Abroad program to Kenya in East Africa, and it was there that she developed the idea for her thesis. Basically, she looked into the historical development of the Christian missions on the Education of this East African country. I was very tough with Tracey, but she was no shirker, and her burning desire to improve her intellectual capacities made her stay the course. The result is that I saw her develop into a self-confident, level-headed person, with disciplined working habits. Her writing, for example, was so improved that even she had to comment on it repeatedly.

And she needed to be disciplined and tough for the kind of job she does. After graduating from Amherst, she entered employment with J .P. Morgan as an Analyst in the Global Securities Product Management Department. Here Tracey was learning new and useful skills: she gained an understanding of the way financial markets operate; the services they rendered both domestically and internationally. But from the outset she became interested not only in the "high finance" aspect of the firm, but also in its social or diversity dimension: "As the only black woman of well over 200 training program participants in 1992, it was immediately apparent to me that recruiting and supporting minorities in the financial services industry would become an important personal goal. Three years later, aiding the development of women and minorities has since become my primary professional responsibility," and this is typical of Tracey who was determined to put her education to the service of helping others.

She was soon able to pursue her diversity goals with a new appointment with Merrill Lynch in New York City, and her title "Undergraduate Diversity Recruiter" unambiguously proclaims its intent. She does this type of recruiting for the Corporate and Institutional Client Group of the firm. In practice, she writes, "I hire and aid the professional development of women and minorities interested in Investment Banking and Debt and Equity Sales and Trading."

Regarding long-term goals, Tracey plans to pursue a graduate degree in

International Affairs, with the intention of using her knowledge of Africa to aid the development of financial markets on this continent. For the moment though, she is "thankful to have the opportunity to educate and challenge undergraduates interested in economic development." Like Lisa Evans of the class of '85, Tracey too is convinced of the dynamic importance of diversity not only in the academy but also in the workplace. She wants to be able to contribute to the understanding "that valuing diversity will create new and evolving ideas which will fuel social and economic development needed for the next millennium."

Very graciously, she ended her letter by thanking me "for recognizing and aiding my personal and developmental needs. I sincerely hope that my accomplishments in life will serve as a tribute to your success as an educator. Please know that you are constantly in my thoughts; your words of encouragement and guidance aid my personal development to this day. THANK YOU!"

ও৲

Key Alexandra Mendes majored in American Studies and Psychology and wrote a Senior Thesis in the American Studies Department, which, she tells me, was an autobiography, between the ages of six and thirteen. The topic, "Pecan Pie Is Not My Pie of Choice," is suggestive. She writes, "My mom is African-American from L.A., and my dad is Jewish, from Brooklyn, New York. We moved around a lot, and I write about my adventures . . ."—after which, a sentence I could not decipher.

On campus, she was involved with the Black Student Union, the Student Senate, was on the Films and Lecture Committee and was a D.J. on a WAMH radio program. Key enjoys running, walking, reading and films. During the spring of 1991 she went on a Study Abroad program to the University of New South Wales in Australia.

After graduating from Amherst she worked as a "Paralegal" with the law firm, Simpson Thacher & Bartlett, between August 1992 and July 1994. As would be expected at this level, her duties involved legal research, assisting in the preparations for trails and depositions, proofreading briefs, maintaining case files, organizing case rooms and writing inter-office memoranda. After leaving this position, she became a Legal Intern with the New York Society for the Prevention of Cruelty to Children, where she became involved in different kinds of conflict resolution and observed proceedings in Family Courts. It is clear that Key is bent on a legal career, and to this end she is now a member of the Fordham University School of Law, from where she is expecting to receive the J.D. degree in May 1997. Here she is already active on campus: she is Associate Editor at the *Fordham International Law Journal*; she entered the William Hughes Mulligan Moot Court Competition (Summer 1995), and is a member of different organizations such as the Black Law Students Association and the Fordham Law Women Group.

In the meantime, she has been Legal and Judicial Intern and in one case, a Summer Associate to different firms, performing the usual entry-level functions. But between June 1995 and May 1996 she was a Legal Writing Teaching Assistant with the Fordham Academic Enrichment Program, where she taught introductory legal writing to incoming first-year law students; she also acted as a mentor and advised students, and coordinated workshops on legal writings.

Key tells us that she has a "knowledge" of French and Spanish, and looks back on her experiences at Amherst with great appreciation: "I wouldn't be the person I am today if I did not attend Amherst College. I learned that its ok to be me, a bi-racial woman who grew up in California and now lives in Brooklyn (New York). The classes I took, friends I made, professors I had and writing my thesis all combined to make my four years at Amherst the most thrilling, challenging and enriching time in my life. It is a time I will never forget."

჻

Nyaneba Nkrumah was among those who responded in a fairly timely fashion to my first letter. Nyaneba majored in biology and upon graduation received an Amherst College Johnson Fellowship to spend the summer of that year in Ghana, West Africa, her place of birth. Here she worked, in her own words, "with a group of doctors from the Noguchi Institute for Medical Research on a rural health and education project. The purpose of the project was to stop the spread of bilharzia by examining and treating children who had been exposed and preventing reinfection by education."

Nyaneba must be a very multi-talented person because while on this highly scientific fellowship in Ghana, she also completed a novel. She said she had started this piece of fiction some years previously and by the end of the summer, "[I] got my first fiction novel for young teens published. A year later I won the Valco Literary Trust Award for the novel."

After her fellowship in Ghana, she returned to the U.S. (September 1992) "and began a job with an environmental group, *Clean Water Action*, based in Northampton, Massachusetts," a group she had already worked for on a part-time basis during her freshman and sophomore years at Amherst. She stayed with *Clean Water Action* for "about four months," after which time she obtained a position as a Legislative Aide with the Maryland Legislature. Here she was working for Delegate Rosenberg, an Amherst alumnus, who was a Delegate to the House of Representatives in Maryland. "At the end of the session," Nyaneba wrote, "I returned to working for the *Clean Water Action* but this time I requested a transfer to their Baltimore office and worked there till mid-August of 1993. Working for *Clean Water Action* exposed me to the environmental field and because most of the job involved meeting and talking to literally hundreds of people at their homes, I felt that we were actually reaching people and making a difference."

But Nyaneba had set her sights on higher goals and in 1993 applied to graduate schools in this country and had the good fortune to have been accepted both at Yale and Michigan. She chose Michigan because "they" offered her a full scholarship. Her aim was to do a Master of Science degree in the field of Resource Ecology and Management. "The highlight of my time at graduate school was being able to go to Ghana to work on my thesis. I worked in the rural areas of Ghana in an area where deforestation was a big problem. My thesis focused on field research that quantified the extent of the deforestation and determined reasons for the deforestation and proposed management strategies for recovery of the area."

She graduated with her M.A. in April and in May started what she calls her first "real" job, working as an environmental protection specialist at the Environmental Protection Agency, National Motor Vehicle Emissions Laboratory.

In response to my question in my first letter regarding job satisfaction, she said she has not been in this "real" job situation "long enough to say whether or not I am satisfied with the job. So far, it's been interesting. It's difficult to work a full day and come back home and want to do anything other than just 'veg': I'm trying to get used to not having much free time and living the more structured 9–5 life."

But I am happy to hear that Nyaneba has not forgotten the literary side of her talents. She writes that she is working on another novel, "this time an adult fiction focusing on African/African American dynamics. I'm not sure how it'll turn out so I can't say any more than that."

Her long-term goals "are aimed at working in the field of development and the environment. Until I've achieved that, I don't think I can truly have job satisfaction. I want to work in an environment where I feel I am making a difference. Not that working in the EPA is not making a difference. I believe that development in less developed countries is often accompanied by environmental degradation and I would like to work to ensure that development occurs sustainably. To me, that's a much more challenging task. It is my dream to eventually work for an international agency such as the UNDP but as yet, that's what it is . . . a dream." One hopes that her dreams will be realized.

Class of '93

⁓

Gertha T. Benoit-Hollis responded to my first letter in good time and was happy to be a part of the project. "I thank you for asking me to be part of this wonderful piece of history and I would enjoy greatly seeing the book after it is completed. I thank you again for your consideration...." She reminded us that her graduation has been only recently, but hoped that what she called her "meager accomplishments over the past two years will be of some use to you for this book...." And yet, already she has a great deal to offer. Although she took only one course with me, she had always been in touch throughout her years at Amherst, and even after leaving. I was always impressed by her commitment to self-improvement and her willingness to take on challenges.

Gertha majored in Black Studies and French and was among those who contributed a great deal to the College community. Throughout her four years on campus she was the Five College Liaison for the Black Student Union and also for the first two years, she was the Correspondent Chairperson for the Black Business Association of Amherst College; she was also the only student representative on a search committee for a Security Chief of the College. It is clear that Gertha's leadership skills were recognized when she was appointed Resident Counselor to the French and Spanish Cultural House. She acted as mentor, problem solver, community builder and her linguistic skills in English, French and Spanish would certainly be useful in this kind of multi-cultural situation. She also acted as a budget director in this situation. In most of her senior year, she helped in the Office of the Dean of Admission, where she interviewed prospective students, conducted information sessions, managed students-of-color weekends, formulated statistical reports for programs dealing with students of color, in addition to which she also traveled with different deans to various college fairs.

But in the spring semester of her senior year she found time to avail herself of a Study Abroad Program. In endeavoring to perfect her French, under the auspices of the Institute of European Studies, she went to Nantes in France, and studied French language and civilization, as well as Russian literature.

Following her graduation from Amherst, she was the beneficiary of the Harvard Fellowship Award and she spent a year attending Harvard's Graduate School of Arts and Sciences, where she studied government. "As you know from the class I took with you, I have a very strong interest in the inner workings of all political systems because I endeavor to understand my own complex, corrupt system of Haiti. My courses in the government department focused primarily on the inner workings of the American Congress and Presidency. I wrote major papers focusing on the socialization of blacks in Congress from 1865 to the later 1960s, and on populist movements in Africa ranging from the Kimbanguists in Zaire to the Mau Mau in Kenya."

After Harvard, Gertha married David M. Hollis, also an Amherst graduate. David also spent a year at Harvard and obtained an M.A. in Education, and they are now living in New York, where David is a social studies teacher at the Webster Junior High School in Port Washington. For her part, Gertha continued her education by enrolling at the Graduate School of Arts and Sciences at Columbia University and from there obtained a Master's degree in Political Science, where she concentrated in comparative and international politics.

As for job satisfaction and contributions to the wider community, she was not yet certain when she wrote to me in July of 1995. She had just started a new position as an associate researcher with KRC Research in New York City: "thus my knowledge of what I will be doing is somewhat limited." But one can be quite certain that this very sociable and articulate person (in both French and English), with her tremendous potential and her serious ambitions for intellectual improvement and community service, will be a success in whatever field she may choose.

༰

Catherine E. Lhamon majored in American Studies and obviously had a very full life on campus. She was a Student Representative on the Faculty Committee on Admissions and Financial Aid, where she helped with policies dealing with financial aid to students. But her activities were mostly centered around campus publications. She was editor of *The Amherst Student* and was Director of Student Darkrooms where she was responsible for the purchasing and maintenance of supplies for all photo publications.

Catherine wrote a thesis with the American Studies Department, with the interesting title, "I Just Knew the Phone Would Ring Someday and Joshua Would Be Dead," where she said she "criticized the reasoning of a Supreme Court decision, *DeShaney v. Winnebago County Department of Social Services*, arguing instead that the state does have an obligation to protect children from abuse and neglect. But I argued also for a principled, nondiscriminatory approach to such interventionist state policy."

At the end of her senior year, Catherine was awarded many honors. She won the Edward Jones Prize in Black Studies, the Doshisha American Studies Prize, and the Ford Foundation Honors Grant, and was also the beneficiary of the John Woodruff Simpson Fellowship in law, and within a year after her graduation from Amherst, under this latter fellowship (1993–1996) she entered the Yale Law School. Here again she became involved in different activities dealing with college publications. As editor of the *Yale Journal of Law & the Humanities*, as would be expected, she was responsible for evaluating and editing articles submitted to the *Journal*, but she soon became a part of the *Yale Law Journal*, as Book Review Editor and Admissions Editor from 1995 to 1996. Her responsibilities included soliciting reviews and editing submissions, as well as helping to set admission standards for the *Journal*. During most of this period she was also the Yale Chapter Secretary of the National Black Law Student Association (1994–1995), where she published chapter newsletters, maintained correspondence and took minutes at biweekly meetings.

Like many other law students, she too was involved in some teaching, as assistant to one professor or another. Between 1994 and 1996 she assisted both Professors Reva Siegal and Burke Marshall: for Professor Siegal she helped to create new courses in feminist and critical race theory and devised readings for them, and for Professor Marshall, she taught legal research and writing to first-year students. Equally, as with all law students she served as legal intern and summer associate on different occasions to various legal firms.

Catherine graduated from Yale, "The Outstanding Woman Law Graduate of Yale Law School" (1996), after having been awarded the Francis Coker Fellow for 1995–96.

This gifted young woman has already published in different law journals. Even before graduating from Amherst, in 1992, she published, "Things That Are Equal to the Same Thing Are Equal to Each Other: The Transitive Property in International Law," in the *Five College Journal of Law & Society*, and in the following year she published in this same journal, "Balancing Acts: Abused and Neglected Children in King Solomon's Court." In the *Yale Law Journal* she published, "Mother as Trope in Feminist Legal Theory," in 1996 (Vol. 105, March 1996, pp. 1421–26).

Fresh with her J.D. (1996) from the Yale Law School, we find her (and will leave her there) working as a Law Clerk with The Honorable William A. Norris, Ninth Circuit Court of Appeals, in Los Angeles, California, with an apparent "contract" for 1996-97. Here she is drafting and revising opinions, and researching cases submitted to her, and is engaged in debating legal analyses with judges.

We are certain to hear much more from this Amherst alumna of the class of '93, who obviously enjoyed Amherst: to my request for a personal statement on her experience here, her reply was simply, "I loved Amherst."

ॐ

Keisha A. Lightbourne apparently majored in Spanish, and in an undated letter to Mrs. Denton she mentioned that she took a year off after graduating in 1993 and then she began attending Washington University School of Law in St. Louis, where she intended to obtain two degrees: a J.D., and a master's in Health Administration.

She also enclosed a five-page essay dealing with, in substance, "minorities" at Amherst College. A part of this essay expressed a view that has suddenly become topical. She said: "In an effort to 'accommodate' minorities the Admissions Office makes a special effort to welcome you, to show you the school, to help you with scholarship money, a summer prep program, etc. Their attempt to forge a sense of belonging between you and the institution you will attend ends up leaving you more frightened with an increased sense of estrangement and the feeling that perhaps you are not worthy of attendance at such a fine institution. This ritual appears to make our skin color a sign that says 'special case: special attention warranted.'"

It is important that this "other" view coming from some blacks be known. Keisha, in her reflective manner, continued: "Assuming," she said, "as most of us do, that we were admitted to Amherst based on our own merits and our own ability to compete with the majority, all of this special attention seems unnecessary. As your classes begin and you meet other people (black and white), you begin to question your ability. . . . You begin to think you were admitted based on the color of your skin, governmental quotas, and . . . you begin to forget the reason you came. You just end up feeling inadequate."

However, with some more acute reflective statements, she concluded her essay on a positive note. After the first emotions of "otherness, inadequacy and unworthiness," she came into a new strength, "that inner strength passed on to me by my ancestors—the very same strength that brought me to this school in the first place." Then she ended this well-structured essay with a beautiful coda:

Reflecting on four years of growth, I have concluded that my ability to succeed here was not a matter of being *allowed* to succeed, but it was based on *my will.* This will was not merely a case of mind over matter, but it was based on a type of example exhibited by the black women who came before me and the duty I had to exhibit this metaphor for black power.

In order to reach this conclusion I had to graduate from a series of stages. I was forced to reconcile my own personal ability: who I was, who I could become, and how all of this related to my gender and race. Janie Victoria Ward in her study on racial identity formation and transformation noted: "This awareness of double jeopardy, because of the additive effect of gender and race, served to heighten levels of introspection and self-examination." This struggle to feel comfortable with a dual minority status affords a sense of inner strength especially when you realize where you are and you actually have achieved just by attending Amherst.

We hope that Keisha will contribute to the updated version of this book later.

ᘒ

Anastasia Rowland majored in Chemistry and Black Studies and was very active on campus, although, "the first year was difficult," she tells me. She had, for example, expected a more united black community and therefore "found it difficult to find my niche." But, from the sophomore year, Anastasia began to settle down nicely for different reasons. First, as she states it, she "had settled into Drew House" and was now involved with the Black Student Union. In addition, and even more important for her in terms of her career goals, she had discovered Professor Patricia O'Hara of the Department of Chemistry, "who had taken her under her wing." She said that during the spring of her sophomore year, she experienced "a shock" when she started Physical Chemistry, was told she was taking the wrong class, and felt "that the two women in the class (50 per-

cent of the class) were ignored. It was difficult to stomach that my department and subject that I loved might be headed by sexists—I even considered dropping my Chemistry major. Luckily, I didn't."

After that semester, she began to feel more comfortable in the department, thanks to Pat O'Hara. On campus, Anastasia soon became an active representative of the Black Student Union; she also participated in the Gospel Choir, and was soon a WAMH Radio D.J. and Curator for the Rhythm and Blues section. She obviously had a strong community spirit combined with good leadership skills. When these qualities were recognized, she was nominated Resident Counselor for the Charles Drew Memorial Cultural House, and was chairperson of the Organizing Committee for Black Alumni Weekend.

Anastasia showed both initiative and foresight when she founded The Charles Drew Pre-Medical Achievers Group—reflecting, doubtless, Drew's brilliance (class of 1926) as a medical practitioner and his initiative in blood plasma preservation. Her group is definitely a support entity for blacks in the sciences, drawing on a network of black alumnae/i and some faculty advisors.

The Charles Drew Pre-Medical Achievers Group must be one of the most important associations formed by blacks on this campus, helping, as it did, to provide a support base for blacks and Hispanics in the sciences. Anastasia would actually hold study sessions in her dorm for students in the sciences to work together on difficult scientific problems. But it appears that this group has changed in different ways since Anastasia's graduation. Now called the Charles Drew Pre-Medical Society, it is currently extended beyond catering only to the needs of students of color. A report of the Student Finance Committee (SFC) in *The Amherst Student* (Wednesday, December 4, 1996, pp. 1 and 2) maintains that "the group has decided to expand and become more inclusive, evolving from a student-run organization to a campus-run organization." A member, apparently of the SFC, described the reconstructed Charles Drew Pre-Medical Society as "a support group which plans to facilitate student attendance at bio-medical conferences and visits to medical schools. The society also plans to have speakers in the medical field, including bio-ethicists as well as doctors, at their regular meetings."

In this same report, the SFC was declaring its intention to fund the Drew Pre-Medical Society. But it is not clear to me whether or not this funding was dependent on its new inclusiveness. I discussed the matter with Anastasia from her new base at Columbia University (May 15, 1997), and she was completely unaware of the changes. She is happy that it will be funded on a regular basis, but is naturally concerned about the original intent of the organization which was primarily a support group for students of color in the sciences. This, perhaps, deserves further investigation. Anastasia was also an active member of The Student National Medical Association.

Despite her impressive contribution to the college community, Anastasia still found time for a Study Abroad Program when, in the summer of 1991, she went to Kishapu, Tanzania, East Africa. Professor O'Hara has related the difficult circumstances under which she went to help in this public health program in Kenya. Anastasia in fact received only modest funds for the program and was therefore responsible for financing most of the trip herself. "With amazing determination and sophistication," O'Hara recounts, "she culled through all possible funding agencies and through her applications and phone calls was able to solicit the remainder of the support from a number of other organizations. She demonstrated a maturity and knowledge of how to work with the system which I have never seen in an undergraduate." At the Kishapu Rural Health Center, Anastasia acted as a Laboratory Technician and Physician's Assistant. In this situation she performed numerous functions, including "lab" tests to determine if patients were infected with malaria parasites, worms, tuberculosis and a host of other infectious diseases. She had also worked at the Harlem Hospital, New York City, as a Research Assistant during the January break of 1990 and a part of the summer of 1991. At this hospital she was equally involved in a number of medical activities. In the summer of 1992, she also served as a Research Assistant at the Massachusetts General Hospital in Boston, where she worked closely with physicians involved in topical issues in this country such as osteoporosis.

Anastasia wrote a Senior Honors Thesis in the Chemistry Department under the supervision of Professor O'Hara. The topic, "Multifrequency Phase Fluorometry as a Means of Determining the Dynamics of Calmodulin" sought to "obtain experimental information to describe the macromolecular dynamics of the protein calmodulin (CaM), an important calcium regulatory protein. The flexibility of the molecule is measured by the changes in the energy transfer from one end of the molecule to the other."

It is certain that at the completion of this thesis, Anastasia would be even more inclined to be appreciative of Professor O'Hara. In a statement to me she said that she was "truly indebted" to this professor:

> When I was a first-year student at Amherst and was having difficulty with some of the concepts of Chem 11, she spent extra time with me and continued tutoring me until I truly felt comfortable with the subject. It is largely because of her that I felt confident enough to declare a Chemistry major as a first-year student, early for most students at Amherst. In all my endeavors Pat was 100% supportive whether it be the pre-med group, my trip to Tanzania, Biochemistry, my thesis or my desire to teach chemistry to high school students, Prof. O'Hara was always in my corner. Despite Pat's hectic schedule as a Professor, member of many committees, advisor to more than her share of students and loving mother she always made time for me. Pat is the personification of a devoted teacher. She is determined to transmit a certain level of understanding of chemistry to students and in the process often infects them with her love of the subject. Once when I was excusing my lack of knowledge, Pat said one of the most important things that anyone has ever said to me: "there is no dumb question, the only dumb question is the one that you don't ask." With that she gave me the freedom to question, to ponder and to dream, for that I am eternally grateful. Now when I am teaching other students, whether it be chemistry or medicine, I find myself

saying what Pat said to me, in the hopes that I can provide that same space that they might find the freedom to learn.

Anastasia has won many honors while at Amherst. In 1990 she received the Hughes Award for Scientific Research, and in 1991 she won both the Johnson and the Peace and World Security Studies Fellowships; in 1992 she won the John Sumner Runnells Memorial Prize, the White Prize for Chemistry and the Ford Foundation Grant for Thesis Research; in 1993 she became a member of Sigma Xi, won the Student Award from American Institute of Chemists, and for the years 1993, 1994 and 1995, has been the beneficiary of the John Woodruff Simpson Fellowship.

As would be expected, following her graduation in 1993, she entered medical school—the Columbia University College of Physicians and Surgeons, New York City, and is expecting her M.D. degree in May 1997. Already she has received different honors from Columbia University. These include the Arnold P. Gold Fellowship in 1994, and she had the distinction of being nominated the Malcolm X Scholar for two consecutive years, in 1995 and 1996—and one can expect to see her receiving many more awards!

This remarkable young woman has even made her mark already in scholarly publications. She, her teacher and mentor Pat O'Hara, and others, have jointly published an article in the *Journal of Photochemistry and Photobiology B: Biology*; 30 (1995) 15–21, and she has submitted another article with a different group of scholars to *AIDS and Public Policy*. Her professional memberships are with The Student National Medical Association, The American Medical Student Association and The American Medical Women's Association. Her numerous interests include herbal medicine, yoga, sewing and bicycling, while her favorite sport is intramural basketball.

Anastasia is certainly an outstanding student and person. It is no wonder that Pat O'Hara seems inspired when she talks about this student of hers. "A shorthand description of Anastasia," Professor O'Hara wrote, "is *competent and committed.*

Those words however do nothing to describe the delightful personality and thoughtful scholar that I enjoy so much. Anastasia is prepared to meet life head-on. She thrives on the most challenging material. This is not to say that she always understands everything that she reads or hears the first time around, but that she confronts the most abstract material in a calm, good-natured manner. I believe she is un-intimidatable. Anastasia is also very good at bringing together ideas from many different fields as well as her daily experience to bear on the problem or concept at hand. . . .

She has also spent part of two of her summers working with children with AIDS at Columbia University Medical School. The fact that AIDS is the leading cause of death in black women of reproductive age is also a problem which I know troubles her greatly. She has mentioned that she would like to return to this problem in the future.

In the research laboratory, Anastasia works extremely hard and takes full responsibility for what she is doing. She learns complex techniques quickly and knows when to ask for further clarification. Her notebooks are thorough, clear, and well organized. When you give Anastasia a problem to tackle, it is usually done thoroughly and carefully before you expect it to be done. She will stay with an experiment as long as it is necessary, and understands how to handle the demands of science. . . . In the teaching laboratory, many of these same qualities are apparent, but what is most striking is her independence, dependability and maturity.

Alain Carmen Sykes is definitely on the side of the angels when she responded in a timely fashion to my first letter. She thanked me for the interest in the project and wished me "good luck with the book."

Alain majored in History and English, and spent the first semester of her junior year studying abroad in Athens, and the second half of this year in Valencia, Spain. She felt that she "might want to become a teacher, but I wanted to gain practical experience before pursuing certification."

Following her graduation, therefore, Alain spent the academic year (1993–94) as a substitute teacher in her home town of Augusta, Georgia, on a preliminary basis, but from January 1994 to June of this year she began working as a long-term substitute teacher. During this period she taught drama to Middle and High School students at the John S. Davidson Fine Arts School, also in Augusta. She was also involved with a parent/teacher committee charged with the task of selecting literature from diverse racial and ethnic groups for use in the classroom.

Apparently Alain must have felt that teaching and/or educational administration might indeed be what her career goals should be, for during the 1994–95 academic year she took a decisive step in this direction. She enrolled at the Harvard Graduate School of Education. Here she focused on their "Risk and Prevention" program, which concentrates primarily on "designing and/or implementing prevention/intervention techniques for high risk children in the schools. The program addresses these issues from a psychological perspective. While taking these classes she was also a counseling intern at a middle school in Dorchester, a community in Boston. She graduated with a master's degree in Education (Ed.M.) in June of 1995, and, she tells us, she also used the year at Harvard "to take a lot of Flamenco dance classes!"

Alain obviously enjoys travel because for the academic year 1995–96, we find her working in Greece where she had already spent the first half of her junior year while at Amherst. On this occasion, she is teaching/counseling for a study abroad program in Crete. When she wrote me, she said that the program was hardly underway; therefore, she did not have much to report. But we do wish her well.

Class of '94

༄

Suzette Duncan—yes, it's she of the "magnetized" letters to the fridge! The secret is out! When Suzette received my letters she was living in Japan, lecturing and promoting international understanding, but returned home less than a year ago. But let us observe sequence here before we go for her!

Suzette majored in Asian Studies and has high praise for this department: "From my friends" she writes, "and from my own experience I feel that the academic experience at Amherst can be shaped by which department you decide to major in. The Asian Languages and Civilizations department is so enthusiastic about the subjects they teach that I think it would be difficult to be an Asian Studies major who disliked Amherst. It was relatively easy for me to find teachers who were willing to help me, advise and befriend me. I often thought that my friends who were not happy at Amherst had majored in the wrong thing."

Suzette was quite active on campus, participating, for instance, in the Amherst College Radio station, WAMH, as a DJ. For the first year she mainly did alternative college rock shows, while from her sophomore year onward she did a more varied show, involving, in her terms, "rap, acid jazz and funk." In addition, she was a producer of the news show, "Off the Record," and curator of the rap collection during her senior year. She also worked with the campus Front Room, choosing entertainers on a weekly basis, as well as some of the acts, and selling tickets for the spring weekends.

As would be expected, Suzette went on a Study Abroad Program, not surprisingly, to Japan. In going to the Doshisha University under the Kyoto Program, she was walking in the footsteps of Karla Fuller '80, the first woman (black or white) to have been so selected. Suzette, too, studied intensive Japanese language and literature as well as its history and the arts.

In Japan, she also taught English conversation as a private tutor to Japanese children, and facilitated cultural exchanges through games and parties. But she was also involved with the Associated Kyoto Program (AKP) Promotional Video Project at the Doshisha University. As Co-Director, she assisted in writing scripts, coordinating activities with Doshisha University Film Club, while managing a budget of some five thousand dollars. This rich experience broadened her experience and almost perilously to the disadvantage of Amherst. She said that after her year abroad, she "found classes and the other students tedious. I'm glad I had the opportunity to study abroad. It helped to put my education in perspective. I guess when I returned to Amherst I realized that it was not what you learned that was important, it was what you did with the knowledge you acquired."

She soon settled down to the business of writing an Honor's Thesis in her senior year. The title, "From a Wordless Land: The Tanka of Ishikawa Takuboku," is about the life and work of a widely read Japanese poet. Suzette chose Takuboku, she tells us, because he was the first poet she read, American or Japanese, "who really moved me, and although he lived (and died) around the turn of the century his sensibilities were very close to those of my generation." It is safe to conclude that this thesis contributed to her having been awarded the Doshisha Asian Studies Prize.

Suzette's professors have a very high opinion of her, and indeed it was Professor John Solt of the Asian Studies Department who helped to get her to respond to my letters. And he has written, in his own inimitable style, a delightful piece about Suzette:

Suzette Duncan '94

at Amherst College found poetry "cool" and started speaking in tongues, including Japanese. wrote a paper elucidating subtleties of seventeenth-century Japanese texts which conflate the sacred and profane. followed that with a thesis on the most read poet, Ishikawa Takuboku (1866–1912). has been living near Takuboku's hometown in northern Japan for the last few years. gives talks in Japanese to descendants of Takuboku's neighbors. in free time teaches basketball to local youth. also does performances at city nightclubs, rapping in English and Japanese. America's finest ambassador-without-portfolio. just by breathing she non-violently smashes often recycled media misperceptions of African-Americans. one day she will return to New York and divulge her experiences for the unborn of the next millennium. suzette duncan '94.

by John Solt

Strategically, Professor Solt and I agreed that perhaps Suzette should see the piece on her and that might well make her respond to my commu-

nications. But it had the opposite effect and it was at this point we heard what she had done with my letters! A part of her letter to Solt reads: "Thanks for the ringing endorsement. Now I'm glad that I never responded to Prof. Campbell's letters. The two that she sent are magnetized to my fridge. Every time I reach in for a beer . . . I feel a twinge of guilt, but no more. How could I have any objections to it"—that is, to Solt's piece on her. We therefore had to try other strategies. More accurately, Professor Solt was marvelous in exerting pressure on her to respond, and since they both could speak in tongues, the Japanese language obviously had the edge and, to shorten a long story, I finally had a response from Suzette in December of 1996.   ·

She thanked me for giving her "the opportunity to contribute" to the book, and was "sorry that my procrastination has inconvenienced you." She also wished me: "Good luck with your book. I can't wait to see the finished product." (Might we find a way to magnetize a copy to her fridge?)

In truth, her reply to me was intelligent and full of important information, some of which we have already entered. In terms of her personal statement of her experiences, impressions of Amherst, that I requested, she has written a long piece but confessed that even though she left Japan nearly five months ago, her "English still suffers a little from two years of infrequent use." But she writes:

> Any statement of my impressions of Amherst has to begin with how I got there. It's not that interesting, but I think it is important. I decided to go to Amherst without ever seeing the campus or meeting anyone who attended the school. I never even had an interview. I had my heart set on going to Oberlin College and once I got accepted I stopped thinking about other schools. My mother, however, had her heart set on me going to an Ivy League school and once I was accepted to Harvard her mind was made up. I never had any intention of going to Harvard. I knew what type of people went to that school. All the people at my high school who I despised went there. All the people who cared more about their grade point average than intellectual curiosity and the exciting challenges involved in learning went to Harvard. At least at my high school. I went to Stuyvesant because I wanted to be with other kids who enjoyed learning as much as me. What I found instead were kids doing anything and everything to raise their grade point average even a few decimal places. I did not want to have to deal with that kind of atmosphere in college and so I wanted to avoid any school that was a popular choice for my classmates. My mother, however, felt that Oberlin was beneath my abilities and refused to pay for me to go there.

After about two weeks of constant arguments we finally agreed on Amherst as a compromise. I got the small, liberal arts, intellectually rigorous college I had always dreamed of and my mother got the (little) Ivy League.

Truth be told I had no expectations when I got to Amherst. I secretly had plans to transfer after my first year. But even before the first semester was over I realized that I wasn't going anywhere. All the students did not sit around discussing obscure 19th-century French Literature, but there existed a spirit of cooperation and desire to learn that was the polar opposite of the atmosphere in my high school. We were free to learn in class and learn from each other because we were not competing with each other for those few decimal places.

I can imagine that Amherst was a very different place when there were fraternities. Some of the people I knew involved in the underground fraternities were interested only in taking the easiest classes and passing them with minimal effort. I always looked at those people and thought they were missing the point and wasting a wonderful opportunity as well.

I feel like I missed out on a big aspect of life at Amherst by not being involved in a team sport. I played rugby for a little while and played volleyball for my dorm's intramural team freshman year, but I was never really part of the whole "Amherst Athletics" culture. I don't really regret it, but I wonder if I did not miss a big part of the Amherst experience by not doing sports. I know I missed out by not being a more active part of the BSU. It is probably the only thing I regret about the time I spent at Amherst. . . .

I know that a lot of my classmates and I sometimes thought that Amherst was not challenging enough, especially because it seemed you could never get below a B-. But with the benefit of hindsight I realize that we took Amherst for granted most of the time. If we did not get everything we could out of Amherst, it was probably because we did not make the effort. Amherst is what you make it. If you wanted to breeze through, it was not too difficult to do; but if you wanted to be challenged, you could be.

Professor John Petropulos has also written a substantial commentary on this very intellectually poised young woman. When I asked Petropulos if he had taught any black female student/s who impressed him, I was not aware that he knew Suzette, but without any hesitation, he wrote a very insightful piece on Suzette. He said that his

> acquaintance with Suzette Duncan '94 was based on only one course that she took with me: my introduction to the history of the Middle East from 600–1300 (History 72f). Even though she took the course with me in the fall of her senior year to fulfill a distribution requirement in her major in the Asian Languages and Civilizations Department, hardly the course where she could be expected to direct her major energies, which were focused on Japanese language and culture, she did a splendid job in my course. Her classroom participation was as impressive as her written work, both indicating a quick mind and an ability to study with effectiveness as well as with skillful management of time. What impressed me as well were the wide range of her interests and the self-assurance and maturity with which she embraced her studies.

Following her graduation, Suzette went to Japan to work with the Takizawa Village Board of Education. Her title, Teacher Responsible for International Understanding, proclaims its intent. In this position, she coordinated and taught English and international understanding classes with Japanese teachers, planned curriculum for and taught adult English conversation classes, assisted in study abroad programs, and was even an interpreter for town officials at international good-will events. She also conducted orientation seminars for students traveling abroad, wrote and presented speeches in Japanese for community organizations, wrote and translated articles for village publications, and coached junior high school basketball teams—among other activities. It is no wonder that John Solt saw her in Japan as "America's finest ambassador-without-portfolio"!

Apart from being fluent in the Japanese language, and familiar with this country's rich culture, Suzette is now skilled in Japanese Word Processor Ichitaro, Japanese Windows '95, Japanese Claris Works and WordPerfect 5.1. And her numerous activities involved traveling, Naginata (Martial Art) and writing poetry.

Whatever is going to be Suzette's next endeavor, we know that it will be done with distinction.

ॐ

Rose Réjouis, left, with Val Vinokurov

Rose Réjouis responded promptly to my first letter. She informed me that she was a graduate student at Princeton University and was "thinking" of studying French Medieval Literature: but she reminded me that she had only been out of college for a year—as if to warn me not to expect too much at this time.

Rose majored in French and English at Amherst and was highly respected for her intellectual strength both by faculty as well as by her peers, so we are indeed expecting a great deal from her.

She also told me that she has been married for "almost two years" (sometime in 1993?) to Val Vinokurov, also an Amherst graduate, who is also a graduate student at Princeton, studying Comparative Literature. We wish them both the very best, and hope to hear much from them in the next edition of this book.

ॐ

Terri Webb would certainly win the "Gold Medal" for having replied to me much before the first deadline of June 30, 1995! Well done, Terri, and your letter was very inspirational. She thinks the project long overdue. "I often find myself complaining," she writes, "to an alumna friend of mine that the term 'women of Amherst' needs a new meaning. Your project is an important step in this direction! I am very interested in participating in it in any way I can." Then, as is usual with the more recent graduates, she too is reminding me that she has not accumulated much yet "with only a year of 'real world' experience under my belt." She could not therefore respond to my questions of jobs and job satisfaction and contributions to society and the like, since she would have no experience on which to base her replies. (This is what happens when one sends out a standard letter to all graduates.) I soon found it necessary to write and/or speak to these new graduates somewhat differently, and when I finally caught up with Terri on the telephone in August of 1996, she was able to send me later some new information.

Terri majored in English and did extremely well in this subject, receiving for example, in her junior year, the Harry Richmond Hunter Junior Prize for creative writing. But, indeed, she was no stranger to receiving awards. While in high school, The Baldwin School, Bryn Mawr, she received the Certificate of Excellence in English (1989) and two others for Creative Writing and Modern European History the year before (1988). She also has become a member of the Editorial Board of her school's paper *The Baldwin Echoes* from 1990 to the present. Equally, from 1989 to 1990 she headed the *Roman Candle*, a literary magazine associated with her school.

At Amherst, Terri became involved in different extracurricular activities, including S.O.A.R. (Students Organized Against Racism), and for the first three years in college she was the chair of this organization; she was also involved with the Middle Alternative Learning Program, which, apparently, helped in developing skills among the underprivileged. On campus, her leadership capacity was recognized when she was elected Resident Advisor, first in a mixed-class dormitory of juniors, and in a senior dormitory the following year. As would be expected, her duties involved mediating difficult interpersonal situations, but she was also expected to help in generating a sense of community spirit in the dormitory. She also advised the students on academic matters and personal concerns; she interviewed prospective resident advisors and planned and coordinated social and recreational activities, and in the process, was responsible for administering a total budget of $1,200.

Terri certainly contributed in meaningful ways to the life of the college community and again this parallels her high school activities where she was honored with the "Outstanding Contribution to the Life of the School Award."

Even before her graduation from Amherst, Terri worked at the Exploration Summer Program at Norwood, Massachusetts, where, during the summer of 1992, she taught jewelry making as well as creative writing. She is excited about her jewelry-making skills. "We worked with saws and torches, and with sheets of brass and silver. It was a class about making jewelry, but it was also a class about process: using one's mind and one's hands to turn something of little value into something of significant— even personal—value: creating something out of relatively nothing." She also did other things at the Exploration during her first summer there, apart from jewelry-making and creative writing. In addition, she also co-ordinated a student art show, led field trips, monitored students' activities at security checkpoints, facilitated workshops and discussions and managed a budget for supplies to the amount of $480.00. She was back at the Exploration during the summer of 1993 where she became Head of House and was involved in numerous activities affecting the program: she addressed parents' concerns, intervened in conflicts among students, provided support for students adjusting to the program, helped to enforce program regulations, adjudicated penalties arising from infractions of rules, and even helped to secure buildings and grounds from undesirable strangers. But she also critiqued and evaluated office staff and teaching faculty, and led discussions and field trips.

After graduation, she took a position, first as Admission Counselor (1994–1995) at *Miss Porter's School* in Farmington, Connecticut, and for most of 1995 was Assistant Director of Admission at this school. Here she interviewed prospective students and their parents; represented *Miss Porter's* at school fairs in several places, including Denver, Massachusetts, New Hampshire, New Jersey, New York, Vermont and Hartford; she planned and organized on-campus events, coordinated and moderated focus groups of students and parents, advised and supervised Tour Guides' clubs and Guide Heads, wrote and edited letters and memos to prospective students and their families, among many other activities.

After returning to the Exploration Summer program for a short period, Terri is now, since August of 1996, working at The North Shore Country Day School, a K-12 private school in Winnetka, Illinois. She is engaged as "Associate Admissions Director" and Assistant College Counselor, where she is working with students and although she has been at this new position for just "a little over a week" (September 1996), she thinks she is enjoying it. "I wouldn't have it any other way. . . . I live four blocks from Lake Michigan, and thoroughly love my proximity to the water. I've found much that is in me in North Shore Country Day School: storytelling is important here, and that is important to me." Terri seems to have found her bliss. She has "experienced many positive changes in the last year," and foremost among them is that she is engaged to be married, and we wish her all the best!

Class of '95

 ❧

Kirsten K. N. Ford majored in Geology and English and was fairly active on campus, at least up to and including her junior year. During her first year at Amherst she "rowed eights in JV crew," and also became an active member of the multi-cultural club, as, she tells us, she "struggled with issues of identity and ethnicity." As a sophomore, she became a tour guide for the College and enjoyed it so much that she continued doing so throughout her years here—that is, when she was not away from campus. Because, during the second semester of her junior year, she did embark on a Study Abroad Program to the University of New South Wales in Australia. Apparently, this was no geological exploration, as was her stint in Canada during the summer of 1993. In Australia she studied Aboriginal History, English, and jewelry making, while in Canada she collected and analyzed field data, and published the report, detailing research and conclusions. As a senior, she found her life "too busy between writing my thesis, my relationship and applying for jobs for much more than quick runs to the Black Sheep for coffee and Judy's for a much needed treat."

Kirsten wrote a thesis for the Department of Geology, and, as I recounted earlier, it was while listening to Professor Edward Belt, of this department, talk about her thesis that I later got the idea about part of the structure for this book. Professor Belt's enthusiasm for her work was contagious, and Kirsten was fortunate to have had him as her advisor. The topic of her thesis, "A Stratigraphic and Taphonomic Analysis of the Bashi Shell Bed at Elba Dan, Southern Alabama, 1995," may sound rather esoteric to the layman but when Kirsten wrote the short description I requested, it became much more accessible. This is what she wrote:

> What is taphonomy? For several months I pondered this very question as I wrote my honors thesis for the Department of Geology under the guidance of Prof. Ed Belt. Taphonomy refers to the processes involved in transporting shell material from the biosphere into the geosphere (Emily CoBabe, UMass., 1994, personal communication). What happens to a clam once it dies? Various external forces, such as the ocean, sand, weather, and other living organisms act upon the surface of the now abandoned shell. Each of these forces is a taphonomic process, and each leaves a distinctive signature on the shell's surface. Such processes continue until the shell is buried and becomes a part of the fossil record. Fifty thousand years later I come along and remove the now fossilized clam shell from an outcrop. As I look at the clam, if I am able to sort out all the various taphonomic signatures, I can begin to reconstruct the clam's depositional history. For my thesis I looked at thousands of mollusk shells from the Bashi Formation shell bed I collected from Elba Dam, Alabama. My objective was to use the taphonomy of the shell as a tool to reconstruct the depositional history of the Elba Dam sequence, which, in turn, could be integrated with stratigraphic correction with other sections.

Professor Belt seems convinced that Kirsten's place of birth and upbringing might well have suggested this topic. She "was born," Ed Belt tell us, "in a house across the street from the ocean in Waianae, Hawaii. Even

when the family moved, the ocean was never more than a 10-minute walk from home. Her mother loved to snorkel, and she and Kirsten would often go on shell hunting expeditions. This early education became an important facet of Kirsten's qualifications when, as a senior at Amherst College, she took on a senior research project that involved identifying 50-million-year-old sea shells."

The process by which Kirsten came to join the Alabama team for her field work must be one of the best examples of how a caring and dedicated professor can assist and facilitate a student—one of course with the capacity to appreciate, to learn and to utilize opportunities. When Belt was asked to be the advisor for Kirsten's senior thesis, he began making contacts with specialists in the field and, by vigorous networking, he soon discovered that a team of experts from the Research Institute of Paleontology at Ithaca, New York, was planning to visit Alabama in December of 1994 to gather fossil specimens, and in response to his enquiry, this team would certainly welcome an addition to the group. The addition was to be Professor Belt and his advisee, Kirsten, and they were given the "go ahead" to study "one of the shell beds, the Bashi," in southern Alabama.

Leaving nothing to chance, Professor Belt saw to it that Kirsten engaged herself in preparatory work throughout the fall semester before going to Alabama. According to him, he wanted her to be able "to recognize the different species of fossil mollusk shells," before the trip. To this end therefore, teacher and pupil went off on a visit to the Museum of Comparative Zoology at Harvard, where she obtained a large collection of fossils for identification purposes. She was also encouraged to read widely on the Bashi shell bed and the strata within which it is found in southern Alabama.

Kirsten must have felt well prepared and excited when she finally landed on site for her field study. This was in December of 1994. Kirsten's obvious meticulousness in approaching her work is quite apparent as is Professor Belt's keenness and fair mindedness in talking and writing about it. He writes:

> We visited numerous exposures of the Bashi shell bed. Outcrops were scattered from southwestern Georgia, across southern Alabama, and into east-central Mississippi, at Meridian. Kirsten quietly took notes and photographs, made many measurements and listened intently to the three "experts" at each exposure. I am convinced at this point that she was not prepared for all the discussion and even the controversy that ensued.
>
> It became immediately apparent to her that the project contained an interesting puzzle that went beyond simply identifying shells and working on their taphonomy. It involved the nature of the contacts above and below the Bashi bed. These contacts seemed to record gaps in the record. The same sort of problem that Charles Darwin wrote about in his "Origin of Species." And here she had three "experts" who would argue (sometimes vehemently) about the nature of the observations that were there. She took copious notes of her own on these exposures and she drew diagrams and photographed the outcrops, but she kept her own council at that time.

In keeping her council, this was largely because Kirsten had not quite seen eye to eye with the "experts" and the result was that she wrote a thesis that Belt proudly considered a breakthrough. It was a breakthrough particularly in her approach to the methodology of the discipline in that she very effectively employed a multiple hypotheses approach to explain certain phenomena where the prevailing approach was usually a uni-variable one. Professor Belt said that she developed this on her own in her thesis: "And that turned out to be the best approach of all. Rather than being assertive about what she supposed to be the one answer, she chose to use the approach of multiple working hypotheses. This approach is particularly fitting for this project because Kirsten has questioned some cherished assumptions on a currently popular paradigm—the concept of Sequence Stratigraphy." Already, Belt said, others in the field have appreciated her new approach, as it opens the door for further research on a matter that was formerly thought to have been closed.

Kirsten is grateful to Professor Belt. In a note to him she said, "Thank you for being a great advisor and friend. Because of you my thesis turned out to be an enjoyable and rewarding experience . . . I could not have done it without you."

In response to my request for a personal statement of her experience at Amherst, Kirsten replied on a very personal level dealing with her identity:

> Before I arrived at Amherst I had always thought of myself as Hawaiian. Though I am only part Hawaiian, I grew up in Hawaii, and attended a school for Hawaiian children for thirteen years. When I arrived at Amherst in the Fall of 1991 I quickly discovered that in the eyes of those around me I was not Hawaiian, I was black. In addition to being Hawaiian, I am also African-American, Cherokee, and Swedish. Given my ethnic background and skin color this new label stuck. Still it made me uncomfortable that in the eyes of my peers I was a black woman. It was uncomfortable because it was an unfamiliar label that I had never really given any thought to. It was uncomfortable because it didn't matter that I thought of myself as Hawaiian; my classmates saw black. It was uncomfortable because being black was outside my experience. It was uncomfortable because I felt ignorant about what that label meant. I knew nothing of black history, culture, or experience. I felt like a fraud, both to other black women and myself. This was the moment at which my whole understanding of self came into question.
>
> My first-year advisor, Tekla Harms, suggested as she tried to round out my schedule, that I take Black Studies 11. It rocked my world. It was a place I could seek information, ask questions, and learn about the world around me. It gave me the courage and the strength to join a multi-cultural club. It was there that my confusion, rage, frustration, and helplessness

found a voice. I took comfort in the echo of my feelings in the experience of others. I was inspired to take more Black Studies courses concentrating on both America and Africa. This line of inquiry lead me to English where I was able to complement my study of Geology with an exploration of African and African-American literature. Over the course of four years I learned how to question assumptions, and how to examine culture and identity.

I learned that I am a black woman. I am also a Hawaiian woman, a Cherokee woman, and a Swedish woman. I am many things. Amherst taught me that identity isn't about what people see. I am not black because someone else cannot get past the color of my skin. I am not black because that is a label someone else chooses to give me. Identity is about what's inside: values, beliefs, experience, family, hopes, dreams, and aspirations. My personal struggle with identity is not over, but I left Amherst with a greater self-awareness, self-respect, and most importantly self-acceptance. I am me.

Kirsten is now teaching at the Punahou School in Honolulu, Hawaii, thus following in the footsteps of both her parents. She is teaching Biology and English for high school students, and, on occasion, substitutes in the history and other science departments. She was also Assistant Kayaking Coach at the school, where she coached "the Girls J. V. and Varsity kayaking team."

Kirsten is happy to be a part of this book. In sending her information to me, she hoped that it was not too late to be included in "Black Women of Amherst."

ॐ

Naya A. Howell responded enthusiastically to the notion of writing a book on black women of Amherst College. She replied in timely fashion, on June 12, 1995, to say that she was "very interested in this project and if I can be of any help please contact me . . . I will do what I can from here

in North Carolina," with her address included. She also enclosed a biographical sketch of herself, which I shall reproduce almost intact.

She was born in Brooklyn, New York, but both her parents were born in North Carolina and exposed Naya to southern culture. She attended Mark Twain Junior High School for the Gifted and Talented and as a result was accepted into the Albert G. Oliver Program. This program takes talented African-American and Hispanic students from public schools and offers them the opportunity to attend Day or Boarding Independent schools.

Naya chose to attend Packer Collegiate Institute in Brooklyn, New York, where she subsequently graduated in 1991. The Oliver Program and Packer allowed her to develop her interest in Dance and education. At Packer she excelled in Spanish and Dance as well as being captain of the Varsity softball team, lay-out editor of the school newspaper and Vice-president of the Minority Students Association. She is also a student mentor for the Oliver Program to other entering students to private schools. She was also able to set her foundation for the study of law while working at a law firm her freshman and sophomore years, as well as the Federal Reserve Bank in the Law Library her junior year. After these work experiences she decided to make the study of law a future goal.

After completing Packer she matriculated at Amherst College. At Amherst she became involved in the Black Student Union, and later became a resident of Charles Drew Black Cultural House during her sophomore year. After becoming very interested in languages and in History, she decided to study abroad in Kenya [during] her junior year. In Kenya she attained a proficiency in Kiswahili and developed the basis for her senior thesis in Political Science. Upon her return to Amherst College she began to develop her thesis based on her experiences of living with nomadic pastoralists in Kenya for one month. After much work the thesis, entitled "Ny'Gombe Nyeusi: The Impact of the Kenyan Colonial Government on the Nomadic Pastoralist. Colonial Rule, Politics of control and Modes of Resistance," was born. She was a double major in History with a concentration in Africa and Black America. Also during her senior year she took on the responsibility of being a Resident Counselor for the Charles Drew Black Cultural House. This proved to be [an] extremely challenging and time-consuming endeavor during this thesis writing time, but proved to be a valuable foundation for her future goals as an educator.

Overall she has been blessed with an atypical education experience for a black American, but as a result she has encountered many racial situations that have given her more of an education outside the classroom than in the classroom. Overall Amherst has been a positive experience because it has opened doors that would have normally been closed, but it has not been an easy seven semesters on campus. Naya's next educational experience finds her at University of North Carolina's Law School. Hopefully this will lead to a Ph.D. program in Political Science and teaching at the collegiate level and will educate minds like those she has encountered at Amherst College.

꒰

Kathy-Anne Rachel Lewis majored in English but took extensive courses in Mathematics and the Sciences, quite possibly because she graduated from the Brooklyn Technical High School with a cumulative grade average of "A" (1987–1991).

During her first summer vacation at Amherst, she took a position at Cornell University with the "Research Experience in Astrophysics for Undergraduates," a program supported by the National Science Foundation, and worked on computer programs. These computers were targeted to map the position of stars, planets and galaxies in the universe. During the following summer, 1993, she became an intern with the Argonne National Laboratory Internship for College Students. She recounts that she worked "with Dr. Bill McCune on OTTER, an automated reasoning program written in C, axiomatized problems in graph theory, abstract algebra and number theory and devised the logical stratagems for the program to follow in its search for a proof"—certainly most complicated!

She obviously had leadership skills for during her sophomore year she was elected Resident Counselor at the Health and Wellness Quarter in Moore Dormitory. Her responsibilities included the planning and coordination of campus-wide non-alcoholic events; she drafted the theme house constitution and defended its objectives and purpose to the Dean of Housing; she organized study breaks and parties for theme house participants, and interviewed prospective members.

This well-rounded student was also Coordinator of the literary magazine, *Madness, This?*, where she selected the poems and short stories to appear in the biannual journal, and, still on campus, she was also Vice President of the Amherst College Student Chapter of the Mathematical Association of America. Here her duties were largely administrative; she planned road trips to mathematical seminars off campus, but she also helped in making decisions about which speakers to invite to the College.

In her junior year, during the spring semester of 1994, Kathy-Anne, went on a Study Abroad Program to the University of Salamanca in Spain where she studied Spanish literature, language and art as well as Spain's colonial history in the Americas. She is also interested in post-colonial literature.

This experience of studying abroad would seem to have been a turning point in her career. According to her, "I came back an entirely different person; happier . . . and more appreciative of Amherst, now that I had lived six months without it. I also came back with a love of language and literature that had been intensified by my having to learn to read and write proficiently in Spanish. I became an English major and wrote my thesis on Jamaica Kincaid's two novels, *Annie John* and *Lucy*. I took French my senior year and loved every minute of it. We had excellent teachers at Amherst and I would recommend it to anyone."

It is no wonder that this all-rounder received the College's John Sumner Runnells Memorial Award for Scholarship and Citizenship for the year 1993–1994. She attended the 1994 Caribbean Writers Writing Seminar in Miami, Florida, and was able to work with some notable Caribbean writers and to attend lectures and readings given by them.

She now works, since August of 1995, as a Business and Finance Legal

Assistant with the firm Morgan, Lewis and Bockius LLP. Here she describes her duties as assisting "in the legal obligations of corporate mergers and acquisitions, initial public offerings, municipal bond offering, leveraged-lease financing and revolving credit facilities with such responsibilities as: conducting due diligence investigations, including analysis of materially binding contracts and risk factors, review compliance with existing credit agreements; draft board resolutions, minutes and various transactional documents; corporate multi-level corporate closings; perform Copyright Trademark-security filings and SEC regulatory findings; review pending litigations and draft responses to audit inquiries."

Kathy-Anne has many skills, including proficiency in Spanish and intermediate knowledge of French, experience with Macintosh and IBM computers, proficiency in WordPerfect and Word, and in the computer language Pascal as well as familiarity with Internet, VAX and UNIX systems. All this is in addition to her major in English with an extensive knowledge of nineteenth-century English and Caribbean literature.

Rebecca Ruth Neubert has a most fascinating life. She states:

> My upbringing was contrary to the norm, having been adopted when I was 10 months old by white parents. (I was given up for adoption at birth by a 15-year-old mother and passed around among 3–4 foster homes for the first 10 months

of my life.) My parents also adopted two other biracial children. I was raised in predominantly white environments in rural upstate New York on the Canadian border. In my high school there were only four non-Caucasian students, three of whom were my sisters and myself. I have never had a problem with this, and I believe it has resulted in my not seeing race as an issue in friendships and relationships. I never really think about the color of someone's skin because I grew up not having anyone think about the color of mine. Consequently, when I arrived at Amherst, being a minority was in no way an issue for me because there were more minorities in my dorm than there had been in a 100-mile radius of my high school. I am grateful that Amherst allowed me to choose who I was going to be and that there was not too much pressure to be part [of] one group or another because that is something I have no desire to do. I have white friends and black friends as well as friends of other ethnicities and as far as I know no one has a problem with that. I am fortunate that at Amherst I can choose my friends by who they are and not just the color of their skin, and more importantly, others do the same for me.

Rebecca is fortunate to have traveled "extensively, worldwide as well as in the United States. I have been in 33 foreign countries, and all 48 states in continental United States, as well as all 9 Canadian provinces." She even attended a school in Malaysia for a time. This was when her father, who is a Professor of Physics at the State University of New York, was on a sabbatic leave there. Here Rebecca attended an international school in Kuala Lumpur when she was still a freshman in high school.

At Amherst, Rebecca majored in Spanish but her interest is broader than in any one language. She is really interested in linguistics and languages. She tells us that 22 of the 32 courses she took here "have been either language or linguistic classes, including studying Spanish, French, and Japanese. My concentration has been Linguistics and I have taken four classes in the nationally renowned Linguistic Department at the University of Massachusetts. I have been especially interested in psycholinguistics and particularly lexical storage and retrieval. . . . "

As would be expected, Rebecca availed herself of the Study Abroad Program of the College, when during her junior year she studied in Seville, Spain, for a semester, living with a Spanish family.

She obviously had a very active social life in college also. She played Rugby and Ice Hockey, but apparently was not as involved in music, singing and acting as she was in high school. She was also involved in community outreach services, when she participated in the Cambodian Tutoring Program.

Her plans upon graduation? They "remain in the air" up to the time she wrote me. Her note was undated but it was not too long after her graduation in May of 1995. She was, though, "currently applying for teaching positions at various prep schools, as well as considering graduate school in linguistics." We wish her well and will guess that she will do the latter. She wished me good luck with the book.

༃

Natasha N. Reed majored in English with heavy concentrations in film studies and the media. With her major in mind, she enrolled also with the Five College Program at Hampshire College, for two spring semesters, studying intensively, screenwriting, film, video and programming productions. She also did some editing and accounting.

At Amherst, despite her concentration, she also took additional courses in Economics and Strategic Business, providing a good balance with her major. Natasha did not write a senior thesis but did a fascinating Special Topics Paper, which she described as "a narrative screenplay. It was a period script (1969) called Black Butterfly. The script was about a young struggling black ballet dancer who travels to West Africa in search of a better life—and to find a mystical Conjure Woman in Nigeria named Black Butterfly."

She was very active in the life of the college community. From her freshman year throughout her period at Amherst, she was actively involved with the outreach program on Cambodia. This program, the Cambodian Tutoring Program, tutored Cambodian children in the Northampton area. She was on the team of the Women's Ice Hockey, where she played left-wing in her sophomore year; she also participated in the Pioneer Valley Film Festival, and assisted in organizing the students and preparing them for the necessary competition. For this she received the Pioneer Valley Film Award and honorable mention in 1993. During most of her summer vacations, Natasha worked as Script Supervisor, Activity Leader in Drama, Production Coordinator and Production Assistant with different small theater or film-producing companies. She also did freelance work in production for small companies.

Since graduating from Amherst in May 1995 she has already done a great deal in her field. In November of 1995, she took an appointment first with Viacom/MTV Networks as Coordinator (Production/Development), and then with the company's Paramount Pictures (Television Group), in New York City, and her duties are many. With the first position, she managed database for legal and production budgets for Viacom Entertainment and MTV Networks, while her production duties include: reading and covering scripts, contacting talents, such as writers, actors and freelance staff, as well as tracking daily production units. As Senior Research Coordinator, she is involved with Television Research and Development, with varied duties, including tracking audience interest by correlating demographic research with script ideas, sales, advertisements and helping with creating daily News Flash for company executives.

Simultaneously, Natasha is also engaged with her own screen writing, and, she told me, "I have sold two short scripts to independent film companies—and I am currently working on selling a narrative script called *The Big Promise*. It is a coming-of-age story of a young black woman torn between two loves—her popular black boyfriend back at school—and a nomadic New Zealand traveler she meets on her summer break in California."

This very productive young woman has many other skills in the computer world, including, Microsoft 6.0, Microsoft Excel 5.0, PowerPoint 4.0, Lotus, 123, Database IV, MovieMagic™ Scheduling/Breakdown, MovieMagic™ Scriptor, and MovieMagic™ Budgeting. In the field of languages, she reads and speaks French.

Yet another black alumna with high praise for Amherst. She writes,

> I genuinely enjoyed my time at Amherst College and would not trade the experience for anything. Academically, I matured as a writer and lover of film, literature, and African Diaspora history. Unfortunately, I did not enjoy my experience with the English department as I had wished. Socially, I was able to deal with feeling "out-of-place" in a very white environment. I never had to sacrifice my personality, culture or differences. In turn, I learned how to tolerate and appreciate the differences between many types of people. In addition, I made some very good friends, and had great relationships with friends of the opposite sex. It was an excellent learning experience—and I miss it dearly!

Class of '96

ॐ

Kim Gittens majored in English and although she did not write a thesis she did a special topic which she considered important to her. This was with "a collection of 10 poems and I worked one-on-one with Professor Cody."

Kim was very active as a student on campus. She was a staff member for two student journals, *The Amherst Review* and *Madness, This?* Between 1992 and 1996; she was Communications Officer for the Black Student Union from 1993 to 1994; an English tutor for A Better Chance (ABC) during 1995 and 1996 as she was, also during this same period, a DJ for the radio program WAMH. Throughout most of her time at Amherst, she also served as group leader for the Outreach Orientation program where she focused on volunteer work in Hartford, Connecticut. She was also employed as a student worker doing jobs on campus with the Office of Career Counseling and the Black Studies Department.

During her summer vacations from Amherst she was employed in some very interesting job situations: for the summer of 1993, she worked as an intern for Penguin Books, USA, in New York City, where she learned about publishing by spending five weeks in Children's Marketing and two weeks in Adult Editorial. She worked also on computer cross-listing on children's catalogue information. The summer of 1994 found her at "Kitchen Table," the Women of Color Press in Albany, New York. As an intern, she was involved with data entry, general office duties, invoicing, packaging and sending off books; equally, she supervised other interns and volunteers, mailed catalogues, participated in selling Kitchen Table Books at book readings and even assisted in the process of selecting a new director.

Her internship with *The Quarterly Black Review of Books* in New York City was in January of 1995. Here she compiled and coordinated the logistics of key events for the *Quarterly* during a two-week road tour; she typed and proofread feature stories, read manuscripts and made judgments on them; as well, she did the mundane things like answering the phone, running errands and distributing copies of the *Quarterly* to various publishing companies and bookstores.

During the summer of 1996, Kim took a different kind of position; she became a Teaching Assistant at the Prep for Prep school in New York City. But she was no stranger to this school; she graduated from it in 1986 before going on to The Chapin School, New York City, from where she matriculated to Amherst College. At the Prep for Prep she assisted in teaching English Literature to fifth-grade students.

Since her graduation (1996), she has been working with Grove/Atlantic, Inc. as an Editorial Intern, doing more or less what she had already done as an intern elsewhere.

Kim has graduated with good computer skills: she is proficient in Page-Maker, Microsoft Word, WordPerfect and Filemaker Pro on Macintosh; she is also familiar with Multimate, Alpha 4 and WordPerfect on IBM.

In her personal statement to me she has already discovered a good working philosophy; that is, the learning process is not just confined to the college institution, but life is all about learning (I think this is what she has written). "Also, having not chosen the investment banking/consulting tack, and having not being simply handed a job, . . . I've realized that an Amherst College education gives you options, the power to choose a path, permanent or not, and the tools with which to do it." Well, we wish her well with whatever pathway she may choose.

ॐ

Elisabeth A. Graves made up her own major based on her fascination with ancient civilizations. It was not just Ancient Rome or Ancient Greece as she would explain, and, in any case, her major could then be accommodated under the Classics, but she was equally interested in non-western ancient histories and for this reason she took Colloquium 12. Colloquium 12 studies pre-Columbian civilizations, specifically, those of the Mayas, Aztecs and Incas, and this was how I became acquainted with Elisabeth. From the start her interest in the course was clear, and her final paper, "Mexican Information Recording Systems and Encounters Between Mesoamerican and European Philosophies of Writing," is easily one of the best papers I have received from any student in my teaching experience here. Professor Don Proulx, with whom I taught Colloquium 12, was also impressed by it, and we both decided to show it to Professor Christopher Couch, whose expertise includes Mesoamerican Ancient forms of writing, and he too (with a few suggestions here and there) found the essay impressive.

For this reason I made the decision to reproduce the paper in this book, and Elisabeth was delighted. "I am very excited that my paper might be published, and I hope that you are still considering it," she writes. Elisabeth's paper, in the main, looks at colonial Spain's attitude to the writings of Mesoamerica—viewing them, as would be expected, through Eurocentric prisms with little or no understanding of the cultural imperatives of these indigenous cultures. As with the early approach to Anthropology (Bartolomé De Las Casas excepted) the Spaniards judged these modes of writing according to evolutionary paradigms, ranging, hierarchically, from pictographic, glyphic, ideographic to the more "developed" language-based alphatethic script—and as for the *quipu* of the Incas that hardly figured at all in this evolutionary configuration! A part of Elisabeth's paper reads:

> When the Spanish came to Mesoamerica, they encountered a
> group of cultures with complex and precise writing systems

structured around direct pictorial representation, indirect ideograms, and phonetic homophonous substitutions. These systems
of writing were completely outside the European sphere of experience, just as the Spaniards' Latin
alphabet was unknown in America. Unfettered by Boazian ideas
of cultural relativism, many of the
Spanish erased the differences between their culture and Mesoamerican civilization, using their
description of themselves as a
universal frame for understand-

ing disparate cultural traditions. Applying notions of the evolution of alphabetic writing and the absolute nature of the
"book" current in Europe, Spanish colonial chroniclers viewed
Mesoamerican writings in European terms and within a European context; and, thus, most often, the indigenous systems
were found to be lacking in efficiency and refinement.

However, regardless of sixteenth-century Spanish perceptions of Mexican writing, indigenous peoples did have unique
ways of encoding and transmitting knowledge, as well as distinct concepts of those activities. Unfortunately, it seems that
many modern scholars and Mesoamerican specialists have
fallen, perhaps inadvertently, into the same or a similar intellectual trap as did the colonial Spaniards, who used universalized Western European standards to judge the validity and efficiency of non-European cultures, and specifically writing
systems, usually to the detriment of the culture in question....

But you can read the paper in its entirety as Appendix E. We—Don
Proulx, Christopher Couch and I—expect Elisabeth to be going to graduate school soon for the Ph.D. degree, and we know that she will be a great
curator of a museum (her career goals) and we will be keeping track of

her. However, I received a note from Elisabeth, just before this work went to press, stating that she is presently the managing editor of *History: Reviews of New Books* and the *Journal of Arts Management, Law and Society*. I think, though, that she will soon be going to graduate school, and pursue her career goals.

How does Elisabeth view her experience at Amherst? She said:

> One of the reasons that I went to Amherst College was the diversity of the student body. Through the years, I found that this commitment to variety and diversity—in people as well as resources—was present in most facets of life at the college. Although the social scene was certainly delineated into close (though not necessarily closed) groups at times, the academic atmosphere at Amherst definitely fostered discourse between opposing opinions and the coalescence of disparate minds.
>
> I never found being black or a woman to be issues in the classroom, except as a matter of perspective. At Amherst, I was taught to view all perspectives as enriching; and I found that the exploration of difference can lead to exciting opportunities for learning. The great thing about Amherst is the number of opportunities, and choices—personal, intellectual, social, academic—, which a student has there. College, for me, was about investigating options, opening up to alternatives, and exploring different modes of learning and of knowledge.
>
> I think that the following paper captures this aspect of learning at Amherst College. It is my final paper from Colloquium 12: The World Columbus Found, a discussion group led by Professors Campbell and Proulx. The class was a synthesis of two very distinct institutions (Amherst and the University of Massachusetts), several different disciplines (history, anthropology, archaeology), and various perspectives (Spanish and native Mesoamerican, modern and historical). The paper itself is about conflicting world-views, and alternative ways of approaching history and the preservation and perpetuation of knowledge.

Class of '97

～

Amani D. Brown majored in Biochemistry and Spanish, and despite her double major, was quite active on campus. In her first year, she was a Tour Guide to the Pratt Museum of Natural History, and Monitor of the Gerald Penny Cultural Center; she played Intramural Soccer, sang with the Amherst College Gospel Choir, was a member of the Further Room Literary Group, and was a volunteer member of the Office of Admission. In her sophomore year, she was a Spanish tutor, and her leadership skills must have been recognized when, in her junior year, she was appointed Residence Counselor to the Spanish/French cultural center, the Newport House. As would be expected, she was also a member of the Black Student Union, serving, in some cases as Cross-Cultural Representative, and as advisor.

She also went on a Study Abroad trip under the auspices of the International Exchange Hamilton Program to Madrid, Spain, where she not only perfected her Spanish but was also involved with her other major when she worked with Spanish physicians in Neurology, Radiology and

Emergency Services at La Fundación de Fernando Giminéz in Madrid. While in Spain, she wisely took the occasion to travel to some other southern European countries, including, Italy, France and Switzerland.

Amani wrote a Senior Honors thesis, "Fluorescence Characterization of Abzymes Binding to Transition State Analogues and Substances," for the Departments of Chemistry and Biology with Professor Patricia O'Hara as her principal Faculty Advisor. "The core of my thesis project," Amani said, "was the use of two fluorescence spectroscopic techniques, steady state and stopped-flow in order to determine binding constants for the reactions between the abzyme TEPC 15 and its transition state analogue, p-nitrophenolphosphoryl-choline. I also determined binding constants for the reaction of another less well-characterized transition state analogue abzyme, NPN43Cp, with one of its hydrolysis products (p-nitrophenol), and amide and an ester substrate."

Amani was fortunate to have "discovered" O'Hara from her first year when she worked in the professor's laboratory. But, perhaps, O'Hara would insist that she also made the discovery, when she wrote: "I worked hard to convince her [Amani] to work with me this semester because of my high regard for her skills and perseverance." Even at this early stage O'Hara was impressed by the kind of work Amani was capable of doing, and the disciplined work habits she displayed. "Amani succeeded," she recounts, "in transforming an E. Coli cell culture with a plasmid containing the cDNA for wild type human liver calmodulin. Amani was responsible for developing the protocol and procedures for cell growth, protein isolation, affinity and gravity chromatography, gel electrophoresis, dialysis and lyophilization. She was successful in finally isolating nearly 50 mg of calmodulin, which she was proud to report has a market value of nearly double her summer salary! More importantly, she showed character and determination in getting a protein procedure to work using molecular biological techniques and classic protein purification technology. There were nights when she was here till the wee hours and mornings she was in before the sun rose. I would like her to continue on in my laboratory and will try to get her to do work-study this fall."

Amani has won many awards at Amherst College: in 1994 she was the recipient of the Howard Hughes Fellowship in Biochemistry, and in her senior year, she received the Amherst College "R" Committee Prize for the fostering of and contribution to the Amherst community through aiding communication among faculty, students and administrators, and she was also awarded the Thesis Research Fellow in Biochemistry by the National Science Foundation. In addition, she graduated a member of Sigma Xi Scientific Honor Society.

Amani also has a very strong sense of public service. Despite the demands of her science program, she still found time to volunteer as an ABC House Tutor in English and Science, to disadvantaged youths. Equally, she has many interests, making her a very well-rounded young person. Fluent in Spanish, she is also a budding poet, having at this time a book of poetry pending publication; and, not least, is her interest in Yoga and native Spanish and ballroom dancing, and she also plays the harp!

What are her experiences and impressions of Amherst College these past four years? She writes to me that:

> The scope of my experience at Amherst College has been as varied as the diverse members of this body. I have achieved a level of scholarship here through methods of learning which have challenged and intrigued me well beyond even the high personal ideal I held Amherst to before walking this campus as a student. As a black woman, a poet, a dreamer, and a lover of God I have faced obstacles of unnecessary difficulty at an institution of the highest learning such as this. However, though still somewhat bruised by battle, I waged a fight with the help of my sister Ashaki Malkia Brown (who is a fellow black woman in science as a Neuroscience Major in the class of 1997 and true Beautiful Queen, as her name indicates in Swahili) to reform some of Amherst's most damaging flaws in academic support, particularly in quantitative disciplines. With special

support from my parents, God, and alumni friends followed by such extraordinary faculty warriors as Professor O'Hara, Professor Rosbottom and Dean Moss, we have begun to see the fruits of our efforts in the planning of a new Quantitative Skills Support Center at Amherst College.

On this, my graduation day from Amherst College, I reflect on the manner by which Amherst has helped to shape me. I have known myself in ways here that reaffirm my belief in a higher power and cause me to rededicate my life to service. I have held hands with some of the best people in the world from every corner of the earth as friends for life and instructors. Two of the most beautiful of these hands and richest of these friends are those of Lionel Legagneur, my future husband and a History Major in the class of 1997. I have anguished here and triumphed here. As I look forward to the next phase of my learning through work in research, health policy, and eventually work as a medical doctor, I am both humbled and exhilarated by the knowledge that Amherst College has been a rocky yet beautiful conduit to that beginning.

Her "future husband," Lionel Legagneur '97, I know very well. I "discovered" him in his freshman year when he took a course with me and thereafter he took many more up to his senior year when I became his Faculty Advisor for his Senior Honors Thesis in History. Lionel has qualities of character that are admirable. He is responsible, trustworthy, mature, and had the unflinching ability to persevere in pursuing his goals with focused attention. In him Amani will find one who will always be there for her, thoughtful and protective, as he will find in her a beautiful, loving and sincere person with pretty ways—a beauty which seems to be illuminated by an inner goodness; of whom Pat O'Hara who knows her well has said: "She has one of the finest characters I have seen in the ten years [writing in 1994] I have been at Amherst. I am confident she will continue to bring delight to those who have the pleasure of interacting with her...."

Lionel has been admitted to the Harvard Law School and Amani will take a year off before going on to a medical school to pursue her goals of becoming a doctor of medicine.

ↄ⌒

Ashaki M. Brown, sister of Amani, who described her as a "true Beautiful Queen, as her name indicates in Swahili," majored in Neuroscience and, like her younger sister, is a member of the class of '97. These two sisters, although not twins like Karla and Tara Fuller of the pioneer class of '80, are nevertheless very close.

Ashaki, too, was very active on campus, and, like her sister, was extremely concerned about women—but particularly black women in the sciences. For this reason Ashaki was one of three students chosen to serve on an ad hoc committee to examine Academic Support in Introductory Science Education at Amherst, instituted by President Gerety of the College. As a member of this committee, she served with Pat O'Hara who chaired it, and Ashaki's contribution was obviously quite substantial. O'Hara recalled her deep commitment and the intelligent approach she brought to bear to the problem, and has paraphrased the centrality of this young student's position: no one, she would maintain, was asking the College to lower standards for minority students, as this would, indeed, defeat the whole purpose "of our coming to Amherst. Instead, we ask that you

give us the tools to be able to tackle this tough, rigorous science curriculum. With your support and our dedication and hard work, we are bound to succeed." One hopes that the College will never forget the urgency of this plea. We know Pat O'Hara will not forget it and she has actually confessed that it has "haunted me since then."

Ashaki also took a course, "Women and Minorities in Science," with Pat O'Hara, and her participation in it was again insightful, intelligent and original. Her final paper, Professor O'Hara tells us, was eventually used as a model for other students: Ashaki developed a curriculum that introduced children in the school system to the contributions of black scientists, including Benjamin Banneker, Henry Blair, Charles Drew, George Washington Carver, among others. With the curriculum, Ashaki also developed "complete lesson plans, including activities, demonstrations and worksheets," to make the course more meaningful.

But, perhaps, her outreach activities were even more impressive. Ashaki is said to have spent one afternoon a week for fourteen weeks with a local kindergarten with a view to exposing these young children to science in general, but particularly the science done by blacks. O'Hara is now using Ashaki's curriculum along with others that grew from that class, "as part of an outreach project for science students at Amherst."

Ashaki did not send me a personal statement of her experiences and impressions at Amherst, but it is probably not very different from her sister's. She too, like Amani, will apply to medical schools next year, and we are happy to hear that she has received a Houston internship involving both clinical and experimental work with pediatricians for the next year.

ﺰ

Rasheema Graham majored in Economics and English and contributed a great deal to the college community. As an active member of the Black Student Union (BSU), she participated in discussions on different themes and assisted in choosing speakers to address the campus. She was also a part of a Black Women's group which, discussed what she calls "interesting and problematic issues regarding women." She was very interested in dancing, calling herself a "Professional Dancer," and even toured campuses doing West African dancing and drumming.

Rasheema is a very poised and reliable young person, who is highly respected by her peers and administrators with whom she interacted. We were very impressed with her charming presentation of a video she herself made on Gerald Penny '77 and the occasion of his tragic drowning at the College. After the video, she fielded questions from the audience which consisted of students, faculty and administrators, and she handled herself with dignity and ease.

Rasheema was the first one of her class who responded promptly to a circular letter I sent out asking them to fill in certain details about themselves, and, under personal statement of her experiences at Amherst she has given some interesting views on a wide range of issues. She said, "I appreciate my time at this school because I know people at big universities that do not receive the attention from professors in office hours or have our resources and networking capabilities of the Office of Career Counseling. If I had to do it again, I would say yes to Amherst all over. My friendships are very rewarding. I am disappointed with the low en-

rollment of black students in the Class of 2000, but I have heard that this is a nationwide phenomenon. The one thing I missed but I didn't realize this until my Junior year, was a film department or a production teacher that did not have to leave every semester. I will know an Amherst student wherever I go. The culture here is very distinct. We ask questions; we fight the points made; we are elite—yes, elite in the way we speak of other schools because we have a sense of pride and we were number 1 for several years.

"I got tired of the usual arguments about blacks in one area of Valentine and the need for Drew House. Amherst get over it! Where I sit is my prerogative. No one questions the football team or soccer players who cling to one another like white or rice. [?] The minority always has to justify its reasoning. Well, I never did—just ask someone else!

"I'm ready and not ready to leave. I'll miss this place—NOT the food however.

"Good luck Professor Campbell"—and I, too, say Good Luck to you Rasheema, we know you will be bringing dignity and intelligence to whatever you decide to do.

Monet Elise Hilson is a very courageous student with a firm determination to succeed even against all the
odds. The greatest odd she had to con-
tend with is the fact that, as she tells
it, she entered "Amherst in the fall of
1991 as a newly diagnosed multiple
sclerosis patient." How did she cope?
Occasionally she had to withdraw as
the "illness became active," but she was
determined not to give up. "It is difficult," she tells us—certainly an under-
statement—"but I am persevering." And so she did, and finally graduated
with the class of 1997E.

Monet was a double major in Black Studies and Women's and Gender
Studies (WAGS), and had planned, she said, to write "a thesis in the WAGS
Department," but apparently this did not happen. On campus she was in-
volved with the Black Women's group.

Now that Monet has graduated, "her future plans include attending
Rutgers Law School in the fall of 1997," and we have no doubt that she will
not only "follow" but will fulfill her dreams. A persistent concern of hers
is the topic of the legal system and rape victims, and had she written the
thesis she had contemplated, it would have been around this theme.
However, after law school she is hoping to work in a District Attorney's
Office where she could "prosecute sex crimes."

Erika L. Butler '95

Debra J. Evans '95

Michelle J. Lomax '95

Ghenete E. Wright '95

Photographs of several other Amherst women who are not profiled in the text

Marsha P. Hampton '96

Melissa D. Alexis '97

Lisa N. Blair '97

Naeemah Clark '97

Candida Haynes '97

Thandeka N. Myeni '97

Logan Nakyanzi '97

Melanie H. Overby '97

Stephanie N. Stone '97

Rachel M. Williams '97

Stacy A. Williams '97

Nichole Taylor '98

Conclusion

⠦

Altogether, I am delighted to have put together *Black Women of Amherst College*, and again I express my gratitude to all those who facilitated its completion as expressed in the Introduction. In a unique way, this work placed me at the center of these black alumnae of Amherst College: I listened to their concerns, their anguish, their confusion at times, but also their good humor, their triumphs and moments of joy even during trying times. Above all, I observed their courage, their unfailing grace and their amazing reasonableness. In Ashaki M. Brown '97, for instance (to mention just one), I saw all these traits in conjunction. With Professor Pat O'Hara, we hear her making a case for a more science-friendly atmosphere for women in general—but particularly "minority" women at the College. She was not, she emphasized, asking for the lowering of standards to accommodate them, because this approach would, indeed, defeat the whole purpose of their coming to a college of quality. What she was asking for instead was more academic support to help in preparing them to tackle the rigorous science curriculum. Such a support combined with their dedication and hard work, she maintained, would certainly ensure success to them—and to the College. One can only hope that the College had listened—and responded effectively.

APPENDICES

Appendix A

Following are the alumnae I could not locate:

Cheryl A. Bailey '90
Patrece M. Bryan '93
Pamela J. Flood '91
Lynn C. Hartfield '85
Elise K. Henry '88
Zenzi E. Gadson '94
Malana K. Moshesh '92
Maria L. Shelton '88
Charmaine C. White '91

Appendix B

May 31, 1995

Dear ————

I am writing to tell you of a project I am working on and to solicit your participation. You may be aware of the book, *Black Men of Amherst* by Harold Wade, Jr., published by the Amherst College Press in 1976, and I am now in the process of doing a companion piece to this on "Black Women of Amherst College." If at all possible, we hope that the publication of this book will coincide with the anniversary marking 20 years since women have been admitted as students to this College. To this end, therefore, I am asking you to take a few moments away from your busy schedule to send me some details of your life since graduation. For example, the positions you held, the length of time in each, the level of job satisfaction, the contribution you think you are making to society and so forth. Your marital status is optional, but a recent photograph that could include your family would be welcome.

The President of the College, Tom Gerety, is most supportive of the work which will be published by the Amherst College Press.

Since time is limited, if the book is to be completed by 1996, I shall have to ask you please to try and reply by June 30 of this year, and your reply should not exceed 2 pages.

I thank you very much for your attention and I hope to hear from you—immediately?

Sincerely,
Mavis C. Campbell
Professor of History

Appendix C

Amherst College
The Board of Trustees
September 14, 1995

To Whom It May Concern:

Insofar as the rights of Amherst College are concerned, permission is hereby given to Mavis C. Campbell, Professor of History at Amherst College, to reproduce for one time in her book *Black Women at Amherst College*, the following texts from the Case Book on Co-Education at Amherst:

> Letter from George L. Shinn '45, Chairman on the Board, to Alumni and Friends of Amherst College, dated November 4, 1974.

> Two Resolutions passed by the Trustees on Saturday, November 2, 1974, regarding admission of women candidates for the academic year 1975–76.

Dorothy W. Hertzfeld
Interim Secretary
The Trustees of Amherst College

cc: Daria D'Arienzo, Archivist
Amherst College

Appendix D

Amherst College
The Board of Trustees

RESOLUTIONS PASSED BY THE TRUSTEES ON SATURDAY, NOVEMBER 2, 1974

VOTED: Beginning with the academic year 1975–76, Amherst College will admit women candidates for the B.A. Degree.

VOTED: The Board of Trustees desires that the College, in carrying out the foregoing resolution, make every effort to do so in the most financially responsible manner and with due consideration to the values which the Board believes derive from the smallness of the College;

The Board, therefore, sets forth the following general guidelines subject to continuing review by the Board, for the direction of the Administration of the College in implementing the above resolution:

1. Beginning with the academic year 1975–76, the College will admit women as transfer students in the sophomore and junior classes.

2. Beginning with the academic year 1976–77, the College will admit women in the Freshman Class. It is anticipated that at first approximately one-third of each entering class will be women. During the period of transition, the College will continue to assess its experience to determine how best to achieve the objective that candidates for admission be accepted without regard to sex.

3. The College will expand gradually from its present enrollment of 1,300 to approximately 1,500, and as part of its continuing review the Board

will consider whether a slightly larger or slightly smaller enrollment would be in the best interests of the College. During the period of transition, as the student population increases, the Administration should bring the budgeted ratio between students and faculty from the present ratio of 8.5 to 1 to approximately 10 to 1, and take other steps to effect economies in operation.

4. The College should increase the number of students permitted to live off-campus from the present 90 to approximately 150. The College should make such modifications in the physical plant as may be necessary to accommodate the needs of women students, but, except for additions to facilities in physical education, will delay other expenditures for plant until experience establishes the necessity and women in the College can participate in the planning.

The Board strongly reaffirms the value it places on the benefits which are achieved through Five-College cooperation, and it will continue to be the policy of the Board that Amherst College will do its part to expand and strengthen cooperation among the educational institutions in the Valley.

రొ

Amherst College
The Board of Trustees
November 4, 1974

Dear Alumni and Friends of Amherst College:

The Board of Trustees of Amherst College, at its Fall meeting, November 2, 1974, voted to admit women to Amherst College. The full text of the two resolutions voted by the Board is enclosed. The first, and central, resolution was voted 15-3; the second, on implementation, was unanimous.

The decision to admit women was reached after long and exhaustive study. The process has involved alumni, faculty, students, and administrators as well as trustees. The Board is grateful to all whose hard work made it possible for the Board of Trustees to reach a decision on the basis of the best evidence and the most complete information.

The Board of Trustees strongly believes that the admission of women to the

College will enhance the central purpose of the College: to provide the best in undergraduate liberal arts education.

The immediate issue was the admission of women. Constantly before the Board, however, was the larger, general question, how best to maintain the preeminence of Amherst College as a place for liberal learning among institutions of higher education in the United States today.

Two considerations were uppermost in the discussion within the Board: first, how to maintain the quality associated with small size and a high proportion of fine faculty to fine students; second, how to manage the financial resources of the College with prudence. The Board's second resolution, the guidelines for implementation of the resolution to admit women, speaks directly to these considerations.

The Board's deliberation on what is perhaps the most important question to come before the Trustees of Amherst College in the twentieth century also brought into sharper focus other concerns central to undergraduate, liberal arts education. The Board deeply believes it has made the right decision, a decision which will strengthen Amherst College for the problems which remain before it in the years ahead.

The Board knows the College will continue to need the strong support of its alumni. The Board is confident the alumni will continue to provide it.

We look forward to seeing daughters as well as sons of alumni at Amherst College among women who transfer into the College as well as in future classes of the College. My letter, on behalf of the entire Board of Trustees, is an attempt to get the news to you quickly. Greater detail will, of course, be forthcoming.

Sincerely yours,
George L. Shinn '45
Chairman

APPENDIX E

Mexican Information Recording Systems and Encounters between Mesoamerican and European Philosophies of Writing

ELISABETH ANDERSON GRAVES
Colloquium 12: The World Columbus Found
9 May 1996

> Aztec writing suffered from one great disadvantage: it was non-alphabetic.... The advantage of an alphabet is that the whole range of language can be precisely expressed by means of a few symbols which are easy to learn and convenient to write.
>
> —WARWICK BRAY, *Everyday Life of the Aztecs*

They had scribes for each branch of knowledge. Some dealt with the annals, putting down in order the things which happened each year, giving the day, month, and hour. Others had charge of the genealogies, recording the lineage of rulers, lords and noblemen, registering the newborn and deleting those who had died. Some painted the frontiers, limits, and boundary markers of the cities, provinces and villages, and also the distribution of the fields, whose they were and to whom they belonged. Other scribes kept the law books and those dealing with the rites and ceremonies which they practiced when they were infidels. The priests recorded all matters to do with the temples and images, with their idolatrous doctrines, the festivals of

their false gods, and their calendars. And finally, the philosophers
and learned men which there were among them were charged with
painting all the sciences which they had discovered, and with teaching by memory all the songs in which were embodied their scientific
knowledge and historical traditions.

—IXTLILXOCHITL, *Historia Chichimeca*

During the first half of this millennium the Mexicans of Pre-Columbian America
developed some very unique systems of recording information that were associated with special structures, techniques, and culture-specific social and political
meanings. A tradition of conventional abstract representation was protected, developed, shared, and highly respected among the Mesoamerican peoples.[1] Figures such as the hieroglyph, ideograph, and pictograph had been created to
record and convey meaning, and diverse forms in which information was tran-
scribed, such as the codex, *lienzo*, and year-count, had evolved to meet specific
cultural needs. These writing forms were closely linked, physically and philo-
sophically, with the two other major styles of expression and communication in
Mesoamerican culture: artistic representation, which was clearly connected to
the painted figural form of Mexican "writing," and oral performance, which involved interpretive and memorized elaboration of recorded information. The
Mesoamerican philosophy of writing was based in these connections, in the in-
terrelated nature of the verbal and nonverbal and the iconic, symbolic, and semasiographic collection and conveyance of knowledge.

When the Spanish came to Mesoamerica they encountered a group of cultures
with complex and precise writing systems structured around direct pictorial representation, indirect ideograms, and phonetic homophonous substitutions.
These systems of writing were completely outside the European sphere of experience, just as the Spaniards' Latin alphabet was unknown in America. Unfettered
by Boazian ideas of cultural relativism, many of the Spanish erased the differences between their culture and Mesoamerican civilization, using their description of themselves as a universal frame for understanding disparate cultural traditions.[2] Applying notions of the evolution of alphabetic writing and the absolute
nature of the "book" current in Europe, Spanish colonial chroniclers viewed
Mesoamerican writings in European terms and within a European context; and,
thus, most often the indigenous systems were found to be lacking in efficiency
and refinement.

However, regardless of sixteenth-century Spanish perceptions of Mexican
writing, indigenous peoples did have unique ways of encoding and transmitting
knowledge as well as distinct conceptions of those activities. Unfortunately, it

seems that many modern scholars and Mesoamerican specialists have fallen, perhaps inadvertently, into the same or a similar intellectual trap as did the colonial Spaniards, who used universalized Western European standards to judge the validity and efficiency of non-European cultures—specifically writing systems—usually to the detriment of the culture in question. This form of scholarship, ultimately based in the philosophical trends of the European Renaissance, has quite recently been challenged by a new school of Pre-Columbian American thought. In the last decade, some Mesoamericanists have debunked traditional Western constructions of language, reading, and writing and have started to create more sensitive, culturally specific, and relativistic models for defining recording systems and specifically American patterns of visual information communication. An entire area of Mesoamerican study has been reopened, and a new focus has been established on analyzing the encounter between indigenous and European philosophies of writing and the effects of that confrontation on modern Mesoamerican writing theory. It is only after the biases of past and present views of indigenous writing are recognized that scholars can begin developing an intellectual appreciation of the history, techniques, forms, and functions of Mexican writing itself.

Persistent European Models of Writing and the "Book"

The basic Western evolutionary model of the development of writing—a "natural" maturation from pictographic, to ideographic, to language-based alphabetic script—was solidly born in the scientific positivism of the late nineteenth century, a time when evolutionary models were being pushed throughout the natural and social sciences.[3] However, the cultural bias of the evolutionary model of writing systems has its beginnings in postconquest and colonial European impressions of the civil barbarism of American nonalphabetic writing forms. In the sixteenth-century European view writing was autonomous from orality, and the "book" took the place of the person (or reader) as the receptacle and source of information. Writing does not necessarily presuppose the book; however, during the sixteenth century, under the influence of the celebration of the letter, its meaning was narrowed down almost exclusively to just that.[4] Writing and the bound book of the printing press were essentially interchangeable.[5]

Europeans took for granted the notions that the book was the authoritative container of knowledge and that writing was the inscription of the human voice in alphabetic script. The ways that missionaries and men of letters perceived Amerindian records were informed by this specific, limited, European definition. The Spaniards thought it only natural that their reading and writing habits, their human and divine books, and their ways of organizing and transmitting knowledge were normative, as well as superior.[6] It is probable that in the latter half of the sixteenth century writing was generally conceived of—by Europeans in Europe and colonial America—exclusively in terms of books, and books in terms of the medieval manuscript and the printing press.[7]

The evolutionary model of writing and the book was the one used by missionaries and educated men to describe Amerindian writing practices and sign carriers.[8] The Europeans in America could not get away from such analogies:[9] For example, Diego de Landa understood Mayan writing only in terms of European books, and Toribio de Benavente, or Motolinìa, projected the cognitive component of the idea of the book onto Aztec writing. So, somewhat ironically, early European chroniclers give the impression that the Mexica were doing well in reading and writing matters, according to their standards.[10] The analogy became fact to them, and the paradigmatic writing model of the Spanish imposed a completely misleading gloss of Western conceptualization over what was basically construed of as a somewhat second-rate indigenous system comparable to European writing.

Inevitably, though, as the writing systems of the Mesoamericans were described in European cultural terms, the systems were found to be increasingly lacking within that European context. Though, for example, the Maya were praised by learned men such as Antonio de Cuidad Real and so on for their book-like writings, the analogies eventually broke down and revealed the (in European terms) limited, primitive structure of Mexican "writing." Under the auspices of colonial acculturation, Mexica writings were translated not only from pictographs and ideographs into script and from indigenous languages (particularly Nahuatl) into Spanish but also into an entirely different, European conceptual tradition. The conception of writing and the book that was imbedded in the mind of European missionaries and men of letters erased many of the possibilities for them to inquire into the Americans' alternative writing systems and sign carriers rather than simply describe them by analogy with their own model.[11] The Spanish imposed their idea of the book and what it meant culturally onto indigenous recording systems rather than trying to understand the culture-specific meaning of, for example, the native Aztec *amoxtli*. This European mind-set virtually eliminated the Andean *quipu* system and led to the degradation of Aztec and Mixtec writings: The Mexica codex became known to history as little more than a bastardized form of the European book; Mixteca histories became crude and skeletal records of past events; and the *lienzo* became simply a painted map of sorts.

Unfortunately, some modern scholars appear to cling to the perceptions and misconceptions of the Spanish colonial observers: They have internalized view-points from a highly prejudiced era and now perpetuate images of the Mexican writing systems as simple and inadequate, virtually incapable of communicating information, and ultimately passive receptacles for the more advanced alphabetic writing system of the Europeans. Gradually, this negative, culturally biased mode of thinking has evolved into a patronizing form of praise, leading some modern scholars to wonder at the thought that such unprogressive cultures had even some form, albeit uncivilized, of writing- or book-like expression.[12]

New Models and Alternative Literacies

If in these evolutionary and Eurocentric views the most developed writing systems replicate speech the most efficiently and completely within the form of a European book, where, then, do the largely pictorial systems of Pre-Columbian America figure?[13]

Usually, all Mesoamerican systems are labeled "nonwriting." Scholars of the history of writing are usually dismissive of the nonlinguistic recording systems in Mesoamerica, and sometimes they are blatantly pejorative.[14] There are divisions even among Mesoamerican scholars as to the "validity" of Mayan and Mexica writing systems. The traditional Western definition of writing can be stretched to include the Maya hieroglyphic system, and many Mayanists consider the language-based glyphs of the Maya as true writing but not the more pictographic style of the Aztec and Mixtec.[15] Meanwhile, modern Mexica specialists often have a more expansive view of writing that is inclusive of the ideographic and pictorial styles found throughout Mesoamerica (including even the abstract, wholly conventional, noniconic, and nonlinguistic system of the Inca).

Generally, writing has been conceived of by the Western European mind as a spoken language that is recorded or referenced phonetically by visible marks.[16] An expanded epistemological view would, and should, allow all notional systems to be encompassed. A more inclusive definition of writing describes a system that communicates relatively specific ideas in a conventional manner by means of permanent visible marks.[17] This definition allows for semasiographic systems, in which meaning is directly communicated on a logical level but is not reliant on spoken language—specifically, Aztec pictographic and ideographic writing.

European distinctions between writing and illustrations were, and are, irrelevant in the Aztec and general Mesoamerican context. Art and writing were essentially the same thing in the context of Pre-Columbian Mesoamerica: for example, *tlacuiloliztli* means both "to write" and "to paint" in Nahuatl. Also, in the Western view of the sixteenth century—and in many ways of today—writing was an instrument for taming, not representing, the voice and language.[18] But just as Mesoamericans did not distinguish writing from painting, they did not consider writing a surrogate or a tool for controlling the voice.[19] Indeed, it seems that the peoples of Mesoamerica used their writing systems more as channels for information than as tools for recording language or mastering orality. The Mexican systems, linked as they were to indigenous background—weaving and agriculture, song and iconography—sociopolitical needs, and cultural milieu, challenged the Renaissance European experience of the alphabet. Even once the adoption of alphabetic writing became widespread among the Aztecs, it cannot be inferred that the Western *philosophy* of writing was adopted or that writing was thus conceived of as the representation of speech.[20] Aztec writing is an alternative literacy that questions and conflicts with historical and contemporary views of information reproduction and communication. It was virtually its own linguistic system, unique to Mexico, independent of any specific spoken language and unrelated to any strategies of intellectual inquiry, politics of information collection and enunciation, or cognitive approach to writing familiar to European thought.

Mesoamerican Recording Systems and Philosophy of Writing

In Pre-Columbian America, glottographic (speech-based) and semasiographic (meaning-based) systems were used at different times and under various cultures. Hieroglyphs, ideographs, and pictographs, as well as more abstract signifiers were all used to some extent, often all together. There is no evidence of the European evolutionary model of the history and development of writing. In fact, the Maya system of strong phonetic elements and well-developed hieroglyphs came before Aztec and Mixtec pictorial systems, and it seems that the peoples of these later cultures actually eschewed the earlier system for their own.

Aztec-Mexica "writing" is largely figural, or pictographic. It involves no distinction between text and pictures; both are parts of an overall visual description,[21] couched within a framework of arbitrary convention. Individual and composite glyphs, and sometimes certain phonetic elements, are used to indicate personal and place names, but they are fundamentally a part of pictorial presentation. Meaning is carried by pictorial and conventionalized images, by their position and color, and by the contexts in which they participate. Pictographic writing is similar to musical notation or quantitative writing in this way, in that position, symbol, and interrelationship all convey information. Far from being limited, such special systems succeed where alphabetic ones do not because of the human ability to discern certain relationships visually at a glance but not to de-

scribe them in words with anything like equal precision.[22] Diagrammatic recording systems can describe, interpret, and communicate complex phenomena: for
example, maps express spatial relationships especially well—they have no equal
in their ability to characterize relative and actual size, form, and placement.[23] Pictorial depictions of meaning can present information in efficient, precise, and
powerful ways, and people have the ability to receive and comprehend such visual
iconic information.[24] Every item in a Mexican composition is there to provide information, either directly or by implication, and the painter assumed that the
person examining the document was familiar with the insignia of rank, the cos-
tume appropriate to various classes, and the iconography of the different gods;[25]
and of course, the specially *calmecac*-educated interpreter would have been.

The graphic components of Aztec writing convey meaning without a detour
through speech: Functioning outside of spoken language, they help to compose a
visual language of graphic convention and spatial relation that is understandable
to those familiar with the pictorial conventions.[26] Different readings and interpretations are possible, and, within the context of a shared general culture base,
the images could operate across languages—such that Nahuatl-speaking scribes
from central Mexico could have read the Mixtec histories of southern Oaxaca,
giving them voice in their own language.[27] Standardization and convention allowed most of the pictorial histories to be intelligible across ethnic and linguistic
boundaries throughout and beyond the realm. Thus Mexican writing, as an
"open" writing system, bridged and unified areas of relative linguistic diversity
and cultural homogeneity.[28]

There are several forms of Mesoamerican written document: event-oriented
chronicles, cartographic (or location/geography-oriented) histories, and time-
line-like year-count forms. All of these forms use graphic and pictographic representation, convention, and description to convey meaning and story and to
record the Mexican experience. The Mixteca are closely associated with the seri-
alized, narrative, event-oriented chronicles and the genealogical-historical maps,
and the Aztec are known for their continuous year-count annals. These associations are significant because recording systems were created out of specific needs:
The Mixtec need to document the history of alliances and wars among a localized
segmentary elite differed enormously from the Aztec need to document the collection of tribute from entire populations of conquered peoples.[29] The various
uses of information and differing needs for documentary strategies to record territory and history gave rise to diverse written forms and their assorted focuses on
action, space, and time.

In the event-oriented histories, which were usually painted on strips of hide or
bark, actions are recorded by arbitrary conventions and by the poses and gestures

of the participants. Location is indicated by place signs, though they are also de-scribed pictorially; time is conveyed by sequence, and often, especially with indi-vidual events, fixed dates are expressed. This codex form is flexible but limited to simple action and ambiguous spatial relations. In contrast, dynamic cartographic chronicles excel both in picturing the whole story as a single statement and in pre-senting spatial relationships.[30] Cartographic forms, widely known as *mapas* and *lienzos*, are extremely similar to event-oriented forms in content and function. They were recorded on large panels of bark, hide, or cloth and were painted with stylized geographic panoramas representing certain landscapes and territories in which historical action took place. They were used as a means of conceptualizing the political landscape, but they also point the way to sites in memory rather than simply to particular locations in the terrain.[31] Artists were often commissioned by members of the elite to create *lienzos* for political and social uses. They show the conquests, intermarriages, alliances, and splittings within a great framework of historical and geographical interplay, informed by political and social needs for aggrandizement and access to knowledge. Dynastic lineages and territorial al-liances are most often shown in the records, in the form of genealogies, confeder-ations, and factions. *Lienzos* combine the features of a map with pictorial history and "ruler lists" and were useful in revealing complex genealogical and historical relationships of critical importance in political decision making: They also dis-play a fundamental perception of nationhood that goes beyond the city-state or "great house" level of elite organization.[32] *Mapas* and *lienzos* provided essential historical support to the political system and the social status quo. Also, carto-graphic forms were ideally suited to portray migration sagas—which are a major part of Mexican history—as well as simultaneous events, though those were somewhat limited in complexity.[33]

Generally a postconquest form, *lienzo* is in fact a Spanish term for a large sheet of cotton or linen sometimes used as a canvas in European oil painting. The de-rivation of the term is revealing, in that the Spaniards must have looked on the Mexican cartographic histories as in some way akin to paintings. Even today this connection persists, and some scholars believe that, "lacking a written language when they developed their *artistic traditions*, [the Mixteca] used visual devices, such as joining lines, footprints, placement of material, omissions, unconven-tional sequences, and the scale of drawing to underline points they wanted to make."[34] Certainly *lienzos* do have an artistic element, as is dictated by the general Mesoamerican philosophy of writing. They are sometimes used not only to illus-trate a phase in the transitional art style that developed in sixteenth-century colo-nial Mesoamerica but also to reflect an earlier stage in Mexican picture writing.[35]

The most prevalent and important form of information carrier, though, and that related most specifically to the Aztecs, is the continuous year-count chronicle. The annals were developed by the Aztecs of Tenochtitlan as an efficient and effective way to accommodate and preserve their official and imperial history.[36] Writing was a prestigious, imperial channel of information, although, ultimately, indigenous cultural emphasis was placed on internal recording of knowledge; the interpretation of painted codices depended on intensive memorization. Oral reading and explication of manuscripts were (according to de Landa, among others) a public event, but popular literacy was probably low, though literacy presumably came in varying degrees. The restriction of access to knowledge and writing can be seen as a means of facilitating social advantage and political power for those in control. Mexican literacy was probably situated within a system of control and exploitation, exercised by the centralized authority that apportioned the privilege of reading and writing with the aim of monopolizing political discourse.[37] Indeed, the Aztec Empire depended on the strict management of the production and interpretation of written codices: Accurate tribute records and, especially, control of a reworked written history that asserted messages of imperial propaganda—for example, stories of Toltec ancestry, the dominance of Huitzilopochtli and his need for sacrificial offerings—were essential to Aztec hegemony. Historical manuscripts, though they served other purposes, were the motivation, justification, and legitimation of imperialist policies: They allowed for the manipulation of alliances, and their use by the rulers generated the need and structure for expansion.

The continuous year-count annals were created under the imperial Aztec to encode political rhetoric and to record and present the Aztec-Mexica story and the mytho-historical events of the past. The file of years provided the structure for the histories, which show all manner of natural, political, religious, social, and martial events and more varied activities than the cartographic forms or even the event-oriented codices. Individual accomplishment is rarely a significant element in the Aztec annals, as it is in the Mixtec codices and in the cartographic presentations.[38] The Aztec-Mexica chronicles are specifically nationalistic, symbolic of the empire. The continuous, monotonous sequence of the years presents Aztec history and destiny as an unbroken line: Time was used as a device to demonstrate the imperial right to rule and the continuity of past to present and beyond.[39]

This year-count form is expressive, though it is limited in showing causality and consequence. The point to remember, though, is that the annals fit the requirements of the Aztec imperial story, just as the event histories allowed the Mixtec rulers to document their lineage, alliances, and territorial claims, and the cartographic forms accommodated migrations. Each recording system has advantages and limitations, and each developed within a certain cultural setting to meet specific needs. Also, sometimes all three forms were blended together, in varying degrees and according to need, to create a highly flexible and even more effective channel for information. Regardless of colonial misinterpretations and even modern, European-based views of Mesoamerican writing systems, these Mesoamerican manuscripts were accepted by their makers and interpreters, as well as the general society, as valid documents that functioned to chronicle the Mesoamerican cosmos, convey traditional knowledge, and establish new ideas. Mesoamerican writing systems were linked closely to every form and function of sociocultural communication, and, in that sense, these systems of writing were much more open and effective than any book of Latin characters.

Conclusion

Colonial writers mention the close relationship of reading, writing, and oral recitation in the indigenous writing systems, though they interpret this relationship as limiting.[40] Spaniards never understood that if the Amerindian lacked letters, they (the Spanish) by the same token lacked *quipu* and *amoxtli*.[41] The limitations of pictographic notation are not incomparable to those of alphabetic script; they are simply different and are culturally accommodated. Just as language itself does not express all of human experience, much as Bray might believe the contrary, neither do European writing or Mesoamerican glyphic presentation. In a way, Aztec writing is more flexible than Western forms because extensive interpretation is allowed and indeed is intrinsically a part of the structure. Painted images privilege certain memories, setting out a visual framework for oral constructions of identity.[42] The Mesoamerican codices, histories, and annals form a dynamic tradition of visual discourse on history, geography, and so on; they are armatures for the native reconstruction of their past and present identity. They may be undisciplined in the European sense, but this makes them much more open to interpretive elaboration and, at the same time, historical authenticity.

The initial encounter between European concepts of the authority of the written word and the Mesoamerican emphasis on the authority of the interpreter cannot be ignored, nor should the dichotomy that that encounter erected continue to surreptitiously impose itself on the history of writing systems and Pre-Columbian Mesoamerican scholarship.[43] The alternative literacies of Europe and Mesoamerica reflect conflicting politics of language and suggest the need for a new history of writing, specifically Mesoamerican writing, that is nonevolutionary and sensitized to Western biases. At the very least, they cast doubt onto modern portrayals of Aztec recording systems as well as current conceptions of the history and development of writing.

The spoken word, written signs, and social roles and functions attached to such cultural constructions were conceived of and articulated by indigenous Mexicans without reference to European standards. Therefore they cannot be adequately translated into Western categories without some misunderstanding and suppression of their value. Scholars must rid themselves of the basic assumption that writing in an alphabetic script is superior to other forms of recording information and communicating knowledge nonverbally. A nonevolutionary (or co-evolutionary) model must be developed, and a broader definition of writing is necessary to encompass all nonverbal systems of graphic communication and the full spectrum of alternative literacies and visual and tactile systems of recording.

Notes

1. Karttunen, 398.
2. Mignolo, "Signs," 243.
3. Boone, "'Art and Writing,'" 6.
4. Mignolo, "Signs," 227.
5. Other, earlier book forms, such as papyrus rolls, and indeed even the idea that writing does not automatically imply the need for a book were apparently forgotten with the coming of the printing press and the new style of printed vellum codex.
6. Mignolo, "Signs," 227.
7. Ibid., 225.
8. Ibid., 228.
9. Because of this widespread penchant for book analogies very little attention was paid to sculptural writings or pottery inscriptions and the like. Similarly, just as elements of Aztec sculptural writing were dismissed, the tactile reality of *quipu* was lost through translation into an analogy system that could incorporate only graphic signs inscribed upon a flat surface.
10. Mignolo, "Signs," 257.
11. Ibid., 234.
12. For example, "[The glyphs used by the Aztec] represent a notable achievement for what was, essentially, a stone-age people, lacking both wheeled vehicles and pack animals" (Ross, in *Codex Mendoza*, 13).
13. Boone, "'Art and Writing,'" 7.
14. See John DeFrancis, Kurt Ross, and so on.
15. The implication is that a pictographic system is indistinguishable from complex iconography.
16. Boone, "'Art and Writing,'" 5.
17. See ibid., throughout.

18. Mignolo, "Afterword," 294.

19 Ibid., 295.

20. Ibid., 296.

21. This is not to say that visual description is the same as artistic representation.

22. Boone, "'Art and Writing,'" 9.

23 Ibid., 10.

24. In our modern, increasingly international and multilingual world, iconic systems and supralinguistic ways of presenting knowledge have been taking over the domains of public communication because they convey meaning regardless of the language one speaks, and they are quickly understood by those participating in the same general culture (Boone, "'Art and Writing,'" 16).

25. Bray, 95.

26. Boone, "Aztec . . .," 54.

27. Boone, "'Art and Writing,'" 19.

28. Houston, 34.

29. Pohl, 138.

30. Boone, "Aztec . . .," 60.

31 Leibsohn, 170.

32. Pohl, 143.

33. Sixteenth-century Spanish chroniclers and modern scholars alike have found it virtually impossible to interpret some of the more crowded and complicated *lienzos*; however, it is, I think, still questionable as to whether an indigenous Mesoamerican versed in interpretation and history would have had such a difficult time.

34. Parmenter, 24 (emphasis added).

35. Ibid., 75.

36. Boone, "Aztec . . .," 64.

37. Houston, 41, note 4.

38. Boone, "Aztec . . .," 66.

39. Ibid., 67.

40. See Gaspar Antonio Chi, Diego de Landa, Sanchez de Aguilar, Bartolome de las Casas, Bernardino de Sahagun, and so on.

41. Mignolo, "Signs," 241.

42. Leibsohn, 161.

43. The following quote is a fine example of conflicting colonial and indigenous philosophies of reading and writing and of the problematic carry-over of biased European sentiments about the validity of indigenous forms into modern scholarship: "[The Spanish scribe working on the Codex Mendoza] points out that the Indians took such a long time to agree among themselves on the exact meaning of some of the pictographs that he only had ten days left in which to complete the task of writing the commentary and the explanatory notes which appear on the illustrated pages themselves" (Ross, in *Codex Mendoza*, 13–14).

Works Consulted

Boone, Elizabeth Hill. "'Art and Writing' in Pre-Columbian America." In *Writing Without Words: Alternative Literacies in Mesoamerica and the Andes*, ed. Elizabeth Hill Boone and Walter D. Mignolo, 3–26. Durham: Duke University Press, 1994.

Boone, Elizabeth Hill. "Aztec Pictorial Histories: Records without Words." In *Writing Without Words: Alternative Literacies in Mesoamerica and the Andes*, ed. Elizabeth Hill Boone and Walter D. Mignolo, 50–76. Durham: Duke University Press, 1994.

Bray, Warwick. *Everyday Life of the Aztecs.* New York: Peter Bedrick Books, 1968.

The Broken Spears: The Aztec Account of the Conquest of Mexico. Ed. Miguel Leon-Portilla. Boston: Beacon Press, 1962.

Codex Mendoza: Aztec Manuscript. Commentary by Kurt Ross. Fribourg: Productions Liber SA, 1978.

Conrad, Geoffrey W., and Arthur A. Demarest. *Religion and Empire: The Dynamics of Aztec and Inca Expansion.* Cambridge: Cambridge University Press, 1984.

Houston, Stephen. "Literacy Among the Pre-Columbian Maya: A Comparative Perspective." In *Writing Without Words: Alternative Literacies in Mesoamerica and the Andes*, ed. Elizabeth Hill Boone and Walter D. Mignolo, 27–49. Durham: Duke University Press, 1994.

Karttunen, Francis. "Nahuatl Literacy." In *The Inca and Aztec States 1400–1800: Anthropology and History*, ed. George A. Collier, Renato I. Rosaldo, and John D. Wirth, 359–410. New York: Academic Press, 1982.

Leibsohn, Dana. "Primers for Memory: Cartographic Histories and Nahua Identity." In *Writing Without Words: Alternative Literacies in Mesoamerica and the Andes*, ed. Elizabeth Hill Boone and Walter D. Mignolo, 161–187. Durham: Duke University Press, 1994.

Mignolo, Walter D. "Afterword: Writing and Recorded Knowledge in Colonial and Postcolonial Situations." In *Writing Without Words: Alternative Literacies in Mesoamerica and the Andes*, ed. Elizabeth Hill Boone and Walter D. Mignolo, 292–313. Durham: Duke University Press, 1994.

Mignolo, Walter D. "Signs and Their Transmission: The Question of the Book in the New World." In *Writing Without Words: Alternative Literacies in Mesoamerica and the Andes*, ed. Elizabeth Hill Boone and Walter D. Mignolo, 220–270. Durham: Duke University Press, 1994.

Parmenter, Ross. *The Lienzo of Tulancingo, Oaxaca: An Introductory Study of a Ninth Painted Sheet From the Coixtlahuaca Valley.* Philadelphia: The American Philosophical Society, 1993.

Pohl, John M. D. "Mexican Codices, Maps, and Lienzos as Social Contracts." In *Writing Without Words: Alternative Literacies in Mesoamerica and the Andes*, ed. Elizabeth Hill Boone and Walter D. Mignolo, 137–160. Durham: Duke University Press, 1994.

ELISABETH ANDERSON GRAVES graduated from Amherst College in May 1996 with a major in history and a special concentration in comparative ancient civilizations. She is presently the managing editor of *History: Reviews of New Books* and the *Journal of Arts Management, Law, and Society.*

APPENDIX F

Class of 1980

Melbia V. Andrews
Lydia I. Blackwood
Laura P. Carrington
Wendy A. (Ross) Drew
Denise M. Francois
Karla R. Fuller
Audrey L. Garrett
Beryl E. Kenney
Tara L. (Fuller) Lamourt
Linder F. Lane
Elaine Levison-Williams
Sheila Y. (Newsome) Maddox
Amina R. Merritt
Susan M. Prattis
Gloriana (Marshall) Sabestian Tecuma
Le Ann Shelton
Berdette E. Thompson
Lynda A. Wright

Class of 1981

Wendy L. Blair
Velna (Jackson) Christopher
Kellie E. Jones
Lisa Llewellyn

Lynn C. Mishoe
Cheryl D. Singleton
Gina M. Stevens

Class of 1982

Frances D. Babb
Janice R. Cook
Ada S. Cooper
Elise R. (Ricks) James
Bonnie D. Jenkins
Victoria F. (Hicks) Kassa
Kimberlyn R. Leary
Allison A. Moore-Lake
Annette Sanders
Angela D. Scott-Henderson
Adrienne E. White-Faines
Alice C. Williams

Class of 1983

Beverley E. Allen
Timolin (Cole) Augustus
Susan E. Byrd
Michele I. Clarke
Kathy L. Frazier
Kakuna N. Kerina

Class of 1984

Janet M. Buckner
Courtney L. Bullard Parks
Rani Lewis
Yvette C. Mendez
Barbara J. (Liggon) Smoot
Margaret R. (Cohen) Vendryes

Class of 1985

Karen E. Cole
Phyllis M. Cureton
Lisa Evans
Christina J. Funderburk
Deborah M. Grogan
Lynn C. Hartfield
Zena M. Martin

Class of 1986

Phyllis R. Barber-Smith
Renee M. Baron
Christine R. Cain
Gabrielle Foreman
Tracy Hughes-Matson
Susan M. Humphrey
Karen R. Jones
Susan L. McKeever
Marjorie Modestil
Anne Marie Pocock
Gwendolyn D. Reeves
Donna-Marie Samuels-Artis
Dana R. Woods

Class of 1987

Niki M. Archambeau
Dahna L. Batts-Osborne

Melanie J. Bingham
Karen S. Gardner-Moore
Carol A. Gray
Joy I. Green-McGann
Wanda Mial
Alice Middleton Merrick
Patricia F. Miller
Etta P. (Johnson) Milton
Melanie A. Posey
Annette M. (Harris) Powell
Lisa A. (Williams) Smith
Esther L. Thomas
Faye E. Walker
Kathryn A. Washington
Sheree D. White
Kimberlee D. Wyche

Class of 1988

Nadia M. Biassou
Gisele F. de Chabert
Patricia (Spencer) Favreau
Davidella M. Floyd
Sherry B. Garrett
Donnella S. Green
Elise K. Henry
Hannah L. Kilson
Suyen M. Lyn
Tracye L. McQuirter
Marylyne J. Moody
Kimberly A. Moorehead
Marla L. Shelton

Class of 1989

Adrienne E. Baker
Crystal R. (Jean) Brown
Sonya Y. Clark
Monica M. Colvin

C. Elizabeth Hollister
Kwai J. Kendall-Grove
Daphnee M. Roy

Class of 1990

Cheryl A. Bailey
Loretta A. Daway
Karen A. Fairclough
Sonja R. Harrell
Angela M. Jackson
Nicole M. Moore
Marylin Pierre-Louis
Julia A. Rhodes
Rachael N. Scott
Keila C. Tennent
Karen A. Woods
Sheryl D. Wright

Class of 1991

Dolores K. Cass
Valerie J. Daugherty
Marvalyn E. DeCambre
Pamela J. Flood
Angela J. Reddock
Kelly M. Robinson
Shelley D. (Dugas) Thomas
Danielle R. Waldrop
Charmaine C. White

Class of 1992

Akinyi A. Adija
Tracey D. Briscoe
Linda A. Lewis
Keisha N. Lindsay
Maritza J. Maxwell

Key A. Mendes
Joy M. Mitchell
Malana K. Moshesh
Nyaneba E. Nkrumah
Angela D. Sloan
Malissa Williams

Class of 1993

Gertha Benoit-Hollis
Lisa L. Biggs
Patrece M. Bryan
Nikki M. Canady
Kimberly M. Davis
Yulanda T. Faison
Carrie J. Green
Nicole C. Harry
Lucinda A. Holt
Catherine E. Lhamon
Keisha A. Lightbourne
Rebecca E. Miller
Nicole D. Northern
Anastasia Rowland
Nichole T. Rustin
Nicole D. Sin Quee
Alain C. Sykes
Kirsten A. Walker
Ericka L. Williams

Class of 1994

Karen Barnes
Angela Bronner
Karlene D. Brown
Nikki R. Brown
Erika B. Clark
Jocelyn D. Collins
Galanne Y. Deressa

Suzette A. Duncan
Tarsha Y. Echols
Zenzi E. Gadson
Chantal E. Kordula
Elizabeth A. Ngene
Rose M. Rejouis
Jocelyn D. Taylor
Kara I. Theard
Terri L. Webb

Class of 1995

Lisa M. Bowman
Erika L. Butler
Debra J. Evans
Kirsten K. Ford
Bronwyn G. Glenn
Donnis D. Glover
Naya A. Howell
Kathy-Anne R. Lewis
Michelle J. Lomax
Rebecca R. Neubert
Natasha N. Reed
Cybill M. Sigler
Vonesca M. Stroud
Ghenete E. Wright

Class of 1996

Alyssa K. Earle
Kim S. Gittens
Elisabeth A. Graves
Marsha P. Hampton
Dana Z. Hopings
Trinda S. Lee
Mirissa M. Neff
Nicole A. Roux
Karima L. Thomas
Tracie L. Yorke

Class of 1997

Melissa D. Alexis
Soyini Baten
Lisa N. Blair
Nichole N. Bridges
Amani D. Brown
Ashaki M. Brown
Naeemah Clark
Elizabeth Fairfax
Rasheema M. Graham
Shana Harry
Candida Haynes
Monet E. Hilson
Nicole Moorehead
Hilary Mosher
Thandeka N. Myeni
Logan Nakyanzi
Melanie H. Overby
Tiffany N. Powell
Nicole Scott
Vicki S. Skovle
Stephanie N. Stone
Rachel M. Williams
Stacy A. Williams

Class of 1998

Janelle R. Alexander
Cymande B. Cannon
Nichelle S. Carr
Stacey J. Dorsey
Marti A. Dumas
Nathalie Elivert
Alicia E. Ellis
Dana W. Gunthorpe
Robynn D. Jackson
Michele A. Jefferson
Valerie Legagneur

Maygen E. Moore
Shaunette R. Richards
Shandra Rowand
Nichole L. Taylor
Dionne A. Thomas
Leza A. Thompson
Brooke L. Warren
Tracey L. Watts

Class of 1999

Jennifer D. Booth
Lashanda Q. Brown
Katherine V. Burns

Katrina L. Burton
Radiah A. Donald
Kimberly J. Duplechain
Emilie P. Eliason
Rebecca L. Foreman
Vanessa Legagneur
Mina L. Lolomari
Rachel H. Nelson
Melanie E. Okadigiwe
Leticia O. Roach
Michelle M. Rousseau
Gisele C. Shorter
Cassandre S. Victor
Jewel S. Younge